PHILLIP TI

THE MONEY MATRIX
— O F   T H E —
NEW WORLD ORDER

WORKBOOK PRESS LLC
187 E Warm Springs Rd,
Suite B285, Las Vegas, NV 89119, USA

Website: https://workbookpress.com/
Hotline: 1-888-818-4856
Email: admin@workbookpress.com

Ordering Information:
Quantity sales. Special discounts are available on quantity purchases by corporations, associations, and others. For details, contact the publisher at the address above.

Library of Congress Control Number:
ISBN-13:   978-1-961845-75-6 (Paperback Version)
                978-1-961845-74-9 (Digital Version)

REV. DATE: 03/08/2023

THE MONEY MATRIX
of the
NEW WORLD ORDER

by: Phillip Tilley

DEDICATION

On the road to riches I encountered an enchanting woman. I learned the secret to happiness isn't being rich, the secret to happiness is being happy, and I've been happy ever since.

This book is dedicated to my wife Christine. Special thanks to my three sons for inspiring this book, challenging my thinking, and assisting me in completing this book.

FOREWARNING TO THE MONEY MATRIX

In the movie "The Matrix," the main character is given an opportunity to make a choice. He can take either the red, or the blue pill. If he chooses the blue pill, he can go on living the illusion, not knowing the answers to the questions that have nagged him all his life.

If he chooses the red pill, the illusions will be removed and he will gain knowledge that few ever possess. If he does choose the red pill, there is no going back. Once your mind expands beyond what it knew before, it cannot shrink back.

I have bad conversations with people where I told them the truth about the money matrix. They became angry with me. They did not want to heart it! They could not handle the truth.

I realized people cannot, or at least should not be forced to see the truth. They should be given the choice to know the truth, or keep living the illusion.

That is why I wrote this book. So you can choose to know the truth, by reading it for yourself. This way, you can see the logic of it for yourself. Learn the facts and free your mind about the money matrix forever.

If you can't handle the truth, it should be your choice not to heart it. You may believe whatever you want to believe, but that does not change the facts or make it the truth. You can choose the blue pill to keep the illusion, happy to live in the system as you have only known it. If that is the case, close this book now and read no further.

This book is the red pill. If you want to know the money matrix, you can choose to keep reading this book.

It will peal back the foreskin of your mind and expose it to the truth, a truth that not everyone can handle. Even if you read a little of this book, it will be too late to go back. How can I be so sure you may wonder? It is because I also understand the phenomenon of cognitive resonance, just as you can not un-ring a bell, you cannot not think about what you have read.

I define cognitive resonance as: a psychological awareness of large amplitude caused by a relatively small periodic stimulus, with the awareness starting small and growing larger and more regular in occurrence.

I will give you an example, I will make the statement; "There sure are a lot of red haired people these days." This is the beginning of the small stimulus. You probably never notice any red haired people. That does not mean they don't exist, it merely means that you never paid attention to it before.

Now, I have made you aware of it. You can try not to think about red haired people, but it is too late. Now you are cognizant of it. Sure, you may soon forget you even read about red haired people. Close this book after reading this section and don't read anymore for a week. Go on about your daily life.

As you go on about your daily life you will strangely begin to notice red haired people all over the place. The waitress at the café you visit, the man using the cell phone, the cab driver, the lady walking her dog, the child on the school bus.

The late night radio talk show host George Noory is another example of cognitive resonance. On his program called "Coast to Coast A.M.," George mentioned that he was seeing the numbers eleven eleven, and one eleven all over the place.

Somehow, at some point, he recognized the seemingly

coincidental re-occurrence regularly of these numbers. He had become cognizant of that fact. When all conditions of a fact are present, it enters into existence.

Then George Noory took it one step further by asking his listening audience, numbering up to fifteen million people, if it was only him seeing this phenomenon, or where they seeing it also? Suddenly, 15 million people were made cognizant of it and the resonating soon began.

Listeners began to e-mail an d call saying that they see it too. Suddenly they were seeing the number 11-11 and 1-11 all over the place.

It is a case of simple cause and effect, where the effect causes the cause. Learning the truth about the money matrix is the cause. The effect is that it resonates into every aspect of your life.

Even though you weren't thinking about it, suddenly you noticed. I didn't put the red haired people there for you to see. They were there all along, just like the money matrix. All I did was make you aware of it.

If you don't believe me, try it for a week and see for yourself. That will give you the time to decide if you want to take the red pill and read the rest of this book.

After, you know the money matrix, every time you use, spend, receive, or observe anyone else using money, you will resonate some aspect of the money matrix. The truth is relentless.

The money matrix is not a concept that is easy to wrap your mind around.

However, once you do comprehend it in its entirety, it will change the way you think, and perhaps change your life forever.

Anurism. Sorry, it just popped in my head.

INTRODUCTION TO THE MONEY MATRIX

It started out innocently enough. Of course, that's how it always starts. I was having a conversation with my oldest son, Jeremy. He told me he was looking for a new job. I asked what was wrong with the job he had. He said it didn't pay enough. He needed a job that paid more money.

I said, "What difference does it make, there is no money." I don't even know why I said it, I just did.

My family is used to me saying off the wall things. I am not used to being challenged about the validity of what I say, but that's what happened next.

Jeremy asked, "What do you mean there is no money?"

Great! Now that I had opened my mouth and said something bazaar, I had to back it up, I said, "After FDR took us off the Gold Standard, our money is no longer backed by gold, it's backed only by faith. So really, there is no money."

Jeremy pulled a $5 bill out of his pocket, stretched it out between both hands, and said, "What do you call this then?" A smirk of satisfaction crossed his lips indicating that he had me.

"It's a Federal Reserve note," I said. Pointing to it I said, "See, it says so across the top of the bill."

Jeremy's mouth gaped in surprise. "What does that mean?" he asked.

"It's not issued by the Treasury Department, or any other government agency." I said. "It's issued by the Federal Reserve, which is a private bank that controls what we think of as the money supply."

Jeremy continued to press me with good questions. Each time he thought he had put a hole in my "theory," from out of the ether, an answer popped into my head that made too much sense.

When he finally gave up, he encouraged me to write down what I had told him. He was certain other people would be interested in it.

I thought about what I had said and wondered what on earth made me give the answers I had. It numbed my brain for three days as it all became so clear to me how much truth there was in it. I was truly in awe.

Then I started doing some research. Three pages of notes turned into seven pages, then thirteen pages, then twenty-eight pages. This book is the results of the conversation that faithful day, and the research that followed.

I will refer in later chapters to the other excellent questions Jeremy asked, and the answers that became a revelation to me. Also, at the back of this book is a glossary of terms and words that I hope will help to re-enforce the statements I make.

CHAPTER 1

A BRIEF HISTORY OF MONEY IN AMERICA

In the beginning there was nothing, and there still is! Before the US was the US, it was thirteen British colonies along the east coast of North America. It was a desperate situation as far as money was concerned. The colonists were always short of official British coins for conducting every day commerce. A diverse variety of money substitutes were used throughout the colonies, but they all shared a common accounting basis in British pounds, shillings, and pence.

Essentially, the money supplies of the colonies fell into five major groups.

1.) The official British coins, which were scarce.

2.) Furs and wampum, which were traditional currencies used by the Indians. Trade with the Native tribes was essential for the survival of the colonists. These items had real value to the Indians. Furs could be made into clothing, or traded to others for goods they needed. Wampum, made from a type of clam shell, was used as jewelry. Holes were drilled in the middle and they were made into beads, which were strung together in lengths of about eighteen inches and sometimes as long as six feet. These were tied into a loop called a hank. The Narragansett tribe specialized in manufacturing

Wampum beads. They were put out of business when the colonists, using steel drills opened a factory in New Jersey and increased Wampum production a hundred times faster. Wampum remained in use until after the Civil War.

3.) Cash crops. The natural commodities of rice, tobacco, beans, wheat, indigo, and corn also had real value. They could be stored for later use, eaten, smoked, or used as dye in clothes. Certain areas of the Southern colonies used tobacco as money for almost two hundred years.

4.) Spanish pieces of eight. Also known as the Spanish milled dollar, were silver, a precious metal and had real value. These coins were sometimes sawed into eight pieces, like a pie. Each piece was called a bit. Cut in half, gave you two halves of the coin, worth four bits each. The half coin cut in half again gave two quarter pieces of the coin worth two bits each. That is why today, you may hear someone refer to a quarter as two bits. The Spanish had beaten the British colonists to the new world, or North America, by over a hundred years. This allowed them to conquer the Aztec tribe in what is now Mexico, and grab control of the substantial gold and silver in the region. As far as silver coins were concerned, the Spanish pieces of eight had cornered the market for over three hundred years. Because of there wide availability, they were accepted as legal tender everywhere. When the US did decide to coin their own money, the dollar was based on the Spanish piece of eight in exact size and weight.

5.) Paper currency. In 1690, the Massachusetts Bay colony issued the first paper money in North America. They were called "bills of credit," and promised redemption in gold or silver. Since gold and silver have real value, so did the bills of credit, and they were accepted as legal tender. Other colonies followed Massachusetts in issuing paper money.

In 1727, Virginia made "tobacco notes" legal tender. This paper money was backed by a quantity of tobacco on deposit at public warehouses. Since tobacco had real value, so did the tobacco notes, and were readily accepted until about 1800.

It wasn't long before banks began to issue paper money in the form of loans. The loans were secured with a mortgage on the land owned by the borrowers. These were known as land banks. Since the money was backed by land, which has real value, these bills of credit had real value and were accepted as legal tender.

The British were not happy with the colonists printing and using paper money. They began to restrict the colonies right to issue paper money, and in 1764 issued a complete ban on paper money in the colonies. The British stranglehold over the colonies with the ban on paper money was a major factor in causing the colonies to revolt.

When the Revolutionary War broke out, the newly formed government did not have any money. They financed the war with paper money, backed by the "faith of the continent." In May of 1775 the first issues were printed of the "Continental" dollar bill. They were to be redeemable in 300,000 Spanish pieces of eight. That soon rose to 9,000,000, and as the war drag on, more and more were printed.

In all hundreds of millions were printed period. By the spring of

1780, the Continental was worth only two cents on the dollar. They were soon worthless, giving rise to the saying "Not worth a Continental."

It was the first fiat currency in the new world; fiat being worthless or backed by nothing of real value.

The two dollar bill was first issued in June 1776. The Continental Congress authorized the issuance of 49,000 two dollar bills as bills of credit for the defense of America. They were backed by Spanish silver.

After the war was over, financial chaos gripped the newly formed United States. Individual state banks began to issue money. This lead Congress to establish the "dollar" as the new national currency.

In 1792, Congress passed the Coinage Act, establishing a Mint, and regulating the coins of the United States. The "dollar" was established as the unit of measure to be the value of the Spanish milled dollar, or pieces of eight already in circulation. All gold and silver coins struck at the Mint were legal tender. However, due to a shortage of gold and silver bullion, pieces of eight were also accepted as legal tender starting in 1797 and remained as such for fifty years. In 1835 the Mint began coining its own silver dollars. In 1857, Congress repealed the legal tender status of all foreign currency, making the US silver dollar, and gold the only official money of account, or legal tender.

In 1848 gold was discovered in California and bullion to min coins with became plentiful.

The Civil War started in 1861. Wars are expensive. Up to that point, the US government collected revenues with excise taxes (also known as consumption or sales taxes), tariffs (taxes on imports), land sales, and borrowing.

President Lincoln wanted to get loans to pay for the war. The New York bankers wanted exorbitant interest rates, as much as 36%. The banks also insisted on being paid in gold. This would have bankrupted the government, which was unacceptable.

Since the coinage act of 1792 gave Congress the power to coin money and regulate its value, President Lincoln asked Congress to print paper currency instead. This idea was hotly debated, as some representatives believed that to be unconstitutional. War, however, caused the rule to be bent. Congress created the legal tender act of 1862, authorizing the Federal Government to issue paper money.

The National Banking act of 1863 established for the first time in America, a single common paper currency. They were known as greenbacks, and they put an end to all the privately owned bank notes.

The Greenbacks were redeemable for gold, and were legal tender. Since they were backed by gold, which has real value, they were readily accepted. Greenbacks were the first paper money issued by the US Treasury.

In July 1862, the economy was so bad, and money was so scarce, Congress authorized the use of postage stamps as money. Copper coins were melted down and used for cannons and cartridge cases. People used postage stamps as small change. Stamps were not made to be passed around as currency, and they wore out rather quickly. After the Civil War ended, so did the practice of using stamps as currency.

In 1873, the American dollar coin was legislated out of existence. America was virtually on the "Gold standard," with gold, and Greenbacks backed by gold as legal tender.

Then, in 1878, the richest silver discover in America occurred at the Comstock mines in Northern Nevada. A million dollars of silver were being mined each week. A market for the silver had to be created or the bustling Nevada economy would collapse.

Congress enacted the Bland-Allison act in 1878. This required the US Treasury to purchase between 2-4 million dollars worth of silver bullion each month, and coin in into silver dollars. Thus, the Morgan silver dollar was born. Morgan dollars were 90% silver and 10% copper. Between 1878 and 1904 over 500 million silver dollars were minted.

By the turn of the century, huge gold deposits were discovered in Australia, Alaska, and South Africa. This huge increase in gold supplies stimulated the world economy, and by 1900 America was officially on the Gold Standard. No silver dollars were minted between 1905 through 1920.

On December 23rd, 1913, during the Christmas break, taking advantage of the absence of Congressmen opposed to the creation of a fiat monetary system, the Federal Reserve act was passed. The Democratic Party hotly opposed the act using the same argument against President Lincoln in 1862, that only Congress has the power to coin money and regulate its value. The Federal Reserve, also known as the "Fed," is a privately run banking enterprise that prints currency backed by credit lines. Money created out of thin air and really backed by nothing. Thomas Jefferson had warned not to let a private bank have control of your money.

In 1914 WWI broke out in Europe. By 1917, America joined the war. On Novermber 11th, 1918, an armistice was signed bringing an end to the war. In 1921 with the war over, the Peace silver dollar was minted. They continued to be minted through 1935.

On October 24th, 1929 the crash of the stock market occurred. The nation fell into financial chaos. When President Roosevelt took office in 1933, his first official action was to declare a bank holiday. For the next four days, the world's largest economy was left bankless as the financial system was formed.

Congressmen Louis T. McFadden suggested that the Federal Reserve deliberately triggered the stock market crash of 1929, in order to eventually force passage of the emergency banking relief act of March 9th, 1933 which suspended the Gold Standard.

The citizens' banks of Tenino Washington failed on 12/05/31. This created a shortage of money in the area. Merchants had to drive thirty miles over narrow and rough roads to get change. For most, it was too difficult a trip to make. The local chamber of commerce met, and decided to have the local newspaper print the first wooden money in America. The wooden money was valued at 25 cents.

Blaine, Washington issued wooden nickels in 1933. Other places in Pacific Northwest also issued wooden money after that. Some were rectangular, like the Tenino wooden money, and some were round like coins, like the Blaine wooden nickels. Most of the wooden money had an expiration date printed on it. They were worthless after that date, or if they were broken, and some were fragile. That is where we get the saying, "Don't take any wooden nickels!"

Franklin Delano Roosevelt was elected president in the 1932 election. On February 15th, 1933, he was nearly assassinated in Miami. Major General Smedly Darlington Butler informed Congress of the plot for a Coup D'etat to overthrow the government. General Butler said it was sponsored by big money interests.

On April 5th, 1933, Roosevelt issued Presidential Executive Order 6120, making it illegal to horde gold. The order read: "All persons are hereby required to deliver on or before May 1st, 1933, all gold coin, gold bullion, and gold certificates now owned by them or coming into their ownership on or before April 28th, 1933. Until otherwise ordered any person becoming the owner of any gold coin, gold bullion, or gold certificate after April 28th 1933, shall, within three days of receiving thereof, deliver the same to the Federal Reserve bank or member bank. Upon receipt of gold coin, gold bullion, or gold certificates deliver to it, the Federal Reserve bank or member bank will pay therefore an equivalent amount of any other form of coin or currency coined or issued under laws of the United States."

Essentially, this order called for the surrender of all private gold holdings. Believing it to be a temporary measure arising out of the "national emergency" of the Great Depression, most citizens complied and exchanged their gold for paper money.

It is understandable that people at the time thought they were doing the right thing. Gold could no longer be used as legal tender. Then exchange value of paper money was greater than the value of gold content of the coins.

On August 28th, 1933, President Roosevelt issued another Proclamation. It read: "After thirty days from the date of this order, no person shall hold in his possession or retain any interest, legal or equitable, in any gold coin, gold bullion, or gold certificates situated in the United States and owned by any person subject to the jurisdiction of the

United States, accepte under license therefore issued pursuant to this Executive order."

The Gold Reserve act on January 30th, 1934 established penalties for anyone who violated these orders. It read: "Any gold withheld, acquired, transported, melted or treated, imported exported or earmarked, or held in custody, in violation in this act, shall be forfeited to the United States, and in addition any person failing to comply with their provision of this act or of any such regulations or licenses, shall be subject to a penalty equal to twice the value of the gold in respect to such failure occurred."

All the gold in the United States was now in the hands of the Treasury. The words, "redeemable for gold" were removed from the paper money. America was officially off the Gold Standard. Paper money could still be redeemed for silver. And since silver has real value, the paper money had real value.

On December 7th, 1941, Pearl Harbor Naval Base was attacked by Japan sending America into WWII. In order to conserve nickel for the war effort, silver was used to mint nickels from 1942 through 1945. The need for copper was so great that in 1943 pennies were minted out of zinc.

As WWII drew near an end, 730 delegates from all forty four Allied Nations met at the New Hampshire resort town of Breton Woods. A system of rules, institutions, and procedures were established to regulate the International Political Economy, Known as the Breton Woods Agreement, they essentially set up the World Bank, and the International Monetary Fund.

This established an exchange rate for currency between nations. Since the currencies were to be redeemable in gold, in 1946 America was back on the Gold Standard as far as foreign governments were concerned. It was still illegal for American citizens to own gold. It was also the first negotiated "monetary order" in world history.

On June 4th, 1963, seeking to head off a financial crisis. President John F. Kennedy issued Executive Order 11110. This order required the Treasury to begin printing and issuing silver certificates backed by the remaining silver in the Treasury's vault.

This was not unusual, as silver certificates had been issued by the Treasury for over a hundred years. What was unusual was the sheer magnitude, nearly 4.3 billion dollars! President Kennedy wanted to stop paying the Federal Reserve banks (they print Federal Reserve notes, then loan them to the US government with interest). This was a return to the Constitution that states that only Congress shall coin and regulate money.

Kennedy was at odds also with Congress, which had earlier that day. June 4th 1963, passed a Congressional act to abolish silver certificate legislation. President Kennedy's Executive order 11110 was never implemented. On November 22nd, 1963. Kennedy was assassinated.

1964 was the last year US silver coins were issued. In 1965 they were replaced with copper nickel slugs. The coinage act of 1965 was designed to reduce or eliminate the amount of silver used in US coins.

In March 1964, the redemption of silver certificates in silver dollar was halted by the Secretary of the Treasury. On June 24th, 1967, Congress passed the silver certificate act of 1967. It said: "Silver certificates shall be exchangeable for silver bullion for one year following the enactment of the act." In June 1968 all redemption for silver was halted.

The only paper money that remained in circulation was Federal Reserve notes. This is the point at which US currency became a true fiat currency. All legislative ties to specie or the "money of account" of the US were severed.

On August 5th, 1971, President Nixon issued Proclamation number 4074. It stated that after that date, not even foreign central banks could convert their paper dollars for gold. America was off the Gold Standard for good and the Breton Woods system collapsed. By this point, all economically developed countries' currencies were fixed to the US dollar.

CHAPTER 2

THERE IS NO MONEY

"It is well enough that people of the nation do not understand our banking and monetary system, for if they did, I believe there would be a revolution before tomorrow morning."

– Henry Ford

In the movie "The Matrix," the main character has to visit a psychic to see if he is the "One." In the waiting room are other hopefuls that live with the psychic. One of those hopefuls is a small child bending spoons with his mind. When the main character asks how the child is able to do that, the child responds that you should not try to bend the spoon, as that would not be possible. Instead, realize that there is no spoon, and bend yourself.

It's a mind bender of extortionist proportions.

The bending of yourself is called inflection. Prepare to be inflected. Just like there is no spoon, I'm here to tell you there is no money! That, my friend, is The Money Matrix.

In chapter one, I gave you a brief history of money in America. I showed you that our money was based on silver and gold, and that any paper money the Government issued was backed either by silver or gold. In the end, we were left with only Federal Reserve Notes, which are backed by nothing and issued from a private bank. There is no money!

After 1971 when President Nixon took us off the "Gold Standard" for good; Federal Reserve Notes became an "I Owe You Nothing" weren't even alive then. You were born into the money matrix never having seen or known what real money was.

The money is gone. We are left with green pieces of paper, that are backed by nothing of real value, and are therefore worthless, or worth nothing. In fact, if you replace the word "nothing," for the word "money," life takes on a whole new meaning.

Nothing! Poor people have it, rich people need it!

What is your problem? Money!

What is your problem? Nothing!

What do you want out of life? Nothing!

Nothing worth having comes easy.

The love of money is really the love of nothing.

I came into this world with nothing, and I still have most of it left.

I did it all for money! I did it all for nothing!

In a perfect world, you should want for nothing. Well, this must be a perfect world then, because there's a whole lot of nothing out there and everybody wants it. He who has nothing has everything! If you lack for nothing, you are truly wealthy.

All of the people that committed suicide at the crash of the stock market in 1929, did so because they had lost everything. They knew there was nothing left, so they had nothing left to live for. They committed suicide knowing full well penalty for suicide is death. They did it all for nothing!

You can't enjoy money. You desire to fulfill your want of nothing. If you ate money for every meal you would die of starvation from eating nothing! That, my friend, is putting your money where you mouth is.

My mother said she wanted to win the lottery. I asked her why? She said she wanted to have more money. I told her that if money is nothing, she wanted to be winning nothing. I asked her what she had won so far. She said, "Nothing."

I said, "You keep wanting to win nothing, you keep winning exactly what you want, nothing, and yet you are not satisfied." It is like a drug addiction. Money is like any other addiction, you only know you have enough when it begins to destroy you!

The least I could do for his birthday was give him nothing, so I did.

A good example of that is Mr. Whittaker, the guy who won $320 million in the lottery. He has since been burglarized several times with a friend having been murdered in one of them. He's been robbed several times. A friend of his granddaughter's died at his house of a drug overdose. The girl's father has filed a wrongful death lawsuit against Whittaker. Whittaker did not give the girl drugs but he has all that money. Whittaker said they will get nothing from him! His only granddaughter died of unknown causes two months later. I suspect it was an overdose of money. Nothing could destroy his life so completely.

Everything is worth more than nothing.

The concept that money equals nothing, should not be very hard to grasp. When you buy insurance, you are really paying for nothing. Were it not for insurance, far fewer buildings would burn down, and far fewer people would be murdered! Paying for life insurance becomes paying for your own hit man. All for nothing!

My mother said "You will never amount to nothing!"

I said, "Thank you for your consideration, but nothing is impossible."

If it takes money to make money, the term, "Nothing ventured, nothing gained." Makes perfect sense.

Expect nothing and ye shall not be disappointed.

Waste not, want not, or waste nothing, want nothing. It seems that everyone who wants money (nothing), wastes their whole life chasing after it. On the road to riches, the race belongs to the swift. Hurry, or there will be nothing left.

The true measure of a friend is someone who will do something for you knowing full well you have nothing to give them in return!

Santa Claus, the Tooth Fairy, the Easter Bunny. Once you knew they no longer existed, it was hard to get excited about them. You can add money to the list because it doesn't exist either. It's hard to get excited about money, I mean, It's hard to get excited about nothing. Anything is better than nothing I always say. Everything is more valuable than nothing.

The truth is, there is no money, and the truth shall set you free.

By now, you are probably feeling "Peripeteia." This is a sudden reversal of circumstances, the feeling you get when everything you thought you knew was wrong. When some people realize there is no money, they go into shock.

I have a question for you. When your shadow goes away, do you feel pain? Of course not. Money is like your shadow. All I did was shine a light on it and it disappeared.

On June 26, 2003, late night talk show host Art Bell was interviewing remote viewer Major Ed Dames. Remote viewers are similar to psychics. Art asked Ed if he could remote view the price of gold in the future. Ed said no, because money is abstract. I guess you can't see something that isn't there.

My mother became angry when I explained the money matrix to her. She said, "Guess what I'm leaving you in my will."

I, said, "I hope you're leaving me nothing."

Shae said, "That's exactly what I'm leaving you, nothing."

I said, "Then you're giving me exactly what I want. I asked for nothing, you're giving me nothing, and I have to say thanks."

She looked shocked. "Thanks for what?"

"Thanks for nothing." I burst into laughter. "If the meek shall inherit the Earth, then I must not be meek, I'm inheriting nothing."

Expect nothing and you shall never be disappointed. Nothing makes more "cents" to me.

Nothing has value, in that you can exchange it for something you need. Money matters is really nothing matters. What's wrong with this world? Nothing!

In the movie "Matchsatick Men." Nicolas Cage plays as a wealthy con man that is miserable. In the end, his own partner takes him for everything he's worth. Suddenly, he realizes what really matters in life, and it's not money. His partner got his money and he got happiness!

In a poker game, when it's over, one person has all of the chips and everyone else has nothing. The fun is over for everyone, even the winner. It's not fun for the losers, they have nothing. It's not fun for the winner because the excitement of the game has come to an end, and he really has nothing either.

You should always leave someone with something. Never take it all away from them, because a man who has nothing, has nothing to lose!

The prostitute said she would do me for nothing.

It's all been taken. We're left with nothing. All around us the nothingness whirls like a big black hole, sucking away at our soul.

"The entire world economy rests on the consumer. If he ever stops spending money he doesn't have on things he doesn't need, - we're done for." – Bill Bonner

CHAPTER 3

SHOW ME THE MONEY

"All the perplexities, confusion and distress in America arise not from defects in their Constitution or Confederation, nor from want of honor or virtue, so much as downright ignorance of the nature of coin, credit, and circulation." – John Adams

When I told my son Jeremy there was no money, he pulled a five dollar bill from his pocket, stretched it out with both hands so I could see it, and asked me, "What is this then, if there is no money?"

"It's a Federal Reserve note." I said. "See, it says so right across the top of the bill."

Jeremy looked astonished as he saw I was right. "Federal Reserve Note, what does that mean?" he asked.

"It means it's issued by the Federal Reserve, which is a private bank. They are not run by the Government in any way, and those bank notes are backed by nothing, making them worthless."

"What do you mean they are worthless?"

"Our money used to be backed by gold, but in 1933 President

Roosevelt confiscated all the gold and eliminated it as a source of backing for our paper money. You see son, if the paper money isn't backed by anything of real value, then it has no value either."

"How could they get away with that?" asked Jeremy.

"Well, it's a little like the Boiling Frog Story." I said.

"Now you're going to tell me what The Boiling Frog Story is, aren't you!"

The Boiling Frog Story goes like this. If you drop a frog into a pot of boiling water, it knows it will be cooked, so it immediately jumps out. However, if you put a frog into a pot of lukewarm water, then slowly heat the water up, the frog won't jump out. It gets comfortable, and as the water heats up gradually, the frog falls asleep and allows itself to be boiled alive.

"So you see," I said, "the Government debased our money gradually and lulled us to sleep."

"Debased, what does that mean?" asked Jeremy.

"Our money system we based on silver or an equal amount of gold as stated in the Coinage Act of 1792. When the Government removed that backing, and stopped making coins of silver, that base was removed. Silver coins use silver as their base metal. After 1964, all coins were minted using a mixture of copper clad between nickel, or copper nickel clad as it's called. The base metal of silver is gone, so the coins are debased." The Coinage Act of 1972 put a penalty of death for debasing our money. The Congress that did it should have been hung in public.

Jeremy took a quarter out of his pocket and examined it. The copper color along the edge of coin was distinct and obvious. "So this isn't money either?" he asked.

"No, it is a slug, a token, like the Federal Reserve Notes, it is only a shadow of real money," I said. "It is like a dream for those that are asleep to the truth, and when they are awakened, it vanishes."

"If there is no money, then what is in my bank account?" asked Jeremy.

"Let's find out," I said.

We got in the car and drove to the bank. There we asked the teller if we could see Jeremy's bank account. She asked for the account number, verified that he was who he said he was, and then punched up his account on the computer. Pointing to some numbers on the computer screen she said. "This is how much is in your account."

I said, "You misunderstand the question. We don't want to see how much is in the account, we already know that. We want to see the account!"

She looked confused, "Is this your account number?" she asked

"Yes." Said Jeremy

"Then this is your account right here." She said, pointing to the computer screen.

"I want to see the money in my account." Said Jeremy.

"There is no money in your account." She said.

"Then where is the money I have deposited into my account?" asked Jeremy.

"It's in the vault." she said.

"Is my account in the vault?" Jeremy asked.

"No, your account is kept on the computer." she said.

"An account is only a record of entries or transactions during a fiscal period. This record of the coming and going of your money from this bank is called accounting. There is no physical location in this bank, like a safe deposit box, with just your money in it. All the money goes into a pool. The dollar amount you deposit or withdraw from this pool is kept track of in your account. Your account on the computer only keeps track of the dollar amount using numbers." She leaned forward, "Do you get it?"

"So I can't hold my account in my hand?"

"No."

"I can't smell it?"

"No."

"I can't see it?"

"No."

"I can't hear it?"

"No."

"I can't taste it?"

"No."

"You can't show me the money in my account?" "No."

"Why not?"

"There is no money in your account, only numbers!" she said. It appeared her patience was wearing thin.

"Well son," I said. "There you have it. they cannot show you something that isn't there! There is no physical money in your account, only numbers."

"If I deposit a two dollar bill into my account, do I get it back when I draw it out of my account?" Jeremy asked.

"No," she said. "We don't keep track of the type of money you deposit, whether it's nickels, dimes, quarters, or paper. We only keep track of the dollar amount of that deposit. It's all electronic these days, almost nobody uses money anymore."

"People don't use money anymore because there is no money." I said.

I deposited my liquid assets in the river bank.

"Money is really a concept, anything used as a medium of exchange value, like the numbers in my computer." she said. "Automatic deposits from your employers account to yours, checks written from your account to pay bills to your creditors accounts, credit card transactions, they're all just electronic funds transfers. The numbers move around from one computer to another." she said with a sigh.

"What if I make a cash withdrawal?" Jeremy asked.

"I'll give you funds from the cash drawer and deduct that amount electronically from your account." she said.

"And this cash would be in the form of Federal Reserve Notes?" Jeremy asked.

"Yes." She said. "Do you want to make a withdrawal?"

"No." said Jeremy.

"Thank you for your time, and for the accounting lesson." I said. As we left the bank Jeremy said, "What difference does it make if our money is Federal Reserve Notes, everyone accepts them as money anyway."

"I don't think everyone has to." I said. "Let's find out." I walked over to the pay phone and picked up the phone book. I looked up the number for a local motel and called them to make a reservation for a room.

A young man answered the phone at the motel. After taking the standard information as to my needs, he confirmed they had a room they could hold for me. Then he asked for my credit card number. "I don't have any credit cards." I said.

"Did you want to pay cash for that?" he asked. "I don't have any cash either." I said.

"Well how did you intend to pay for the room?" he asked. "I have Federal Reserve Notes." I said. "Do you accept them?" "I don't know." he said. "Let me ask my boss."

The phone was silent for about 30 seconds. Then the young man came back to the line. "I'm sorry sir, we don't accept those here." "Thank you." I said and hung up the phone.

"There you have it son, not everyone accepts Federal Reserve Notes as payment." I said.

"I don't think he knew what you were talking about." said Jeremy. "He is ignorant like most people, when it comes to coin, credit, and currency." I said.

"If you were at the motel and handed him the Federal Reserve Notes, he'd have to take them then though." Said Jeremy

"No he wouldn't." I said.

"Why not? They say right on them that they are legal tender." Said Jeremy

"Yes, but what does legal tender mean?" I asked.

"I don't know." Said Jeremy "I guess I'm ignorant too."

So when we got home, we looked up legal tender at the United States Treasury Bureau of Engraving and Printing. They are the ones that actually print the Federal Reserve Notes. This is what it said. Legal

Tender: A definition

Section 102 of the Coinage Act of 1965 (Title 31 United States Code, Section 392) provides in part:

"All coins and currencies of the United States, regardless of when coined or issued, shall be legal tender for all debts, public and private, public charges, taxes, duties and dues."

This statue means that you have made a valid and legal offer of payment of your debt when you tender United States currency to your creditor. However, there is no Federal Statue which mandates that privates business must accept cash as a form of payment. Private businesses are free to develop their own policies on whether or not to otherwise. accept cash unless there is a State law which says o

We then web surfed to the Federal Reserve web site. There, in the frequently asked questions section, was this question. "Is U.S. currency legal tender for all debts?" Answer: According to the "Legal Tender Statue" (Section 5103 of title 31 of the U.S. code), "United States coins and currency (including Federal Reserve notes and circulating notes of Federal Reserve banks and national banks) are legal tender for all debts. public charges, taxes, and dues." This statue means that all U.S. money as identified abore, when tendered to a creditor legally satisfies a debt to the extent of the amount (face value) tendered. However, no Federal law mandates that a person or an organization must accept currency or coins as payment for goods or services not yet provided. For example, a bus line may prohibit payment of fares in pennies or dollar bills. Some movie theaters, convenience stores and gas stations as a matter of policy may refuse to accept currency of a large denomination, such as notes above $20, and as long as notice is posted and a transaction giving rise to a debt has not already been completed, those organizations have not violated the legal tender law.

Back at the Department of the Treasury web site in the frequently asked question section, I found this.

Question: I thought that United States currency was legal tender for all debts. Some businesses or government agencies say that they will only accept checks, money orders or credit cards as payment, and others will only accept currency notes in denominations of $20 or smaller. Isn't this illegal?

Answer. The pertinent portion of law that applies to those questions is The Coinage Act of 1965, specifically section 102. This is now found in section 392 of Title 31 of the United States Code. The law says that: "All coins and currencies of the United States, regardless of when coined or issued, shall be legal tender for all debts, public and private, public charges, taxes, duties and dues."

This statue means that all United States money as identified above is a valid and legal "offer" of payment for debts when tendered to a creditor. There is, however, no Federal statute mandating that a private business, a person or an organization must accept currency or coins for payment for goods and or services.

So there you have it. Nobody has to accept Federal Reserve notes as payment. They are only a tender in payment, they are not payment unless acknowledged as such.

Also at The Department of the Treasury web site was this question: What are Federal Reserve Notes and how do they differ from United States Notes?

Answer: United States Notes were issued by the Treasure Department directly and were redeemable in gold until 1933 when the United States abandoned the gold standard.

Federal Reserve notes are not redeemable in gold, silver, or any other commodity, and receive no backing by anything. This has been the case since 1933. Federal Reserve notes have no value for themselves, but for what they will buy.

So there you have it friends. Even the Treasury Department admits Federal Reserve Notes are worth nothing!

Another interesting thing is the motto, "In God We Trust," which is on all coins and paper currency. It did not appear on U.S. Federal Reserve notes until 1963. After all, if they are not backed by silver, gold, or anything of value, we better trust in God because you sure can't trast the Government. There is no money! I took out a dollar Federal Reserve Note and wrote with a black marker. "No Money."

Jeremy said. "You just defaced that money."

"How can I deface money if there is no money?" I asked. So we ran down the law on defacement of money at the Bureau of Engraving web site. This is what it said: Defacement of currency is a violation of Title 18, Section 333 of the United States Code. Under this provision. currency defacement is generally defined as follows: Whoever mutilates. cuts, disfigures, perforates, unites or cements together, or does any other thing to any bank bill, draft, note, or other evidence of debe issued by any national banking association, Federal Reserve Bank, or Federal Reserve System, with intent to render such item(s) unfit to be reissued shall be fined not more than $100 or imprisoned not more than six months, orboth.

Defacement of currency in such a way that it is made unfit for circulation comes under the jurisdiction of the United States Secret

Service.

So, it's not money that is illegal to deface, its currency. And the key term, "with intent to render such item(s) unfit to be reissued." leaves the Secret Service to prove that's what I intended. I don't suggest t everyone writes "No Money" on all their Federal Reserve notes, but wouldn't that be funny? Imposter Dollar!

My currency is a doppelganger.

Incidentally, the Secret Service is also in charge of investigating counterfeit currency. Making a fake of the Federal Reserves fake money is not legal, and is punishable by a $5,000 fine and 15 years in prison. They will accept Federal Reserve notes as payment for the fine. I asked. I am reminded of the famous bank robber Willie Sutton. He robbed banks mostly in the early 1930s when gold still backed our paper money. When he was asked why he robbed banks, Willie Sutton said, "Because that's where the money is."

Willie Sutton died in 1980. Before his death, he co-authored a book

"Where the Money Was." I think the key word here is "was." After the gold confiscation, and debasement of our silver coins, the money was gone. Willie didn't rob banks after there was no money.

Our money is an optical obtrusion. It is naught money. Tainted money. Taint gold, taint silver, taint backed by anything of value, taine in your bank account, because taint money!

If money talks, Bill Gates must be affluent in over 200 languages.

CHAPTER 4

THE VALUE OF A DOLLAR

A man was talking with God. He asked. "God, how long is a thousand years to you?"

God said, "To me, that is only a second."

The man then asked, "God, how much is a million dollars to you?"

God said, "To me, that is only a dollar."

The man asked. "God, will you give me a dollar?"

God said, "Sure, just a second!"

That's a funny story, but it helps to illustrate the value of a dollar. If ask anyone what a dollar is, almost everyone tells you it is a dollar bill. That is not the truth though. That dollar bill is a Federal Reserve Nore, backed by nothing of value. So just what is a dollar and what is its value?

There is no law that says a "one dollar Federal Reserve Note" is a dollar in any way shape or form. Furthermore, United States Code states that Federal Reserve Notes shall be redeemed in lawful money on demand at the United States Treasury Department. So, Federal Reserve Notes are not "lawful money," but a dollar is.

When our Founding Fathers started the United States, they knew they needed to establish a stable monetary system to measure wealth. The U.S. Coinage Act of 1792 defined the dollar as the unit of measure. This dollar was specifically to be a coin containing 371.25 grains of pare silver. Therefore, a dollar is really a unit of weight, the weight of 371.25 grains of pure silver. This means that only a Silver Dollar is a dollar. All other currency is measured against the dollar unit.

Before the confiscation of the people's gold, our paper currency was printed with these words: "Redeemable in gold on demand at the United States Treasury, or in gold or lawful money at any Federal

Reserve Bank." After 1934, these words were printed on our paper "This note is redeemable in lawful moncy at the United States Treasury, or at any Federal Reserve Bank." In 1963, with plans to stop minting silver coinage, which is lawful money, our paper currency was printed with these words: "In God We Trust."

Federal Reserve Notes after 1963 not only were not money, they were no longer redeemable for lawful money. Federal Reserve Notes are not dollars, which are what we use in place of what would otherwise have been dollars. Imposter dollars. The last real silver dollars were minted in 1935!

I saw an article in the paper that said the value of the dollar had fallen against foreign currency. That is hog wash. The value of the dolla "an ounce of pure silver," has remained the same. It is still worth an ounce of silver.

What has really happened is currencies have fallen against the value of the "real dollar." That includes our own Federal Reserve Note currency. This means it takes more Federal Reserve Notes, or other currency, to equal the value of the one ounce silver dollar. Currency inflation causes the illusion that the value of the dollar has fallen.

This confusion is caused by people thinking or believing that a one dollar bill is a dollar. Completely different things of unequal value are treated as equivalent in value. The lack of purchasing power of Federal Reserve Notes in no way lowers the value of a silver dollar, which is our unit of measure.

Objective values do not exist in the economy. A dollars value is constant. It must remain constant or we do not have a true unit of value to measure any things of value against. Money cannot be pulled from the ether, and a silver dollar is the U.S. unit of money.

This being said, let me remind you that we no longer use silver dollars as money. Furthermore, in 1963 President Kennedy wanted to issue silver certificates backed by the Treasure Departments 4.3 Billion ounces of silver. That silver reserve no longer exists. The Treasure Department sold off the silver reserve years ago, and now it is all gone.

Without any real dollars we are left with nothing. How can the value of nothing fall against the value of anything? It can't! There are no dollars; there is no money, so the value of the dollar cannot fall!

Alexander Hamilton, our first secretary of the Treasury understood the need for a constant value of the money unit. He said, "There is scarcely any point, in the economy of national affairs, of greater movement than uniform preservation of the intrinsic value of the money unit. On this the security and steady value of property essentially depend."

If the "Dollar" is really a weight as defined by the Coinage Act of 1792, then what we think of as a dollar today is weightless. Space age money for the "New World Order." The more money you earn, the more weightlessness you gain.

The government has reduced our currency to the same abstract that money itself represents. Without linking Federal Reserve Notes to silver, gold, platinum, or anything else of real value, the government has empowered itself to print limitless amounts of money with currency inflation causing limitless debasement of our currency. I point out that once again that in 1792 Congress affixed the death penalty for debasing the coinage.

The value of money is perceived. You did not perceive it on your own. It was taught to you by your parents or at school. You are never too young to learn the value of money. Enslavement of your mind begins at an early age indeed.

Let's begin your re-education of the value of money and the value of a dollar.

A dollar is Money

$ = Money

A dollar is an ounce of pure silver.

An ounce of pure silver Money - Dollar

Federal Reserve Note is Currency

Federal Reserve Note - Currency

Federal Reserve Note Debt

Federal Reserve Note does not equal a "Dollar" and can therefore not be money.

Using this equation, it is plain to see that currency is not money. Since only Federal Reserve Notes are in circulation, we have no money!

A silver dollar is a "Dollar." Anyone who has ever held a silver dollar in their hand, and could feel its weight, and the way is sparkles and glints as sunlight flashes off its surface, knows full well it has real value.

Anyone who has ever held a paper Federal Reserve Note in their hand, felt it's near weightlessness, its dull green and gray surface, knows

it is a piece of paper with no real value..

A silver dollar is a dollar. A Federal Reserve Note in a $1 denomination is a representation of what would have otherwise been a dollar. Mirage money, when you grasp for it, it disappears.

Analogy of a Dollar: Let's say the leader of a country is a "Dollar." If the leader cannot attend a function, he sends an emissary or Ambassador. Here, the emissary represents currency. Currency is not the Dollar anymore than the emissary is the leader. It merely represents it.

So if the leader goes to the function, he is his own emissary. When the leader stays back and the emissary goes, he is backed by the leader, or the currency is backed by the "Dollar."

Since we have no "Dollar" anymore, only the currency, then what can this currency represent if there is nothing backing it? Logic dictates that if nothing backs the currency then there is no money!

This brings us to Gresham's Law. This is defined as an observation in economics; when two coins are equal in debt-paying value but unequal in intrinsic or real value, the one having lesser real value tends to remain in circulation, and the other to be hoarded or exported as bullion. Bad money drives out good money.

In the case of U.S. Currency, gold was confiscated, silver coins were no longer minted, paper money was not backed by gold or silver, thus gold and silver were hoarded while worthless Federal Reserve Notes are circulated in the economy.

I asked my Dad if I could have $5 and he told me there is no money.

CHAPTER 5

THREE TYPES OF MONEY

They say money talks, but I haven't heard mine say any thing. That's because they are Federal Reserve Notes, not money.

There are really three types of money. The first of these is "hard money." Hard money is gold, silver, platinum, or anything else with intrinsic or real value. They are called hard money because they are precious metal and they are hard, and heavy.

I put my money in the freezer so I could have cold hard cash! I ended up with frozen assets.

Hard money is an asset, a hard asset. It is limited to the quantity that exists. It is universal money. Anywhere on this planet, if you offer gold or silver as payment, it will be accepted. Its value is universally known. Hard money occurs in nature.

The second type of money is soft money. This is paper money that is backed by some form of hard money. Silver certificates and gold certificates were a type of soft money. The original Green Backs were backed by silver, so they were soft money. Treasury Notes were abo backed by gold and silver, so they were soft money.

Any paper money that is backed by anything of intrinsic or real value is soft money. That would include paper money issued by land banks using land as the real value backing it. Soft money has to be backed by hard assets and is limited by the quantity of hard assets that back it. Soft money is man made.

The third type of money is Fiat Currency, or no money. currency is paper money that is backed by no hard assets or anything of real value. Fiat currency is by itself worthless. It is unlimited in its quantity that can be printed, since it is only paper, and lots of it can be produced without any cost. How much could it cost to make something worth nothing?

Fiat currency is man made. It would not exist at all were it not forced on the people by their governments by legal tender laws.

Federal Reserve Notes are the no money paper Fiat Currency that we use today. Furthermore, Federal Reserve Notes are "debt money." This means that every dollar has to be borrowed from a bank before it is born into existence. This is why people say it is created from thin air, pulled from the ether. A friend of mine said "What difference does it make if I use hard or soft money, or whether I use Federal Reserve Currency? You are trying to compare apples to oranges."

I said "No, I'm not comparing Apples to Oranges. We are comparing apples to pictures of apples. I can smell a real apple. I can feel it, and when I bite into it, I can taste it. If I eat it, it will be fulfilling my bunger."

"A picture of an apple doesn't smell like an apple. I cannot feel it. If I bite into it, I get an awful taste, not the taste of an apple. If I eat the picture, it has no nutritional value. My hunger is unfulfilled."

That is why you can never get enough money. It is like eating air. You will still be hungry because you are full of nothing. Fiat Currency equals nothing, and its nothingness cannot fulfill you. No matter how much you have, you always have an empty feeling.

Hard money has matter. Federal Reserve notes are anti-matter.

To further prove there is no money. I will use the example of digging a hole. Our currency of Federal Reserve Notes is a debe currency. That means that for any amount of currency to exist, someone had to go into debe. Going into debt is commonly called "Going in the Hole."

Imagine that on a level piece of ground you dig a hole. The dirt you remove from the hole is debt currency. To create that currency, you had to go in the hole, or into debt. The more dirt, or debt currency, you dig out, the bigger and deeper the hole. The hole itself is nothing. This is to go in the hole, or into debt. The more dirt, or debt currency, you dig the nothing that backs our currency.

When you are in your hole, there is only emptiness and nothing Getting more dirt, or debe currency, only puts you deeper in the hole, and your emptiness grows. It forms a void, a black hole sucking at your soul.

You cannot fulfill the emptiness with more debt currency. That only

makes the void grow larger. The more debt currency you have, the more nothing you have. It cats on you.

That is why rich people are so miserable. The Martha Stewarts of the world try to fill the void with more money. There is no money, only debe currency, so no matter how much they have, it is never enough. They can never be satisfied by nothingness. Nothing cannot satisfy them.

The only way to fill the void with a debt currency like Federal Reserve Notes is to not have any. As you put the dirt, debt currency, back in the hole, the hole gets smaller. The less debt currency you have the better you feel.

When you have no more debe currency, the hole is filled in, and you are once again even. You broke even and are on level ground. You have leveled the playing field, and you are broke.

Now you have no debt currency, no money, and no void. That's not really very satisfying either. Your happiness is dirt cheap.

This brings me back to Gresham's Law. Where legal tender laws exist, bad money (debt currency) drives out good money (gold, silver, platinum). Gresharn's law applies essentially only when two forms of money are in circulation with different real values, but legal tender laws force you to respect them as having the same face value in the marketplace.

I thought my money was two faced.

Good money has a face value equal to the intrinsic value of the material it is made of. A real Dollar is an ounce of pure silver and is worth the value of an ounce of pure silver.

Bad money has a lesser intrinsic value or no intrinsic or real value at all. When we used silver coins, counterfeit coins made of steel would be bad money. Federal Reserve Notes with no value are bad money.

When we were forced by legal tender laws to use Federal Reserve Notes as money, the real money quickly disappeared. In the absence of legal tender laws, Gresham's Law works in reverse. In a free society with the freedom to choose, the value of real money dominates in the open market. Bad money becomes unpopular and is driven out of circulation.

Paper currency is only a tender in payment, unless it's acknowledged as payment and accepted as payment, it is not payment, because it is not money. We have already discussed the "Legal Tender Statute" which states that no Federal law mandates that a person or organization must accept currency or coins as payment for goods or services not yet provided. Why do we accept them then? Because at this point there is no real money and we have nothing left.

We have a currency, we don't have any money. People confuse currency and money thinking they are the same thing. They are not Like an insult, a Federal Reserve Note only has value if you accept it. In the game Monopoly, the money has no monetary value, and neither does a Federal Reserve Note.

CHAPTER 6

CURRENCY VS MONEY (WE USE DEBT CURRENCY)

"I knew of only two men who really understand money, an obscure clerk in the Bank of France and one of the directors of the Bank of England. Unfortunately, they disagree."-Baron Rothschild, French Financier

"I bave studied fiancé and economics and international trade all ray life, and now, after these recent events, I have come to the conclusion that I know nothing whatever abost any of them." -Paul Warburg, Chief Architect of the Federal Reserve System

True money, such as gold or silver or platinum, has real value. When these heavy metals are used as money they serve as a store of weakh Currency on the other hand serves in commerce as a store of value, although that value is both negative and imaginary.

The low corrosion rates of the noble metals and their durability make them excellent stores of real value. If the Government defaults, the holder of the coins can melt them down to recover the valuable metals. Melting them at any other time was defacing the coinage and was illegal.

When specie or real money, (noble metal coins of real value), are used to purchase goods and services, you are exchanging wealth for wealth directly. No debt is created. Federal Reserve Notes are only tokens of intent, they only have the perception of value. If fiat currency (debt currency), is used, the buyer does not pay the seller, he only tenders his debt. When a buyer uses fiat currency or credit as purchasing power, the exchange establishes a debt, since the currency is borrowed into existence.

Because debt is essentially unlimited, the quantity of fiat currency available in our debt money system is also limitless. As the quantity of fiat currency in circulation increases compared to the total of goods and services in our country, its unit exchange value decreases. This is currency inflation. With an inflated fiat currency, you receive less actual compensation while your efforts and income remain the same.

Money is defined as: an accepted medium of exchange, unit of account, and has a measure of value. It is a store of value, usually a valuable metal such as gold, silver, or platinum, in the form of a coin.

Currency is defined as: anything circulating as a medium of exchange such as coins, government notes, and bank notes. A standard of deferred payment. Anything used as money which is generally accepted, portable, durable, and has a stable exchange value. Paper currency is only a tender in payment, it is not payment unless acknowledged as such.

Currency is not money. Just because a Federal Reserve Note says "One Dollar" on it does not make it a dollar. If I wrote "Aspirin" on a sugar pill and gave it to you for your headache, you might think the aspirin I gave you didn't work because you still have a headache.

In fact, you did not get an aspirin at all, and that's why your head still hurts. You can't expect currency to cure your money ills because it's not money any more than the sugar pill was an aspirin. The ill persists because the real problem with money is there isn't any!

The concept of money is man-made. It truly is an abstract, a mental image of value. The value only exists, and changes to more or less valuable, in our minds. Money is a measure of value. Truly you cannot touch money any more than you could touch an inch, or a second.

A bull in the field doesn't pay for the grass it eats. It might be said that it exchanges fertilizer which helps the grass grow. Our Politicians are familiar with this. There can be no growth without a lot of bull shit!

Currency is the thing that represents money in the physical form. When gold and silver were used as currency, they had real value as a commodity. It was this commodity value that made them synonymous with money. Fiat Paper currency has no commodity value, therefore it has no value at all.

All of our Federal Reserve Note Currency is borrowed into existence. So if all the debts were paid off all at once, currency would cease to exist.

This of course would not happen with the noble metals used as money. Once the debts were paid off, the metal would still be there, and it would still have real value and plenty of real uses. Anything can be used as currency.

Only commodities can be used as money.

It should be re-noted here that the value of the Dollar has not fallen, as a dollar is a silver one ounce coin. What has fallen is the value of the fiat currency against the "Real Dollar." When people say the Dollar fell in value against other currencies, what is really meant is that the value of the "One dollar" denomination of Federal Reserve Note fiat currency has fallen. The Government and Federal Reserve attempt to confuse people into believing that they are the same thing. They are not!

The value of the 1960 Federal Reserve Note dropped in value to just 21 cents in 1992.

The Fiat currency we use today is all created by monetizing debt Monetization is simply generating currency and introducing it into circulation through another person's willingness to go into debt. Debt has a negative value in the form of unclaimed wealth. Gold, silver, and platinum coins have a positive commodity value.

When the US. switched to a fiat paper currency, purchasing power began to erode. The physical ties to real money were severed. Had the paper fiat currency maintained its exchange value nobody would have complained. Once the link to the noble metals was broken the decline began, and it continues to this day.

I deposited money in my memory bank.

Common people need borrowed currency to support a reasonable lifestyle. Small businesses also need borrowed currency to start-up, and stay in business. As interest rates rise on this monetized debt, the small business and common people have their wealth siphoned away by financial institutions and affluent investors. The rich get richer while the poor get poorer.

This creates public debt. People created the currency for this debt by borrowing at a local bank. The additional currency created by this borrowing cause's currency inflation which drives down the purchasing power of the currency you just borrowed. You suddenly already have less than you need, and you will have to labor more hours of your life away to pay it back plus interest. You have just become a slave to your job! You should make it a point to go into debt at an early age. The sooner you get behind the more time you will have to catch up!

On the other hand, if real money is in the banks instead of worthless fiat currency, things would be different. When the common people or small business borrowed from a bank, they would be borrowing money that already exists. The act of borrowing money does not create inflation like the creation of currency out of thin air does. No additional money is added to the money supply. Zero inflation.

Even with interest you would be able to pay back the loan quicker because you're not working harder for less. And the goods and services you create add to a building economy. Growth would be slower than it is today, but it would be solid growth, with fewer people defaulting on their loans. They wouldn't have to default because they would be able to pay it back, and faster, with real money.

When the Government borrows currency, which creates what is called "National Debt." This is debt that our Government, as leaders of our nation, created. The Government gets all its income from some form of taxes. The largest of these taxes is the personal income tax, which is deducted from your pay check and sent to the Government.

When the Government goes into debt, they don't worry about paying it off because they don't pay it. You pay it in the form of your taxes. The deeper in debt the Government goes, the higher your taxes to pay the debt off plus the interest on that debt. The deeper into debt the Government goes, the more it has to borrow, which creates more worthless fiat currency, which creates more currency inflation, which means you have to work harder for less so you can pay more to the Government. Why doesn't the Government fix this? Because they don't care. They don't have to pay it. It's not their "money." It's your money. Or, at least it would be if there were money. Really it's your worthless fiat currency Federal Reserve Notes!

On the other hand, if we were using real money, things would be different. It is my opinion that the Government should not spend any more money than it has. There are occasions when an emergency, such as war, causes the Government to spend more money than it has.

When the Government borrows, it sells bonds or Treasury Securities. With real money, they could sell no more bonds or securities than there is money in the private sector to buy them. The real money supply is finite, not infinite like fiat currency. National debt would be small if it existed at all. This would cause no inflation to occur. The Government would run more efficient because, just like you and me, they would have too!

We would not have to work harder for less. Once debt free, we would be able to enjoy life, we could work to live, instead of living to work.

This would cause the United States to see the largest economic boom you have never seen.

Without the limits of the noble metals as a reserve, the temptation for the Federal Reserve to issue additional paper fiat currency always wins over prudence.

Currency is an unnatural resource. Currency has no value; it is only a measure of valuable things. True wealth are the valuable things. Currency represents a claim on the wealth of society. If you hold currency, society owes a debt to that person. Society owes a great debt to Bill Gates. How do you repay your debt to society?

When money is used, you get something for something and something for something. Because true money has tangible and intrinsic value, you are exchanging wealth for wealth. You are paid money (something) for working (something), you use the money (something) to buy a new car (something).

When currency is used, you get nothing for something and something for nothing. Because paper fiat currency has no tangible or intrinsic value, it is only a tender in payment. You work (something) and are paid currency (nothing), you buy a car (something) and pay using fiat currency (nothing). Anytime you use Federal Reserve Notes you get something for nothing. Anytime you are paid Federal Reserve Notes you get nothing for something, Currency is catalyst for commerce.

CHAPTER 7

NOBODY IS RICH

My son asked me, "If there is no money then why are there rich people?"

"Nobody is rich." I answered. "Some people think in their own minds they are rich, and they try to project that illusion on us so we will believe it. If we do not see that truth, if we see the illusion and believe it in our own minds, then our minds make it reality. Einstein said energy follows thought."

My son was looking confused, so I asked him "What makes you think they are rich?"

"Well, for one thing they have lots of money!"

"Son, here is a riddle for you," I said. "Poor people have it, rich people need it, what is it?"

"Nothing!" he said.

"That's right, nothing. Money equals nothing, son in reality they don't have more money than you, they have more nothing!" I smiled and said. "How many times have you heard someone we think of as rich, that just lost a bunch of money gambling or something say, 'Oh, it's only money,?"

And since money equals nothing, hoarding money is like drinking air. You're still thirsty, so you keep wanting more. There will never be enough, and you will never be satisfied. Greed has no upper limit. The people we think of as rich are usually miserable. The love of money is really the love of nothing, and what could be more miserable than that?

"What about millionaires?" my son asked.

"There are no millionaires, they are million errors!" I said. There is no money, so what are they millionaires of? A millionaire is defined as one whose wealth is estimated at a million or more (as of dollars or pounds sterling). Since we know the dollar, defined as a silver one ounce coin, no longer is used as money, there are no dollars and there is no money. They are millionaires of Federal Reserve Note Debr currency. Holding a large quantity of debt in reality is not rich, it is in fact poor.

"Then why do rich people have such nice houses?" my son asked, Really though, what is a house? It is shelter at its most basic factor A tent, a mobile home, a log cabin, a house, a mansion, those are all shelter. The person you think of as rich that has a nice house has no more shelter than you do in your apartment.

"What about the guy with the $100,000 Mercedes?" asked

"What is that Mercedes?" I asked.

"It's a very fancy Luxury Car," said my son.

"More basic than that it's transportation," I said "My $600 Torino is transportation, the only real difference is the Mercedes owner gave a whole lot of nothing for his transportation and I gave a little bit of nothing for mine!"

"The Mercedes is fancier," my son demanded. "What does it have that my Torino does not?" I asked.

"It has air conditioning."

"So does my Torino."

"It has a good stereo and sound system."

"So does my Torino,"

"It rides smooth."

"So does my Torino. The only difference is the name on the transportation," I said. The value of any form of transportation is in the mind of each individual. If you believe the brainwashing of the advertising industry, it becomes realty for you. Again, energy follows thought.

"The perceived value of transportation reminds me of a couple of stories. The first one involves a friend of mine named Bob. Bob had a black Silvarado pick-up truck. While at Bob's house for a bar-b-q, r were talking next to Bob's truck. I leaned against the truck at some point. Bob got upset. He pointed out that I was wearing jeans with rivets in them and I should get away from his truck before I scratched it.

I said. "Bob, it's only a truck."

"If you scratch the paint it will ruin its trade-in value." He yelled at me.

"Is a scratch going to make your truck mechanically unsound?" I asked.

"No you idiot." He yelled. "It ruins the paint job which drives down its value."

I got away from Bob's truck. I also got away from Bob. He obviously valued his truck more than our friendship. You can get another good truck for a little bit of nothing, but good friends are priceless! I hope Bob is happy with his truck.

The other story involved a lady who had parked her Cadillac Escalade in the parking lot at the local mall. The problem is, she took up two parking spaces with her Escalade. How rude. Not being able to find another open parking space, I squeezed my car into the piece of space not occupied by the Escalade. I could scarcely open my car door more than seven inches to squeeze myself out.

Suddenly the ugliest woman I have ever seen in my life was in front of me barking at me. "You scratched my truck with your car door you idiot!" she yelled.

"You took up two parking spaces with your truck." I replied. "Either you can't drive this truck very well or you are the idiot!"

"This is a very expensive truck." The ugly woman yelled. Her red curly hair began to resemble the snakes on the head of Medusa. "I parked in two spaces so nobody would put a scratch on my beautiful truck, and now some idiot had to scratch my truck anyway." She funed.

"Well if you didn't want a scratch on your truck, you should have parked in only one space you idiot!" I countered. "You are inconsiderate of other people that need to park." I said.

"If I park in only one space, idioes like you park on either side of me and open their car doors into the side of my truck causing dings in the paint job!" she hissed. It might have been my imagination but she seemed to grow taller.

"What difference does that make?" I asked.

"Dings and scratches in the paint job lower the value of my you idiot!" the gorgon screeched.

"It seems to me that your fancy Escalade truck is only transportation, and a scratch or ding in the paint doesn't affect its ability to transfer you around." I said.

"It lowers the value!" she screeched at me again. Her eyes were wild and she was huffing and puffing and clinching her fists, 1 flame to spew from her mouth the next time she opened it. She actually believed that her truck had value other than transportation.

I tried to defuse the situation. "You know, they make extra wide rubber molding as an after market product that prevents dings and scratches, maybe you should get some if you are so concerned abou your truck's paint." I suggested.

"Those things are ugly." She yelled. "This is a beautiful truck and don't want to uplify it."

"This is a beautiful truck." I said, as I took a few seconds to truly look at it. "Did it ever occur to you that this beautiful truck might n want some ugly bitch driving it?" I normally have a pretty long fast, but she had used it up and I was no longer in the mood to deal with her insults.

"You're an ass." She hissed.

"Well at least I've got one." I said. "The only thing not flat on you is that giant honking nose taking up half your face."

"I need a new paint job and you're paying for it." She yelled. "You could use a new paint job, but your truck's fine" 1 countered.

"You scratched my truck you idiot." She hollered.

"I don't see any scratch." I said. "Where is this scratch?

She stormed towards me, bent over and glared angrily at the side of her precious truck. I opened my car door forcefully, striking her in the leg. As she dropped to the ground clutching her leg I got back into my car.

"My leg, my leg." She screamed

"Now what's more important, your trucks paint job, or your leg?"

I asked.

"My leg, my leg," She shouted as she wreathed in pain.

"Good." I said. "At least now you know what is really important is life." I drove home and waited for the cops to arrive, none did.

If the cops had of shown up. I would have pleaded self defense. Mrs. Medusa tried to petrify me with her hideousness, but one look at her and no part of me could turn hard.

If money were free we'd all be rich, but then it wouldn't be worth anything.

My son's next question was Rolex watches that rich people wear. A Rolex watch is a timepiece, it does not keep any better time than my Timex. Again, they paid a whole lot of nothing for the Rolex, I paid a little bit of nothing for my Timex.

"Rolex watches are really jewelry as well as a time piece." My son

"Rich people are like an Easter egg" I said. "All pretty on the outside, hollow or rotten on the inside." Keep your caviar and shrimp. I'd rather have a Big Mac and fries.

You can't own money. Money, if there were any, would be issued by the Treasury Department of the Government. It would really be the Government's money. Federal Reserve Note currency is issued by the Federal Reserve and leased to the government, so it really belongs to the Federal Reserve. You can't own something that isn't yours.

We exchange it and use it among ourselves. In God We Tra because you can't trust the Government. If you can't even own money. what makes a rich person rich? Nothing!

When you try to tell someone who thinks they are rich, that they aren't and there is no money, at first they get angry. Then denial follows "I don't believe you." Translation: I don't want to believe you. They want to keep living the illusion. It is a drug that makes them feel good about themselves. Why wouldn't they want to keep living the illusion? Otherwise, they have nothing and have lived their whole life for nothing.

The Government likes us living the illusion. It keeps everything in balance and "under control." If we are awake from the illusion and realize we have nothing to lose, the Government loses control, and that is dangerous! Once I discovered this, I could hardly wait to tell no one about it.

I was once told by an executive that if I were rich, I would be called eccentric and I could get away with my odd behavior. However, since was poor they had a different word for me.

"If I'm not eccentric, what am I?" I asked.

"You're fired!" he said.

I said, "I am neither rich, nor poor, I am me, and if you can't accept me for what I am, that is your loss!"

Incidentally, a year later that company went bankrupt and the executive was out of a job. Funny, how hard the might hit when they fall.

Any person who is out of control is threatening. If we realize we have nothing to lose, the Government loses power over these individuals If a person is eccentric in a way that shows disregard or contemp for current customs or restraints, other prople become frightened and understandably so. It's scary. If you don't rebel with a cause, you shouldn't rebel at all. I guess that's the difference between being a or being revolting. I rebel cause there is no money.

If you rebel you should have a cause, because a rebel without a cause is just revolting!

My son asked me. "Couldn't I take my Federal Reserve Notes, buy gold which is real money, and then use the gold to buy stuff?"

"Son, why would you want to the real money to buy anything that you already get for free using worthless Federal Reserve Notes? I asked.

"It's the Golden Rule." My son said. "He who has the gold rules." You cannot cat money. You cannot have sex with money. What good is it? People do not want money for the money, they want money and to be rich because of the power associated with being rich and having lots of money.

Poor people don't want to hear that there is no money because it destroys their hopes of some day being rich and having lots of money It crushes their dreams. On the flip side, it also crushes the nightmare they live every day. Rich people aren't rich and poor people aren't poor, it levels the playing field when you realize there is no money.

These people think that money equals power, and power equals control. Money really equals nothing. If everyone realized this, it would be total chaos as these in control, wouldn't be. People aren't rich or poor, they are people.

We don't need money to be rich. We only need what we need. Why does anyone need more than they need? They don't. No one needs to control your life more than you do!

Money seems to work like keys to the Merovingian, opening doors of opportunity for those we think of as rich. It allows them to go where they want, when they want, and get other people to do what they want.

If you realize there is no money, you can act like a lock picker. opening a lot of the same doors to opportunities that are normally reserved for the "Rich." You too can go where want, and d get what you want. You just need to create your own illusion that eludes the illusion.

A good example of this is the movie "A Million to Juan." Juan is given a check for one million dollars. Although he never cashes or deposits the check, everywhere he goes with that huge check, people treat him like he is a millionaire. If you've never seen the movie I recommend it.

I would have found the storyline a little hard to believe had I not had such an experience myself. I don't believe in coincidences. Everything that happens does so for a reason. I believe that experience was to teach me a lesson in what it feels like to be "Rich."

This is the story. I was working at a hospital as an assistant supervisor of the janitorial department. One of our supervisors took a job at the medical center in town. I ended up on the day crew as a supervisor. Shortly, the supervisor that went to the medical center called me with a job opportunity.

She was short handed and I had the skills to help her out on the Evening shift at the medical center. I worked there on a call basis when Shelly needed me for several years. Then I went six months without being called.

Then Shelly called me back to work at the medical center on a Friday. I had just cashed my paycheck before going to the medical center that evening, I had over seven hundred dollars in my wallet, which normally would never be the case.

At break time, we all went to the snack bar to eat, and I was really hungry. I loaded up my tood tray and went to the register to pay for it. The girl at the cash register was new, so she didn't know me. She asked

to make sure I was an employee.

My good friend Sionè was next to me in line. He learned over and told her I was a millionaire. Her eyes widened.

I said, "Please don't believe him, he is making that up."

Sione said. "Try to pay with something other than a hundred dollar bill if you can."

I opened my wallet and pulled out a hundred dollar bill. I put it back and each bill I pulled out was another hundred dollar bill. The teller at the bank must have loaded me up with hundred dollar bills when I had cashed check. I looked up astonished. Everyone around me had their mouths hanging open.

"You see, I told you." Sionè injected quickly. "He is a millionaire." The girl at the cash register told me I didn't have to pay. I couldn't believe it. She repeatedly refused to accept my payment.

The next day she again refused to take my offer to pay, even though I had smaller bills and could have paid. Then she sat with us as we ate. Stone asked me. "How many houses does your mother own?" "Seven." I said.

"You see," Sionè said. "I told you he was a millionaire!"

I said. "Please don't believe him, they are all really small houses." "Yes," said Sione. "The bungalow on the beach at Waikiki, the two bedroom house in Miami, the penthouse in New York!" Sione thought it was funny, and the snack bar girl was eating it up.

"Please don't believe him." I pleaded. "He is making that up." In reality my mother had paid no more than two thousand dollars for any of the places. They were in bad shape, but she fixed them up and rented them out.

The girl asked Stone why I was working as a janitor if I were a millionaire. Sionè told her I was looking for a wife that would love me for who I was, not for my money. He told her I was incognito, posing apoor janitor to meet the right girl. He also told her I was a friend of Shelly's, which was true.

All of my money is in a trust where there is no trust there is no love.

I didn't realize it at the time, but Shelly was a millionaire. She had a house in town, a huge cabin in the mountains, drove a Cadillac, wore diamonds, took lavish trips and cruises and ate regularly at all the fancy restaurants in town.

That girl refused to accept any money from me for the next two months I worked there because she thought I was a millionaire. I wasn't rich but I got the same perks a rich person would have. I was rich by association, and because my friend had spun a believable illusion that I was.

Again, I recommend you watch the movie "A Million to Juan." We really do "treat" rich people differently. There are techniques you can use to create the illusion that you are "Rich."

It does not change the facts. There is no money! Nobody is rich! It reminds me of the children's story "The King Has No Cloths." Revealed for who they really are, rich people are naked and helpless. All the more reason to keep the poor people enslaved in the system.

John D. Rockefeller when he was the richest man in the world was asked how much is enough. He replied, "Just a little bit meee" You can never have enough nothing!

The high cost of living has not discouraged its popularity.

CHAPTER 8

YOU CAN'T OWN LAND

"If the American people ever allow private banks o control the use of their money, first by inflation and then by deflation, the banks and corporations that will grow around them will deprive the people of their property until their children will wake up homeless on the continent their fathers conquered."-Thomas Jefferson

You came into this world with nothing, and when you leave, you take nothing with you. If this is true, then how can you own anything? The Indians understood that men could not own land. When white men first arrived in America, they asked the Indians, "Who owned this land?" The Indians said, "Don't be ridiculous, nobody owns the land, you can't own land."

To the Indians, the land, like everything else, belonged to the "Great Father in the Sky." The Mannitoo or Supreme Being only allowed the use of the land and everything else if you showed good stewardship over it. If you respected it and took great care of it, generations would be allowed to use it, but no man owned land.

The white man had a similar belief that everything belonged t God, except the Earth. White men believed that God had given there ownership of the Earth and all things on it. Ownership of land of the own was a dream come true. It remains the American dream to own place of your own.

It is taught in the History books that the Dutch bought Manhatta Island for about four dollars worth of glass beads. We were taught that the Indians must have been gullible to sell their land so cheap. The is no evidence that this is true. Assuming it were true though, the Indians could buy it back today for a stack of worthless Federal Reserve Notes.

It's almost funny that four hundred years ago the Indians knew men could not own land, but you go on the Reservations today they say, "Get off my land." They have been cultured in the teachings of the white men, and their clear vision has been corrupted. Now, they see only the same illusions the rest of us do.

In March of 2005, the Onondaga Indian Nation laid claim to the City of Syracuse, N.Y. as well as thousands more square miles of upstate New York, in a federal lawsuit.

Leaders of the 1,500 member tribe say they want the state to clean up hazardous sites in the land-claim area, specifically a lake they consider sacred that is among the worlds most polluted bodies of water.

"Our concern is for the water, the land, the air. They are not well." Said Sid Hill, the tribe's spiritual leader. "It is the duty of the nation's leaders to work for a healing of this land, to protect it, and to pass it on to future generations."

The lawsuit lays claim to Onondaga Lake, regarded as the birth place of the Iroquois Confederacy. It appears they can see past part of the illusion of ownership, and they wish to show stewardship over the area. Maybe there is hope for all of us.

All the wealth on this planet has always been here, and after we are gone, it will still be here. What fools we must be to think we can own it.

Rich people do not like being told they're not rich, and they especially don't like being told they don't own the big houses and land they think they do. If you think you own that house just stop paying the property taxes on it and see how long you keep control of it. Every one of the 50 states has some kind of property tax.

Tax Americana!

This tax is really the rent you pay the Government for the use of the land. The land you think you own really belongs to the city, country, and state, and country that really control it. Don't think this is true? Just try to build what you want on your property.

You will find out that what you can build, where on your parcel of land it can be built, is all controlled by ordinances. These are local laws that govern what you thought was your property. Want to build an eight foot high privacy fence? Sorry, city ordinance says you can only build a six foot high fence, and that is in the back yard. Front yard fences are to be no more than four feet tall.

What? If it's truly yours, you should be able to build on it what you want, but you can't. Why can't you? It isn't really yours.

This reminds me of a story. A man bought a spot of land on a hillside. He built what is known as an earth home. It was built in two weeks, mostly of cement, and buried on all but the south side by four feet of dirt. It was so super insulated and efficient with passive solar design, that it cost only eight dollars a month for heat in winter.

When he went to pay his taxes on the property he was asked if he had made any improvements. He told them yes, that in fact he had built a house on it.

The clerk did not find any building permits, no inspection reports from the building inspector, or any other paperwork to indicate a house had been built. An inspector was immediately dispatched to the address. The house wasn't built up to code.

In that area, 75% of the house must be above ground level. Each structure must be at least 1750 square feet, this was less than 800 square feet, and it was nearly all below ground level.

Not only was the man given a fine for building without a permit (city permission), also not building to code for that rea (city instructions on what you can build), he was ordered to tear the house down. The city condemned the property immediately. How ridiculous, a perfectly good, high efficient, inexpensive house, had to be torn down. Why? You didn't ask the city how you could build it, or if you could build at all, on "your land."

If It were really yours, you could do with it what you want. But you can't. If it isn't the government its environmentalists or some other puppet group that stops you. You can't put a gold mine here, you'll ruin the environment. Translation, you can't put a gold mine here, you'll have gold.

Incidentally, I pay more every year in property taxes than my mother paid for a four bedroom house in 1970. If property taxes continue to rise at current rates. I will have paid the Government the same amount of money I paid the bank for my property.

Here's another thing. We already know that there is no money. Money equals nothing. So if you gave money (nothing), for your property, how can you own it? And it's useless to complain about the high property taxes, since you also pay with worthless Federal Reserve Note currency. Really you pay nothing for the property or the tax, so don't sweat it. Just understand it's part of the money matrix. Looks good, works well, has flaws, now real.

I live in the state of Montana. The state government just passed a law to make it a crime to smoke in publick buildings. To me, public buildings are buildings owned by the public, we the people. To the government, public buildings are any buildings open to the public, such as stores, bars, café's etc...

It seems to me that buildings owned by a private enterprise for making a profit is their business and government has no right to tell them what they can or can't do in their own building. All except for two things, there is no money so how can a private business earn a profit? Secondly, you can't own land, so the government can tell you what you can or can't do in the building they lease out to you.

A friend of mine runs a micro business out of this own home. I pointed out to him that the new law makes his house a place of business, therefore it is a public building, and he can no longer have a cigarette in his own home. It seems the term, your own home, is really an oxymoron! Being king of your castle becomes a moat point.

A friend of mine pointed out that in the bible, people had an absolute right to their property. The Law of Moses said, "Thou shalt not steal." I asked my friend how can you steal something that doesn't belong to anyone? It becomes a matter of, don't steal, the government hates competition.

Then there is the story about my brother. My mother contacted me, urging me to talk to my brother Herb. It seemed that he was going crazy. He had taken out a loan on his house, and was giving the money away.

I told my mother, "There is no money, so how can he be giving any away?"

She told me Herb was buying poor people food and clothing, paying for them to take trips to visit relatives in other states, buying gas for strangers at the gas station, and other crazy things.

I said, "It looks to me like he is doing a lot of good, so what's the problem?"

"Your brother took out a loan on his house and he'll have to pay it back." She yelled.

"Pay what back?" I asked

"The money!" she insisted.

"There is no money." I said "How can you give nothing back for the nothing you got in the first place?"

My mother said the sheriff would go to the bank and draw all my brother's money out.

I said, "Is there a law against giving away Federal Reserve Notes? Hey, you can't give that away, I'm taking it!" That's ridiculous!

Mom said, "They'll take his house away if he doesn't repay the loan."

I said, "He didn't own it in the first place."

Mom said, "Don't you understand? In the end, your brother will have nothing!""

I said, "In the end, we" all have nothing, Herb realizes it now!"

My mother was mostly upset because Herb wasn't giving his money to her.

My friend Clyde told me his ex-wife was the best house keeper he ever met. They had five houses, and when they got divorced she kept four of them.

Then there is Eminent Domain. The government reserves the right to take your property for the public good. This usually occurs when a road is built through your property. More recently, in June 2005, the U.S. Supreme Court decided the Government can seize property to be turned over to private contractors or developers, if what they would build would be a benefit to the public more than your house. How could they do this if you owned your land? You can't own land, and

Eminent Domain is the proof of it.

With Eminent Domain, you must be given just compensation for your property, This is usually one fourth of what it would have sold for on the open market, not very just.

One fellow asked where the Judge lived. He said, "If you want my house so bad, I'll trade my house for yours."

The Judge said, "That's ridiculous, my house is worth much more than yours."

"Apparently not," the man said "Nobody wants to take your house away."

The Judge didn't want to lose his house, but it was alright to take someone else's. What a hypocrite. It sounded like just compensation to me, a house for a house.

I'm not saying that land isn't valuable, because it is. It has value for raising food and lumber and grazing livestock and to build buildings on. Land has real value, thus, the name "Real Estate." What I'm saying

Is, you can't own its value. You may only use it for the time you are alive here.

The prostitute said it was her streetcorner. Land Ho!

CHAPTER 9

YOU WORK FOR NOTHING

"While boasting of our noble deeds we're careful to conceal the ugly fact that by an iniquitous money system we have nationalized a system of oppression which, though more refined, is not less cruel than the old system of chattel slavery." – Horace Greeley

"To be controlled in our economic pursuits means to be controlled in everything." – Fredrich August von Hayek

When my son told me he wanted to get a different job so he could earn more money, I told him, "What difference does it make, there is no money." WE already know that there is no money. The unit of account of the United States is a unit of weight. The weight is measured as a one ounce silver coin called a dollar.

We no longer use silver dollars; we use worthless Federal Reserve Note fiat currency. Federal Reserve Notes are a space age currency, weightless, and valueless. So if you are being paid in Federal Reserve Notes, you are working for nothing.

This is a free country. You work for free. That's the bad news. The good news it, so does everybody else. Why would you want to pay real money to people if they are willing to work for nothing? It's a free market economy. They don't call America the land of the free for nothing.

The flip side of this is that everything you buy, you also get for free. Free market. Get it? You take the Federal Reserve Notes (nothing), you earned and spend it on food at the local market. You also pay Federal Reserve Notes (nothing), for your electricity, water, car gas, rent you name it. If you give nothing for it, you get it for free.

At the job interview, I asked what the pay was. They said it was ten dollars an hour. I asked if they paid in Federal Reserve Notes, or silver dollars, because if it were silver dollars, I'd work for two dollars an hour. They laughed and said they would too! It just goes to show you that inflation is as artificial as Federal Reserve Notes.

In my early years, I was up for promotion. I had more education and experience than any of my competitors, so I was sure I would get promoted. I worked my butt off. The promotion went to the young lady with the nice butt. I was upset at the time naturally. My good friend Lou Crouch told me, "If at first you don't suck seed, suck again, only harder."

I'm sure she worked her butt to the bone, the boss' bone.

My friend Higgins told me, "Time is money."

I said, "It, must be, I work for eight hours a day."

He said, "If you give me a minute, I'll share a secret with you."

That caused me to spend a lot of time with Higgins, learning his secrets. Higgins asked how much money per hour I was making at the time. It was $5 an hour. So in an eight hour day, I earned 40 dollars

Before taxes, 5x8 = 40. Higgins asked how much I would like to earn, $6 an hour would be nice. Higgins told me to be at work for 8 hours, but only work 7 hours. That way I still got 40 dollars a day, but I worked one hour less to get it, which gave me a raise to almost $6 an hour, 40 +7 = 5.71 per hour.

Higgins encouraged me to screw off on the job for an hour each day. If you work too hard, you're hard to replace in a production job. Produce less and your chances of moving up in a company improve. Although you have no more money at the end of the day than you ever did, you didn't have to work as hard for it.

I was warned by another person in management that if I screwed off on the job it would be theft of time, and that could make me lose my job.

How can you steal time? You can't hold time in your hand. Time is a continuum which lacks spatial dimensions. It is a unit of measure between events, like an inch is a measure of distance, but you can't hold an inch. Money is not wealth, but is a measure of valuable things. In truth, you can't hold money either. Coins or Federal Reserve Notes are like a ruler, a thermometer, or a watch. They are the measuring tools, not the thing they are measuring.

I told the manager that if I were fired for theft of time, I would sue the company for theft of service for accepting my labor and giving me worthless Federal Reserve Notes (nothing) in return!

Think about it. The doctor will see you now. He sees you for about a minute and you get a bill for sixty dollars. Psychiatrists charge hundreds of dollars an hour to listen to you talk. Nobody would listen to you for free? A supervisor sits at a desk or walks around, and to anyone's perspective work less than the workers, and yet is paid more money.

Since money = nothing, they are really only getting more nothing than you are. Why would you work harder if you're getting more nothing for it? IF you're going to pay me more nothing, I'm going to do nothing more for it!

Higgins said time is money, so be careful how you spend it. You can spend it working yourself to death, miserable all the way. Or you can spend it laughing with friends and family. It's your decision.

You get your money for nothing and your checks for free. I got my bonus. A bonus is free nothing. You go for the green and end up in the hole. A penny saved is a penny earned, if I only had a penny to save.

So why do people really want more money? They don't. They want to work less. Hell, I can do that now! People like being the boss for the power it gives them over the other workers. "Do as I say or I'll fire you," they say.

Go ahead and fire me, if I'm being paid nothing (worthless

Federal Reserve Notes) anyway, what difference should it make to me? I'll get another job or start my own business doing what I want to do.

Some people told me, "I can't do what I want, I can't afford to go to college!" Go get a student loan. If there is no money, don't let the lack of nothing keep you from learning what you want. When you graduate and get a job or start a business in your new field that you enjoy, pay the loan off with the nothing you'll be earning.

If you're being paid nothing anyway, you should at least be doing something you enjoy. Don't stay in a rotten job just because it "Pays well." They all really pay the same nothing. Want to make a little nothing or a whole lot of nothing, it really doesn't make you happier. Do what you like doing.

Some people told me they couldn't start their own business because they didn't have enough money. Again, get a bank loan. That's what banks are there for is to create out of thin air fiat debt currency. They have nothing to lose. If you succeed, you'll pay them back. If you fail. They will take your business, which wasn't really yours in the first place. At least you get to work doing what you want. The bankers will lend you the money (nothing). Nothing ventured, nothing gained!

The prostitute said she had sex for money. If you give Federal Reserve Notes for it, it's free sex. He told the hooker, "Please accept this $100 as a 'token' of my appreciation." When the prostitute tried to deposit the $100 bill into her bank account, the teller said, "We can't accept this it's counterfeit!"

The prostitute said, "Oh my God, I've been raped!"

The thousand dollar a night hooker showed him a grand time.

The porn starlet said her job was a labor of love. The man who sold sperm to the sperm bank liquidated his liquid assets.

Will work for Federal Reserve Notes!

CHAPTER 10

RELIGION AND MONEY

"Woe unto you, ye blind guides, which say, whoever shall swear by the temple, it is nothing; but whoever shall swear by the gold of the temple, he is a debtor!" – Jesus of Nazareth

It seems that every time I get into a discussion about money, someone quotes the "Bible." Some of the time they are correct, and some of the time they are quoting a movie line or someone elese, truly believing it is in the "Bible." Therefore it is only fitting that we take this opportunity to see just what The Bible does say about poverty, greed, and wealth or money, and gambling.

My mother always told me not to gamble, because gambling was a sin. The word "Gambling" is not used in The Bible. Scripture does however condemn the practice of gambling in many passages.

Gambling is defined in the dictionary as: To play a game of chance for stakes or money with an element of risk. In Mark 12:31, Jesus commanded, "Love your neighbor as yourself." Gambling is based on loss and pain and suffering of the many losers, so that the few may win.

Exodus 20:17, The 10th Commandment, "Covetousness," prohibits coveting another's possessions. Gambling is the attempt to get the resources of others without providing anything of value for them. It could be described as consensual theft. It is the desperate poor, those who earn less than $10,000, that buy the most lottery tickets. According to the IRS, this same low income group donates a higher percentage of their earning to charity than any other income group.

Gambling is based on greed, with the false hope of getting rich without effort. We are to invest our energy and time into labors that supply our needs and those of our families. (Proverbs 31,2 Thessalonians 3:10, 1 Timothy 5:8) Abundance allows us to share with others, Ephesians 4:28.

It is our responsibility to invest the resources God has entrusted to us, as the parable of the talents makes clear. (Matthew 25:14-30) Money spent on gambling is money that should have gone to provide for the well-being of our family, or at least the advancement of a worthy cause. Gambling is an unwise investment with an almost certain guarantee of loss.

I call the lottery the Stupid Tax!

Gambling is an addiction. "For speaking our arrogant words of vanity they entice by fleshly desires, by sensuality, those who barely escape from the ones who live in error, promising them freedom while they themselves are slaves of corruption; for by what a man is overcome, by this he is enslaved. (2 Peter 2:18-19)

Gambling leads to many other vices to support the addiction. "Evil companionships corrupt good morals." (1 Corinthians 15:33) "Avoid every kind of evil." (1 Thessalonians 5:22)

God ordained the purpose of government to protect the welfare of the citizenry and to suppress evil. (Romans 13:1-5) Many states have become more and more dependant on the taxes and revenues from gambling.

If you walk with the Devil, you will certainly go to hell!

One thing I should like to point out on this subject is that by definition, gambling is trying to get something for nothing. Since we don't have money anymore, only worthless Federal Reserve Notes, which equal nothing, when you gamble using Federal Reserve Note debt currency, you are really trying to get more nothing for nothing. So, in the absence of real money, it's not gambling! Nothing ventured, nothing gained, nothing lost. Money as we know it equals nothing.

Gamble your Federal Reserve Notes all you want, it means nothing to me.

So, what does the Bible say about the poor? "For ye know the grace of our Lord Jesus Christ, that, though he was rich, for your sakes he became poor, that ye through his poverty might become rich." (2 Corinthians 8:9) Few people realize that Jesus was born into one of the wealthiest families in the Middle East at that time. Joseph and his brother ran a shipping business with large camel caravans and boats.

Jesus traveled the known world from Rome to India. Yet Jesus after having it all, gave it all up. Less than three years later Jesus was crucified. They had to make an example out of him for setting a good example.

God commanded his people to care for the poor. Those in poverty must be treated with kindness. Deuteronomy 15:8, "You should rather open your hand, willing lending enough to meet the need. Whatever it may be." Leviticus 19:10, "The poor must be allowed to glean in the vineyards."

The year of Jubilee was intended to be of great benefit to the poor by restoring to them possessions which they, by reason of their poverty, had been compelled to deed over to creditors. (Leviticus 25: 25-54, Deuteronomy 15: 12-15) This was in fact the basics of modern day bankruptcy laws. Jubilee occurred every seven years. Once you file bankruptcy, you are not allowed to discharge your debts with bankruptcy again for seven years. Sadly, the greedy bankers have bought enough of Congress to make it harder for people to file bankruptcy.

I looked at the rich man and said, "There but for the grace of God go I."

God required certain tithes of his people which were to be devoted to the helping of the poor and needy. (Deuteronomy 26: 12, 13) The New Testament teaches the Christian to give of his free will unto God and the church. (1 Corinthians 16: 1-2)

This reminds me of a couple of stories. Years ago, my wife and I attended church regularly. The church elders noticed we rarely paid tithes or put money into the offering plate that was passed around. We explained that we barely had enough to make ends meet as it was, without giving 10% to the church. We thought we were too poor to pay the tithes.

The elders of the church said that if we paid the tithes the Lord would bless us and we would prosper. I asked them why the Lord didn't bless us with prosperity so we could pay the tithes. They didn't like my attitude, so we stopped going to church.

About two months later, an elder from the church called my wife and asked why we hadn't been to services. She explained that we were embarrassed by not having the money to pay tithes. This was an excellent opportunity for the elder to say. "We don't want your money, we want your souls. If you are in need, the church will help see you through this rough time."

That's not what happened though. The elder said, "Oh, that's too bad. Well, when you get some money don't forget where we are."

My wife said, "I won't forget this!" We never returned to church.

It seems that all denominations were welcome. Hundreds, fifties, twenties, tens, fives, one! Whatever happened to each should give according to their abilities?

FRN are an obligation of the U.S. Govt., but what are they obligated to pay them with? Faith! Which faith pays best, Catholics or Protestants?

Another story is when I worked at a church run hospital. That year, the Nuns had decided that for Christmas, they would get names from the local charities of poor families, with the intention of helping them. TO their surprise, half of the names on the list were employees of their hospital.

When they showed up at my mobile home with the food and clothing and gifts, the Nuns were as surprised to see me as I was to see them.

I said, "You know Sister, If I were paid more, I could support my own family."

Things changed after that. We all got substantial pay increases. The hospital didn't go broke, in fact they prospered.

Another story involves my brother Herb and his girlfriend. They traveled from Minneapolis to New York in the winter in search of jobs. They didn't find any employment and their funds ran out after a couple of weeks. They were stranded. Herb suggested they ask for help from the church so they could go back to Minneapolis.

His girlfriend was a Catholic, and insisted that if they went to a church for help, it should be a Catholic church. At the church, the Father told them that the church didn't have any money. Even if they did, they wouldn't give it to strangers not of their own congregation. The Father would say a prayer for them though.

Herb found a Baptist church run by a Reverend that was black. After hearing their story, and how the Catholics would not help them, they got help. Even though they were not black, or even from the local congregation, the Reverend fed them, gave them new coats, bought them bus tickets to Minneapolis, gave them money for food on the trip, and saw them off at the bus station.

Thank God that Catholic Father said a prayer for them! Otherwise that Baptist Reverend might not have helped them. Tithes are given to help the poor and needy.

And the Bible does not say that the helping of the poor and needy is limited to the local congregations, to any specific religion, political belief, country, or skin color.

A friend of mine that used to help me, stopped because I didn't attend the same church he did. I guess the true meaning of a friend is someone who will help you knowing full well you have nothing to give them in return. I had nothing, only friendship. Sorry folks, the friendship sailed without me.

Here are some other scriptures concerning the poor. Galatians 2:10, "They asked only one thing, that we remember the poor, which was actually what I was eager to do." Proverbs 10:15, "The wealth of the rich is their fortress; the poverty of the poor is their ruin."

Matthew 5:3-9 "Blessed are the poor in spirit, for theirs is the Kingdom of heaven. Blessed are these who mourn, for they will be comforted. Blessed are the meek, for they will inherit the earth. Blessed are those who hunger and thirst for righteousness, for the will be filled. Blessed are the merciful, for they will receive mercy. Blessed are the pure in heart, for they will see God. Blessed are the peace makers, for they will be called children of God."

Luke 1:53, "He has filled the hungry with good things and sent the rich away empty." Job 5:12, "He frustrates the devices of the crafty, so that their hands achieve no success." Job 5:16, "So the poor have hope, and injustice shuts its mouth. "Deuteronomy 15:8, "You should rather open your hand, willingly lending enough to meet the need, whatever it may be."

Psalms 70:5, "But I am poor and needy; hasten to me O God! You are my help and my deliverer; O Lord, do not delay!" Romans 12:6, "We have gifts that differ according to the grace given us: prophecy, in proportion to faith."

Matthew 6:3,4, "But when you give alms, do not let your left hand know what your right hand is doing, so that your alms may be done in secret; and your Father who sees in secret will reward you."

Proverbs 14:20-21, "The poor are disliked by even their neighbors, but the rich have many friends. Those who despise their neighbors are sinners, but happy are those who are kind to the poor."

Proverbs 19:17, "Whoever is kind to the poor lends to the Lord, and will be repaid in full."

Psalms 40:17, "As for me, I am poor and needy. But the lord takes thought for me. You are my help and my deliverer, do not delay O my God."

Psalms 9:18, "For the needy shall not always be forgotten, nor the hope of the poor perish forever."

Ecclesiastes 9:15, 16, "Now there was found in it a poor wise man, and he by his wisdom delivered the city. Yet no one remembered that poor man. So I said, 'Wisdom is better than might, yet the poor man's wisdom is despised, and his words are not heeded.' "

"You always have the poor with you, but you do not always have me."
— Jesus of Nazareth

Here is a good question for you. What makes people poor? Bankers with their excessive interest on loans are one cause. This was called usury (Nehemiah 5:1-5). Glutton brings on poverty, (Proverbs 23:21). And greed brings on poverty.

So what does the Bible say about greed, money, and the rich? Plenty! The dictionary defines greed as: excessive or reprehensible acquisitiveness. This reminds me of the "7 Deadly Sins."

1. Pride - The excessive belief in one's own abilities also known as vanity.
2. Envy – The desire for other traits, status, abilities, or situation.
3. Gluttony – An inordinate desire to consume more than that which is required.
4. Lust – Craving for pleasures of the body.
5. Anger – Instead of love, one manifests fury and wrath.
6. Greed – The desire for material wealth.
7. Sloth – The avoidance of work.

At a recent conference it was determined that greed is by far the worst of the 7 deadly sins, and the root from which the others spring. It is my opinion that greed and gluttony walk hand in hand.

Luke 1:53, "He has filled the hungry with good things and sent the rich away empty." It is obvious that if money equals nothing, then the rich are empty. With all their nothingness how could they be anything except empty?

Psalms 39:6, "Surely every man walks about as a phantom, surely they make an aproar for nothing. He amasses riches and does not know who will gather them." Again, money equals nothing and it says men will make an uproar for "nothing."

Proverbs 11:6, "The treacherous are caught by their own greed." Jeremiah 6:13; 8:10, "Everyone is greedy for gain." Luke 12:15, "be on guard against every form of greed; life is not in possessions."

Hebrews 13:5, "Keep your life free from the love of money, and be content with what you have." Money equals nothing, so the love of money is the love of nothing! What could be worse than that?

Psalms 37:7, 16, "Rest in the lord and wait patiently for Him; Do not fret of him who prospers in his way... Better is the little of the righteous than the abundance of many wicked."

Proverbs 23:4-5, "Do not wear yourself out to get rich, have the wisdom to show restraint. Cast but a glance at riches, and they are gone, for they will surely sprout wings and fly off to the sky like an eagle."

Don't spend all your time working to get rich or you'll certainly miss the riches of your children growing up and your own family. A rich man is an empty man, but a poor family man is full.

Proverbs 30:8-9, "Give me neither poverty nor riches, but give me only my daily bread. Otherwise, I may have too much and disown you and say, 'Who is the Lord?' Or I may become poor and steal, and so dishonor the name of my God."

Philippians 4-11-13, "For I have learned to be content, whatever the circumstances may be. I know now how to live when things are difficult and I know how to live when things are prosperous. In general and in particular I have learned the secret of eating well or going hungry, of facing either plenty or poverty. I am ready for anything through the strength of the One who lives within me."

Mark 10:21-27, 31, "Jesus looked steadily at him and loved him, and he said, "There is one thing you lack. Go and sell everything you own and give to the poor, and you will have treasure in heaven;

then come, follow me.' But his face fell at these words and he went away sad, for he was a man of wealth. Jesus looked around and said to his disciples, 'How hard is it for those who have riches to enter the kingdom of God?' The disciples were astounded by these words, but Jesus insisted, 'My children,' he said to them, 'how hard is it to enter the Kingdom of God? It is easier for a camel to pass through the eye of a needle than for a rich man to enter the Kingdom of God.' They were more astonished than ever."

"In that case, "they said to one another, "Who can be saved?"

Jesus gazed at them. "For men," he said, "it is impossible, but not for God: because everything is possible for God... Many who are first will be last, and the last first."

Acts 4:32, 34-35, "All the believers were one in heart and mind. No one claimed that any of his possessions was his own, but they shared everything they had... There were no needy persons among them. For from time to time those who owned lands or houses sold them, brought the money from the sales and put it at the apostles' feet, and it was distributed to anyone as he had need."

Acts 2:44-45, "All the believers joined together and shared everything in common; they sold their possessions and goods and divided the proceeds among the fellowship according to individual need."

Proverbs 11:4,28, "Wealth is worthless in the day of wrath, but righteousness delivers from death.... Whoever trusts in his riches will fall...." Maybe this is why on Federal Reserve Notes it says "In God We Trust."

Luke 8:14 "And the seed sown among the thorns represents the people who hear the message and go on their way, and with the worries and riches and pleasures of living the life is choked out of them, and in the end they produce nothing." Money equals nothing.

Luke 9:25, "What good is it for a man to gain the whole world, yet lose or forfeit his very self?"

Luke 6:30, "Give to everyone who asks you, and do not ask for your property back from the man who robs you."

Luke 3:11, "John answered, "The man with two tunics should share with him who has none, and the one who has food should do the same."

Luke 14:33, "Concluded Jesus, 'None of you can be my disciple unless he gives up everything he has."

I gave all my money to the church because they told me only Jesus saves.

Luke 16:9-11 "Now my advice to you is to use money, tainted as it is, to make yourselves friends, so that when it comes to an end, they may welcome you into the houses of eternity. The man who is faithful in the little things will be faithful in the big things. So that if you are not fit to be trusted with the wicked wealth of this world, who will trust you with true riches?"

Matthew 6:24, "No one can serve two masters. Either he will hate the one and love the other, or he will be devoted to the one and despise the other. You cannot serve Both God and Money."

Luke 12:15-21, "Be on your guard against covetousness in any shape or form. For a man's real life in no way depends upon the number of his possessions... A rich man's farmland produced heavy crops. So he said to himself, 'What shall I do, for I have no room to store this harvest of mine?' Then he said, 'I know what I'll do. I'll pull down my barns and build bigger ones where I can store all my grain and goods and I can say to my soul, Soul, you have plenty of good things stored up there for years to come. Relax! Eat, drink, and have a good time!' But God said to him, "You fool, this very night you will be asked for YOUR SOUL!..." That is what happens to the man who hoards things for himself and is not rich in the eyes of God."

Luke 16:19-31, "There was a rich man who was dressed in purple and fine linen and lived in luxury every day. At his gate was laid a beggar named Lazarus... The beggar died and angels carried him to Abraham's side. The rich man also died... In hell, where he was in torment, he looked up... 'I am in agony in this fire.' But Abraham replied, "Son, remember that in your lifetime you received your good things, while Lazarus received bad things, but now he is comforted here and you are in agony..." "Then I beg you... I have five brothers... warn them so that they will not come to thi s place of torment.' 'They have Moses and the Prophets, let them listen to them.'"

Psalms 49:16-19, "Do not be overawed when a man grows rich, when the splender of his house increases; for he will take nothing with him when he dies, his splender will not descend with him. Though while he lived he counted himself blessed, and men praise you when you prosper, he will join the generations of his fathers, who will never see the light of life."

Hebrews 13:5, "Keep your lives free from the love of money and be content with what you have, because God has said, 'Never will I leave you; never will I forsake you.'"

Corinthians 6:10, "Nor thieves nor the greedy nor drunkards nor slanders nor swindlers will inherit the Kingdom of God."

Ecclesiates 5:10-15, "Whoever loves money never has enough; whoever loves wealth is never satisfied with his income. This too is meaningless. As goods increase, so do those who consume them. And what benefit are they to the owner except to feast your eyes on them? The sleep of the laborer is sweet, whether he eats little or much, but the abundance of a rich man permits him no sleep. I have seen a grievous evil under the sun: wealth hoarded to the harm of its owner, or wealth lost through some misfortune... Naked a man comes from his mother's womb, and as he comes, so he departs..."

1 Timothy 6:5-9, "Men who have been robbed of the truth and who think that godliness is a means to financial gain. But godliness with contentment is great gain. For we brought nothing into the world, and we can take nothing out of it. But if we have food and clothing, we will be content with that. People who want to get rich fall into temptation and a trap and into many foolish and harmful desires that plague men into ruin and destruction."

1 Timothy 6:10-12, "For the love of money is a root of all kinds

of evil. Some people, eager for money have wandered from the faith and pierced themselves through with many griefs. But you, man of God, flee from all this, and pursue righteousness, godliness, faith, love, endurance and gentleness."

James 1:11, "For the sun rises with scorching heat and withers the plant; its blossom falls and its beauty is destroyed. In the same way, the rich man will fade away even while he goes about his business."

James 1:9-11, "It is right for the poor brother to be proud of his rank, and the rich one to be thankful that he has been humbled, because riches last no longer than the flowers in the grass; the scorching sun comes up, and the grass withers, the flower fall; what looked so beautiful now disappears. It is the same with the rich man: his business goes on; he himself perishes."

It is like I said earlier, all the wealth on this planet has always been here, and it will be here after we are gone. We are only stewards of it while we are alive.

James 5:1-3, 5, "And now, you rich people, listen to me! Weep and wail over the miseries that are coming upon you! Your riches have rotted away, and your clothes have been eaten by moths. Your gold and silver are covered with rust, and this rust will be a witness against you, and eat up your flesh like fire. You have piled up riches in these last days...Your life here on earth has been full of luxury and pleasure. You have made yourselves fat for the day of slaughter."

Matthew 19:23, "Then Jesus said to his disciple, 'I tell you the truth, it is hard for a rich man to enter the Kingdom of heaven.' "

Revelations 3:17-19, "While you say, 'I am rich, I have prospered, and there is nothing that I need,' you have no eyes to see you are wretched, pitiable, poverty-stricken, blind and naked. My advice to you is to buy from me that gold which is refined in the furnace so that you may be rich, and white garments to wear so that you may hide that shame of your nakedness, and salve to put on your eyes to make you see. All those whom I love I correct and discipline. Therefore, shake off your complacency and repent."

1 Timothy 6:8-10, "Surely then, as far as physical things are concerned, it is sufficient for us to keep our bodies fed and clothed. For men who set their hearts on being wealthy expose themselves to temptations. They fall into a trap and lay themselves open to all sorts of silly and wicked desires, which are quite capable of utterly running and destroying their souls. For loving money leads to all kinds of evil and some men in the struggle to be rich have lost their faith and caused themselves untold agonies of mind."

Luke 12:47-48, "That servant who knows his master's will and does not get ready or does not do what his master wants will be beaten with many blows. But the one who does not know and does things deserving punishment will be beaten with few blows. From everyone who has been given much, much will be demanded; and from the one who has been entrusted with much, much more will be asked."

So why are we so obsessed with greed? Part of it is simply that it is thrust in our faces on a daily basis. The tabloids follow celebrities and inform us of the extravagance of their lives. The TV used to show

"Lifestyles of the Rich and Famous." It makes poor people want to be those people.

At this time, I am going to pick on some of these rich public figures. At the top of my list is Martha Stewart. She got caught cheating with insider trading on stock. It's not enough that she is a billionaire, after you amass your greed you have to protect it. Heaven forbid that she might lose a million or two.

Greed is a powerful motivator, but fear is ten times as powerful. Fear of losing a little of her fortune made her do a bad thing. She of course said she did nothing wrong. Of course she did something wrong, she cheated, and when you cheat for financial gain you are stealing from other people who will lose because of the cheating.

Someone that "rich" finds it necessary to steal from the poor to maintain her lavish lifestyle. And then lie about it, and then say she did nothing wrong made me lose all respect for her.

Now, if she would have said, "I didn't do anything any other greedy bitch wouldn't have done," I would have some respect for her telling the truth. That didn't happen though.

Next on my list is Shaq, with his extra-large garage full of luxury autos. Why does anyone need more than one luxury auto? You can only drive one at a time. Some people don't have one auto, and other people don't have a garage. In my opinion he is driven. His chauffer is called greed, and he is driven by greed to hoard luxury autos.

Why does Oprah need eight mansions? You can only live in one at a time. In my opinion she suffers from greed and gluttony. And that stunt of giving away cars to needy people on her show, those cars were donated by Pontiac. She didn't use her Federal Reserve Notes to pay for them, but in a public relations coup they were handed out on her program.

Nice move Oprah, make people think you are so generous by giving away cars to needy people. If Oprah really wanted to help the needy, she wouldn't have eight mansions. Instead she should build apartments in Chicago for low income people, or what about the Oprah homeless shelters?

Oprah is the queen of self help, but what it seems she's best at is helping herself. In my opinion, Oprah is a "Wealth Monger!" The black hole of greed inside wealth mongers has them sucking up every available resource whether they need it or not. After you have more than you will ever need, why would you need more than you will ever need? It is greed at its ultimate ridiculousness.

Oprah says she needs these resources to help other people to reach their dreams. Has it ever occurred to her that while she was sucking up more resources than she needs, she was preventing other people from achieving their dreams and goals for lack of resources that she was sucking up more than she needs?

It was pointed out to me that Oprah even created her own religion. This can be found on the internet at "Oprah's religion.com." It states that Oprah is not a Christian and does not believe in hell. This is her way of clearing her conscience so she doesn't feel shame or guilt for her excessive greed. Instead of donating to a church, she can donate to herself and feel good about it. How greedy do you have to be to put yourself before God and start your own religion so you can keep more of your greed for yourself?

If Oprah is an anti Christian, doesn't that also make her an "Anti-

Christ?" How many of Oprah's 20 million viewers are Christian? I'll bet they don't know the truth. It is obvious the Money Matrix has her!

And another thing that bothers me is the way Hollywood throws Federal Reserve Notes at people that are already filthy rich, like Paris Hilton or Anna Nicole Smith. There are good actors and actresses starving while rich people who can't act get a TV series.

I don't want to see any of those videos of rich celebrities having sex with their ex-lover, like Paris or Pamela Anderson with her perfectly fake body. Instead, how about a video of these people taking a crap, or throwing up after a night of boozing it up just like normal people. I'm sure it would gross millions! Feed more greed to the greedy.

The late Linda McCartney said in an interview before her death, that when she was younger she was a very material oriented person, wanting many nice things. But at that point in her life the material things didn't mean anything anymore.

That's easy to say once you already have everything. That's just logic. You want something until you get it and then you don't want it anymore because you have it. The want urge is satisfied. That's like saying, "I used to be hungry, but after I ate till I was full I suddenly didn't feel hungry anymore!" Duh!

On the flip side of all this greed by the rich and famous, there are also excellent examples of giving. Ted Turner gave a billion dollars to the United Nations to help the needy. Wow!

Angelina Jolie is an activist to the poorest of peoples in the world. She puts her Federal Reserve Notes where her heart is, and her heart is in the right place. My hat is off to her and all the good she does. She gave 1.5 million to Cambodian Vision in development for environmental protection. She wants to build schools in Africa because education is important.

Singer songwriter Billy Joel got a standing ovation from the graduating class at Syracuse University. He told them, "Don't do it for security or status, prestige, money, or for crying out loud, don't do it for somebody else. Do it for love. Because if you love what you do, you'll always do what you love." In one of his early song he sings about greed.

Bill Gates, the "richest" man in the world as of this writing, donates to many good causes. Not only are his products responsible for the productivity gains, and thereby the economic gains of the U.S. for the past 20 years, he is also generous. He gave 104 million dollars for AIDS research. Donald Trump also gives millions to AIDS research.

It reminds me of Andrew Carnegie when he was the richest man alive. He said before he died, he intended to give it all away. And he did! He built libraries and hospitals and other good works that carry his name even today.

In a country with as much abundance as the United States, it should be a crime for anyone to go to bed hungry. Yet sadly, 20% of Americans don't get enough to eat on a daily basis. Think about that, with nearly three hundred million people in the United States that means that nearly sixty million people go hungry every day!

Why? It certainly isn't from a lack of food. We throw away more than enough food to feed these people. I'll tell you why, they didn't have the money to buy the food. Plenty of food, but the plenty of poor lack the means to pay for it. Sorry folks, we'll have to throw it away because it rotted while you starved for a lack of money.

Then there are the poor that deserve to starve. These are the people who waste their resources on drugs, alcohol, cigarettes, gambling, and other foolishness. It's hard to feel sorry for those who bring the lack of abundance on themselves with foolishness.

Then there are the lazy who will not work. I have a brother like this, living in a house for free that my mother provides for him. His girlfriend supports him as he sits at his computer all day trying to find just the right get rich quick scheme to blow her Federal Reserve Notes on. He can't seem to figure out why after five years of trying every plan every thought of, that he still hasn't gotten rich quick.

I recommended that after five years of using a computer he must have acquired rather handy computer skills and could get a job using those skills. He got mad at me.

"If I got a job I'd have to pay taxes and I wouldn't earn enough money." he said.

A thousand dollars a month minus two hundred for taxes leaves eight hundred. Multiply that by sixty months (the estimated five years of doing nothing), and you have $48,000. Wow, I'm getting rich already. Yet he keeps throwing away currency on silly, foolish, get rich quick plans.

"If you are going to give your money to some asshole, you should use it as toilet paper." I told him.

It is my opinion that the biggest problem with greed is that there just isn't enough greed to go around.

How much greed can I have for me?

Speaking of taxes, what does the Bible say about taxes? Almost without exception when asked this question, the clergy refer to a passage in the Book of Matthew where Jesus tells people, "Give to Caesar what is Caesar's, and to God what is God's." The church always uses this to say that Jesus is telling us to pay tithes to the church in the, "Give to God what is God's," part. The Government always uses this to say that Jesus is telling us to pay taxes to the Government in the, "Give to Caesar what is Caesar's," part.

Some background needs to be examined as well as the full passage, to get a real grip on what Jesus was really saying. Jesus had to be careful what he said because a lot of the powers that be at the time wanted him dead. To avoid being arrested and executed before his mission was complete, he talked in parables and riddles.

The Pharisees were the enforcers of Jewish laws. One of these laws was that every Jew above the age of 20 was to pay for the support of the Temple in Jerusalem. This "Temple Tax" was called "Tribute." The tax was a Jewish half-Shekel, so money changers set up the tables in the Temple. When Jesus saw the unscrupulous dealings in the Temple, it resulted in his only recorded act of violence.

Mark 11: 15-17, "And they came to Jerusalem. And He entered the Temple and began to drive our those who sold and those who bought in the Temple, and He overturned the tables of the money-changers and seats of those who sold pigeons; and He would not allow anyone to carry anything through the Temple. And He taught, and said to them, 'Is it not written, "My house shall be called a house of prayer for all the nations?" But you have made it a den of robbers.'"

With this in mind, the Pharisees were out to get even with Jesus. He had told people not to pay the Temple Tax to these Pharisees who were lining their own pockets. They corrupted the meanings of the scriptures to enrich themselves. Now let us look at the infamous passage from the Book of Matthew.

Matthew 22: 17-21, "The Pharisees asked Jesus a question, "Tell us then, what is your opinion? Is it right to pay taxes to Caesar or not?' But Jesus, knowing their evil intent, said, 'You hypocrites, why are you trying to trap me? Show me the coin used for paying the tax. 'They brought him a denarius, and he asked them, 'Whose picture is this? And whose inscription?' 'Caesar's' they replied. Then he said to them, "Give to Caesar what is Caesar's, and to God what is God's."

It is easy to see that a connection could be made from this that Jesus was saying to pay tithes and taxes. However, Jesus had already turned the tables on the Temple money changers showing by his action that you should not be forced to pay Tribute. Also remember that Jesus used riddles when he spoke on tricky subjects that could have gotten him executed.

What might his riddle have really meant? To figure it out, we need to examine some other Bible passages.

The God-ordained purpose of Government, as outlined in Romans 13:1-5, is to protect the welfare of the citizenry and to suppress evil. Proverbs 29:4 remarks, "By just government a king gives his country stability, but by forced contributions he reduces it to ruin." This shows that forced taxation was regarded as unjust.

It reminds me of Winston Churchill's quote: "We contend that for a nation to try to tax itself into prosperity is like a man standing in a bucket and trying to lift himself up by the handle."

On the other side of the coin we have Haggai 2:8, "We are custodians of the goods of the world. The silver is mine, and the gold is mine, saith the Lord of hosts." All things belongs to God and out of his grace we are given use of them. 1 Timothy 6:17, "Command those who are rich in this present world not to be arrogant not to put their hope in wealth, which is so uncertain, but to put their hope in God, who richly provides us with everything for our enjoyment."

Ecclesiates 12:7, "Then shall the dust return to the earth as it was, and the spirit shall return unto God who gave it."

If we believe the Bible, God created every thing! Therefore, everything is already God's, even our spirits. And, God has provided us with everything for our enjoyment. How can you give God anything if it is all his already? You can't! You owe nothing but your love.

If everything is already God's, what is Caesar's? Nothing! So you owe Caesar nothing. In his little riddle, Jesus may well have been saying, don't pay taxes, and you can't give God what is already his, which he allows you to use so you can live an enjoyable life, so don't pay the church tithes either.

That's what I think. I would also ask the question today that Jesus asked them. Show me the money, oops! We don't have any money, only Federal Reserve Note debt currency, which is worth nothing.

Money can't buy you love, and it doesn't buy the miserable rich people happiness. It says in the Bible you reap what you sow.

II Corinthians 9:6, "He who sows sparingly will also reap sparingly, and he who sows bountifully will also reap bountifully." Luke 6:38, "Give and it shall be given to you... With the same measure that you use, it will be measured back to you."

Galatians 6:8, "For he who sows to flesh will reap corruption, but he who sows to the Spirit will reap everlasting life." Romans 2:5-6, "Paul taught that, 'In accordance with' the Jew's hard and impatient heart they were 'Treasuring up' the wrath of God. After all, God will 'render to each one according to his deeds.'"

This is Gods pure-positive law. Don't like your situation? Look in the mirror, because we are all a reflection of ourselves. Nobody loves you? How can they if you love nobody? Don't believe me. Try this. smile at someone and they smile back. Wave at someone and they wave back. Give them the finger, and they give you the finger back. Don't wait for them to go first, you go first. Be proactive.

We are really a simple organism with basic needs. You can't buy love, but you can give love. Give love and you become loveable. It's tough to be mean to a nice person. You have the power, whatever your situation, to change it by changing the way you treat the world first. Good things really do happen to good people.

If money is truly the root of all evil, and there is no money, the more people that realize this, the sooner evil will wither and die. If we are doing all the bad things to one another for something that doesn't exist, we are doing it for nothing. And if we're doing it for nothing that's just ridiculous.

Consider this, 90% of all arguments between couples are over money, 90% of all the deaths in the U.S. are due to heart attacks and strokes. Stress is a major factor in heart attacks and strokes. What causes 90% of the stress? Worry over money problems.

A friend of mine said the cure for the world's problems can't be that simple. Achoms Razor says that the simplest answer is usually the correct answer. Yes, it really is that simple.

There is no money! Stop killing one another for nothing! A friend of mine said that if there is no money and you can't own land, then he wanted control over it all.

"Why?" I asked. "What would you do with it?"

"I'd make farmers farm the land and workers work in the factories." He said.

"They already do that." I said.

"Yes, but it would be for me." He said.

"You cannot consume more than you already do." I said.

No one needs more than they need. Greed is stupid. There is no money, and we can change the world by changing ourselves. If you understand this, I have a message for you. Love your neighbor as you love yourself!

Perhaps money is God. It exists in our minds and is indestructible.

If you worship money, then FRN are a false God.

CHAPTER 11

CREDIT, WHAT CREDIT?

"Banks lend by creating credit. They create the mess of payment out of nothing"-Ralph M. Hautrey

"This is a staggering thought, we are completely dependant on the commercial Banks. Someone has to borrow every dellar we have in circulation, cash or credit. If the Banks create ample synthetic money we-are prosperess; if not, we starve. We are absolutely without a permanent money stem. When one gets a complete grasp of the picture, the tragic aburdity of our hopeles position is almost incredible, but there it is. It is the most important subject intelligent persons can investigate and reflect upon. It is so important that our present civilization may collapse unless is becomes widely understood and the defects remedied very soon."- Robert Hemphill

It's the truth even if it sounds pretty gloomy. The illusion that we have money has a shadow, and that shadow is the illusion that we have credit!

When I was a child, my mother taught me an important lesson about credit. If you can't afford to buy something now, what makes you think you will be able to pay more for it later? That's really what happens when you use credit, you delay paying for what you want, and pay extra in interest for the time delay! It's tough to get ahead when you use credit. To get credit, you have to go into debt. The debe you owe is your credit.

With that in mind, I began life not using any credit. I paid cash for everything, and if I couldn't buy it with cash I just didn't buy it. Live within your means, stay in the black, save 10% of your earnings every payday and you'll do fine.

I went to buy my wife a new washer and drier from Sears. It turned out I only had enough cash to buy half a washer. The salesman suggested I apply for a Sears charge card, get the washer and drier and pay later in monthly installments. My red flag was up, but what the heck, it was worth a try.

Twenty minutes later the salesman told me my credit application was denied. I asked why and he gave me the address of the credit agency they used. I could write them a letter within 30 days and they would tell me why they denied credit to me. Why was I not worthy?

The response from the credit bureau was that I didn't have any previously established credit. I was a credit virgin and they did not want to take the risk of popping my credit cherry. It's strange really when you think about it. If I can't get credit because nobody ever gave me any, and nobody will give you any until someone else does, how does you get any?

My worthiness was discredit.

I had watched my finances carefully and lived within my means only to find out that no credit is worse than bad credit. No debts and steady job made me a good risk in my mind. Credit to me, always seemed like a get poor quick scheme. Getting into debt is quick and easy compared to paying it off. Unless you're a credit virgin, then you can't get in.

So just what is credit anyway? As far as finance is concerned, the dictionary defines credit as:

The balance in a person's favor in an account/an amount or sum placed not a person's disposal by a bank/time given for payment for goods or services sold on trust/an entry on the right-hand side of an account/a deduction from an expense or asset account/any one of, or the sum of the items entered on the right-hand side of an account/ a deduction from an amount otherwise due.

Did you understand any of that? No wonder it is confusing and people don't understand the nature of credit, It6 seems to be liquid, solid, gas, plasma, visible, invisible, deadly in inhaled, oh, you get the idea. It is many things that are opposite of one another and seem contradictory to any reasonable human being.

Credit is sometimes referred to as money but it isn't. To qualify as money there are three criteria that must be met.

1. It must be a medium of exchange, a tool used to repay debt. Credit is debt so how can it repay itself?

2. It must be a unit account. The unit of account for the United States is "Dollar." The "Dollar," is one ounce silver coin. So, neither Federal Reserve Notes nor Credit in any form is a unit of account.

3. It must be a store of value. Debt, or Credit, has a negative value. Incidentally, we also know that Federal Reserve Note Currency is debt currency and also has negative value. So, we know credit is not "money" by any definition.

The world's fiat debt currencies are all born of credit. Credit creates currency when banks lend to someone and borrow the currency into existence. Historically it was the Catholic Church's Knights Templar who created the system of credit accounts. They were required to keep a reserve of fiat currency to back their deposits. This is a ridiculous thought. They had money worth nothing to back their money worth nothing.

You see, it really is quite invisible. Or maybe you don't see because it really is quite invisible. Oh hell, there just isn't any. Get it? I'll try to break this down into terms even I can understand.

A bank takes your promise to repay (this is your debt), and create currency by monetizing your debt. Thus, the term debt currency, as your debt creates the currency the bank loaned into existence.

Credit must be established; it cannot be loaned. When your credit was established, the bank loaned an equal amount of currency into existence. Banks don't say they are loaning you money because that would be a lie. They say they are extending you credit. In this case, credit means the repayment of your debt has been postponed. You will likely pay it a little at a time until it is paid off, plus interest.

Accountants, like Attorneys, have their own language. For an Attorney, it doesn't have to be fair, it only has to make their books balance. They do this by using double-entry bookkeeping. This is a method of recording financial transactions in which the transactions are entered in two accounts and invokes two-way, self-balancing posting. Total "Debits" must equal total "Credits." A debit is the opposite of a credit. Don't confuse debits with debt, debt is your credit, the debit is the currency your credit caused to exist when the bank established your credit and gave you a loan.

Double Entry Example:

Date	Accounts	Debit	Credit
Aug 1	Accounts Receivable	82.00	
	Revenue		82.00

You will notice that debits are in the left column and credits are in the right column. For each debit, there is an equal and opposite credit and the sum of all debits must equal the sum of all credits. Assets must equal liabilities. Debits are considered assets and credits are liabilities in this system. You will notice that in this case revenue, or the currency created by your debt is a liability. That is because there is no money. I'm calling a positive so that it balances out! You will also notice that the bank didn't loan money that already existed in their bank because there is no money. They can't loan something that doesn't exist, so they take something that doesn't exist and loan you that instead and charge you interest for this nothing they created with the hocus pocus of their pen. Harry Potter, eat your heart out!

Credit—I'll loan you my nothing and you can pay me back when you get some nothing of your own plus more nothing as interest.

Ridiculous!

I wanted to be a credit to my race, so I went into debt.

The Bank creates currency out of the ether simple by making the bookkeeping entry that says it now exists. The banks admit the currency they loan is not theirs, but they benefit generously from the compound interest from loans of currency which they never had. They never had it because there is no money.

The quantity of currency banks can create is virtually unlimited. This is due to the fact that debt is unlimited. Debt is sustained by ever increasing debt. The currency for the interest has to come from somewhere. The banks just manipulate more debt rather than generate real wealth. The volume of currency increases as the nation's wealth decreases. This is a root of inflation.

You would think that everything must equal out in the end with debits and credits equal, that you cannot return more currency to its point of origin than was created. When you dig a hole and fill it back up with the dirt you removed, you do not end up with extra dirt. Yet, the currency loaned into existence and used to pay interest charges carries its own debt burden. The madness never ends.

There is a continuous flow of currency to creditors from debtors. The cost of living increases with the generated and continuous inflation while the standard of living declines. More than half the families in the U.S use credit cards, and an estimated 80% of the population uses credit of some form.

My FRN's were debt incarnate.

This reminds me of Rosa, a lade that worked at a Taco Hut. Rosa made the best tacos and everyone encouraged her to quit her job at the taco hut and open her own taco café. Rosa didn't have aby funding to start a business of her own, so she applied for a bank loan.

Banks don't loan people; they loan credit scores. Rosa had a low credit score and the bank was reluctant to give her a loan. If Rosa's taco café went belly up, the bank would take possession of its assets, but banks aren't in the café business, they are in the banking business.

If Rosa would put her house up as collateral, the bank would loan her the funds. She went for it. Now Rosa had to succeed. If her business failed, the bank would take her house as well as her business.

You will notice the bank put nothing of value into his equation. Rosa put up a house, real property with real value, her promise to repay with interest the currency she be loaned, and all the know-how and effort in running the Tac Café.

The Bank would do the paperwork to create currency and collect interest for the nothing they created. This creates a society of slaves working to pay banks for nothing. All their efforts and labor is to keep the bankers paid and satisfied. If that isn't being a slave to the bank then what is?

The bankers and the Government all say that credit is important for you, and you should use your credit responsibility to keep a good credit score. The truth of course is that credit is important to bankers and Government. You should live without credit, they can't.

Without the creation of credit and debt, the banks would not have a job. The Government wouldn't have any currency without credit and debt creating it. The Government has a budget to meet every year. That much credit plus more to run the private sector economy must be created every year.

No credit equals no debt equals no currency equals no economic activity which equals a depression. The Government builds its own debt and calls it the National Debt. The Government usually spends at a deficit. A deficit is less than there is. The Government spends not only the debt currency it collects in tax revenue, it spends even more nothing that hasn't even been created yet.

Credit is not good for you, it enslaves you.

The banks are licensed by the Government to create debt currency. Don't try this at home. A group of patriots on Montana calling themselves the "Free-men" tried this. They created currency from nothing. The Government called this bank fraud and these individuals are like no longer free-men, they are in prison. The Government doesn't like competition in the imaginary money-making business.

With Credit being called important, and credit scores a determining factor in establishing credit, just what are credit scores and how are they determined? If you do wish to establish credit, a good score can determine if you get a low interest rate or a high interest rate. The higher the interest, the more you pay! Your credit score is on your credit report.

What is a credit report? It is a report containing information about your identity, credit relationships with anu creditors you have or have had in the past, any court actions, consumers' statements and any previous inquiries into your file. These reports are compiled by agencies that collect information about your credit. There are three main agencies known as bureaus. They are Equifax, Experian, and Trans-Union.

You are eligible to obtain a free copy of your credit report once a year. If you have a computer, you can go to www.annualcreditreport.

<u>com</u>. You can call 877-322-8228 and ask for an "Annual Credit Report Request Form." That's what I did.

What is credit score? It is system used by lenders to determine if you are worthy of credit being established in your name. Information is collected from your loan application and your credit report. This includes your bill paying history, how many loans you already have and how you pay them on time or not, anything that has been turned over to collections, the age of your accounts, outstanding debt, and credit cards.

Creditors take this information and run a statistical analysis to determine the amount of risk you pose. This information is compared to other people with similar profiles to yours. A scoring system awards points for each factor that predicts who is most likely to repay a debt.

The most common risk assessment program of this type is "Fair Isaac" or FICO. Scores run from a low of 300 to a high of 850. The higher the score the less risk to the lender. My score was 512.

My credit was so bad I couldn't even charge a battery!

I tried to find out exactly how the score is determined. It is a closely guarded secret, like the seven herbs and spices in Kentucky

Fried Chicken, and the formula for Coke. This is what I was able to find out.

Five main factors are used to determine your score. The largest of these is your payment history or how you pay your bills, if you pay on time that is good thing, paying late is bad. This amounts to about a third of your score. How many bills have gone 30 days, 60 days, or 90 days past the due date? Accounts sent to collections weigh heavy against you.

In my case, I had doctor bills that went 45 days before they were paid. That is because I waited for my insurance company to pay their part, then I said what was left. The insurance company was slow, so I was also slow. This counted against me. I got dinged responsible, they mark me as dead-beat.

I also paid my electric, gas, and water bills every 90 days. When I got a notice that if I didn't pay I would notice no services, I paid. This way I only had to write and mail a check every three months. I'm busy person and this was easier for me. I get dinged again as a dead-beat.

A friend of mine is a contractor. He doesn't get paid every two weeks like most people; he gets paid at the end of the job. And when the job is done, the people he worked for have 30 days before they legally have to pay him. This causes him to run a large balance on his credit cards for long periods until he gets paid. Then it doesn't make any difference if he pays them off in full, he is already dinged as a dead-beat.

The second largest factor, again about a third of your credit score, is the amount of debt you owe, and the amount of available credit you still have. If you are already paying a $20,000 car payment, and you still owe $10,000. Then your available credit is $10,000 on that account. If you have four credit cards and the available credit on each of them is $1,000 that adds up to $4,000. If you owe $600, your available credit on the cards is $3,400.

In my case I had no car loans and no credit cards. This counts against me because I didn't have any available credit. Again, to my way of thinking, I was being responsible by staying out debt. If the creditors don't have their hand in your wallet, they hold it against you. "What, I'm not making any profit at your expense?" They yell. Ding! Ding! Ding!

The third largest factor, about a sixth of your credit score, is the length of your credit history. That's not inches or feet, it's how long of time you have had credit in years. The longer you have had established credit, the more points you get.

In my case, I was a credit virgin without history. By staying out of debt, that is a major ding to your credit score. If we had real money, staying debt-free would be a good thing, but we don't have money, we have a debt-based currency.

With a debt currency if you don't go into debt no currency is created. Not only are you not helping the economy to grow, you are not enriching the bankers with the fruits of your labor. They hold this against you. Again, you are encouraged by the lenders and the Government to go into debt responsibly. Anything less is downright un-American.

I don't want no sound like conspiracy theorist, but the Government does license banks and lenders to create currency. That's the facts! That's why they punish you with a bad score if you're debt-free, and reward you with a good score if you get into debt. A twisted and warped system of punishment and reward designed to enslave you into playing the game.

Once these financial vampires sink their fangs into you, they will suck you financially dry until death do you part. It's easy to get into debt and tough to get out. Like financial quicksand, the more you struggle, the deeper you go!

I use one credit card pay my other credit card bills. You have to give credit where credit is due.

The fourth factor, about a fifth of your credit score, is your mix of credit. Do you have credit cards, a mortgage, a car loan, and a major oil company gas card? Good for you and your credit score if you do. That's pretty complete mix so the lenders can see how well you handle your credit.

My good friend Rocco was late with payments on a consistent basis. The lender said, "Rocco, you don't know how to manage your money."

Rocco said, "That's not true. I don't have any money to manage!"

I thought he should get points for being consistent. If you are a credit virgin like me, you don't have any mix and that lowers your credit score. All things in moderation, including credit. I just can't find logic in paying service fees and interest to five different creditors for the privilege of them allowing me to have credit. To me, that us mismanaging your finances.

If everyone stopped paying 10% of their earnings to creditors, the economy would prosper. Sure, leaders might go out of business, but if it keeps the economy moving, I'm in. "What's in your wallet?" asks a major credit card company.

"You're not!" I respond. They try to make you feel barbaric if you don't use credit cards. Barbarians didn't accept paper or plastic; it was gold or silver or off with your knob. Ok, call me barbaric, but I much prefer heavy metal to a magnetic strip.

I grabbed my credit card and charged to the rescue.

The final factor, again about a fifth of your credit score, is new credit applications. If you start filling out applications for credit all at one time the lenders get suspicious. You may be in a financial bind. or maybe you intend to charges up a huge debt and go bankrupt. This lowers your credit score.

If you're a credit virgin like me, applying for your mix of credit all at one time is like banging the football team. All that credit at once is too much for a credit whore on crack. Too much risk. Ding dong ding!

As you can clearly see, what goes in to your credit score calculation looks more like a witch's brew than Science. And the best question I can think to ask about this while risk assessment process is, what is the lender risking?

It's not like they are loaning you anything real. If you borrow a tool from your neighbor, you give the toll back when you are done with it. The bank does not loan you a tangible asset, it creates a debt liability out of nothing to loan you. They risk "Nothing!" So where is the risk? Truly if they gave you nothing and you give them nothing back what difference does it make? If you give me nothing, and I'm unable to give none of the nothing back, what happens?

You dug a hole, and if you don't fill the hole back up, it will remain a hole. This cannot happen in double entry bookkeeping. Everything must balance. The hole must be filled. The risk to the lender is that if they make loans that don't get paid back, the Government may take away their license and privilege to create currency.

Credit then is really the currency that is created by debt. Federal Reserve Note has a credit value at its creation as cash. If you already have currency has a credit value at its creation as cash. If you already have currency, it is credit. This is what sets your credit rating. The more currency you have, the better your credit rating. A simple question to determine credit worthiness would be, "Do you have any currency and if so, how much?"

No cash = no credit. If you don't have any then you're not worthy. You are obviously poor and are therefore a poor risk!

Ever notice when you "need" a loan they won't give you one

because you lack credit, which is really currency.

If you have lots of currency you have lots of credit, and that is good. You must be rich and rich people are not a poor risk. Giving credit to someone who does not need it is pretty safe.

We have been taught to believe that money, credit, and currency are synonymous. They're not! Money has real value; currency has no value and credit has a negative value.

This brings us to bankruptcy. Just what is bankruptcy?

Bankruptcy is a federal court process designed to relieve the honest but unfortunate consumers that are in debt over their heads and provide them fresh start. The debts of someone declared insolvent are extinguished after their assets are liquidated to satisfy creditors. A trustee is appointed by the court to handle the process so creditors will not harass you while you get back on your feet.

This is a tough decision to make. It is depressing to think that you are a failure and you are unable to manage your finances. There is also the guilt factor of not paying your creditors. In reality, most people who file for bankruptcy protection intended to pay their bills, but because of some hardship they just can't. Under bankruptcy protection, you can start over from scratch.

Another reason the decision is tough is that bankruptcy proceedings may cause you to lose any property you have. Once the process is set into motion it cannot be stopped. If you have two cars, you may keep one, but the other may be sold to pay some or part of your old debts.

There are two main types of bankruptcy. Chapter 7 bankruptcy is liquidation bankruptcy. This will cause your nonexempt assets to be sold to pay some of your debts, and any remaining debt is discharged or permanently eliminated. Then you can start over fresh.

Chapter 11 or Chapter 13 bankruptcy are recognition bankruptcies. With these you file a plan to recognize and discharge some or part of your debts, or reduce excessive interest so you are able to pay most of your debts. This keeps creditors from seizing your assets while you pay off your debts. Chapter 11 is mostly used by business because it allows them to continue to operate rather than go out of business.

Bankruptcy is a good system that allows you to keep your dignity and your exempt assets. As I said before, you should never take so much from someone that you leave them with nothing, because someone with nothing has nothing to lose. In 2004, more than a million consumers filed for bankruptcy. If you go bankrupt, your debt is written off and that is good thing for you. It is bad for the banks and the Government. Under double entry book keeping everything must equal out. When the debt was created, so was currency to back that debt. If the debt is extinguished, the currency it created must also be extinguished and it disappears from the economy.

Bankruptcy laws were recently changed to keep some people from abusing the system. Essentially the exempt assets are now under tighter scrutiny. You might get to keep a TV set, but not a giant flat screen plasma TV. People who abused the old system consumed more than they contributed.

As you may remember I started earlier that credit seems to be liquid, solid, gas, plasma, visible, invisible, and deadly if inhaled. I will now elaborate on that statement.

When credit is established by a bank loan currency is created, it is pulled out of thin air, the ether, or plasma, credit is established, but you cannot see it. Credit is an invisible gas. Credit is weightless, tasteless, and odorless because it is really nothing.

After establishing your credit, the bank issues you a check. The check metamorphosis into liquid credit. When you deposit the check into your account to someone else's account without taking on solid form of Federal Reserve Notes, your credit has taken on the solid form of Federal Reserve Notes now has become visible.

Since we know that credit is really nothing, if you breathe it, it is deadly. This is because you must breathe air, breathing nothing would suffocate you, and you would die.

Just like there is no money, there is no credit!

When they said it's not the money, it's the principal, I lose interest.

Chapter 12

FRACTIONAL RESERVE BANKING

"The modern Banking system manufactures money out of nothing. The process is perhaps the most astounding piece if sleight of hand that was ever invented. Banks can in fact inflate, mint and unmint the modern ledger-entry currency." – Major L.L.B Angus

"The bold effort the present (central) bank had made to control the government... are but premonitions of the fate that await the American people should they be deluded into a perpetuation of this institution or be established of another like it." – Andrew Jackson

"I believe that banking institutions are more dangerous to our liberties that standing armies. Already they have raised up a moneyed aristocracy that set the Government at defiance. The issuing power should be taken from banks and restored to the people to whom it properly belongs." – Thomas Jefferson

After talking about credit in the last chapter it is only fair that now discuss Fractional Reserve Banking. Just what is Fractional Reserve Banking?

Fractional Reserve Banking bis the current system of banking used in the United States. It refers to the fact that Federal law requires banks to hold currency reserves equal to a percentage of its customers' deposits.

These reserves are a combination of cash or currency in the vault, bonds, notes, United States Treasury bills, certificates, and the bank's deposits at a Federal Reserve Bank. The Federal Reserve sets the percentage of required reserves. The average is about 6%.

Banks are limited to making loans only up to total excess reserves. Excess reserves are any amount on deposit in excess of the required reserves. IF the reserve ratio were 5% and the bank had deposits of $1,000, the reserve would be $50, and the remaining $950 is the excess reserves.

Some people think that banks keep currency in the vault up to the required reserve and then lend the rest out. Banks have a license from the Government to create currency out of nothing. Banks don't need depositor funds to loan out, out they merely create new currency based on the amount they can, in relation to their excess reserves. Banks could loan out other peoples' funds or deposits, however that is unnecessary. People think other people's money is being loaned out, but there is no money.

What is the capital of the U.S.? Federal Reserve Note

The Federal Reserve impose a limit with the reserve ratio for a reason. Debt has no upper limit. If the Federal Reserve did not impose one, there would be no limit to how much currency banks could create. None of the banks' own funds are at risk, and the peoples' funds are insured by FDIC (Federal Depositors Insurance Corporation), against loss.

If there were real money, gold, silver, or platinum, fractional reserve banking could be a problem. In a crisis like the stock market crash of 1929, people would rush to the bank to draw their money out. The banks would not have enough money, only a fraction would be in the vault. This is called a "bank run."

Stealing FRN from a Bank is centless.

With a fiat debt currency, there is no real money, only numbers in the banks' computers. 95% of the currency in circulation is "invisible", numbers in a computer. 5% of the currency is Federal Reserve Notes. The Federal Reserve Notes make visible the invisible currency that is already not there!

Our banking industry is built solidly on nothing, which is clearly obscured.

If the bank run started today, the Government would order more of the invisible currency to be made visible in the form of Federal Reserve Notes. As long as people had that worthless piece of green paper in their hands, their brain would tell them they were satisfied, the bank run would soon stop.

Fractional Reserve Banking with a fiat debt currency does tend to be inflationary. Some argue the Government is the culprit and there is evidence the Government is at least partly to blame.

The Government raises the funds it needs through taxes and by borrowing of currency that is already in circulation. This borrowing is through the sale of bonds and treasury bills. When this is not enough currency for the Government, which is always, the Government borrows from the Central Bank.

The currency created by this loan to the Government is usually earmarked for existing commitments and does not contribute to the productivity. If currency is created and productivity does not rise along with the additional currency, inflation results.

The Federal Reserve is partly to blame as well. When the Government needs, or should I say wants additional funds to spend, the Federal Reserve can purchase Government bonds and Treasury bills. The Federal Reserve creates the funds out of nothing, and writes a check or checks, which are deposited at commercial banks.

This deposit or these deposits. This increases the reserves at the commercial banks. This increases loan activity as people and business borrow the newly created additional funds. And because of fractional reserve banking it continues to grow as the borrower's deposit and the funds in their local banks, and those banks now have increased reserves to loan out.

This inflation of the currency was created by the Federal Reserve. When banks or treasury bills are purchased by individuals it is not inflationary because currency already in existence is used.

As we discussed in the last chapter on credit, any one who uses a credit card essentially creates currency the instant they use them. The credit card is not currency in and of itself, but with a debt-based currency, anytime anyone goes into debt, currency is created.

This is one reason banks put a limit on your credit cards. Without a limit, people would cause currency inflation which would diminish the volume of the currency they just borrowed into existence.

Don't forget about the interest on all the debt currency that has been borrowed means more debt must be established to create more currency to pay interest. People end up one hole to fill another. Debt sustained by ever increasing debt.

Bankers and bacteria multiply by dividing

Compound interest is the worst. You enslave yourself to a lifetime of labor trying to pay off compound interest. It mimics debt currency in that it tries to create something out of nothing. It is a drag on society, sucking away our productivity as a few rich bastards at the top get everything.

Fractional Reserve Banking in action works like this. Imagine you get a loan from you bank for $1,000. They create the currency out of thin air and write you a check. You deposit the check into your account. At an average reserve rate of 6%, $940 of your deposit is now in excess of required reserves and can be loaned to someone else.

Someone else borrows the $940 dollars. The bank writes them a check which they deposit into their account. Again 6% reserve ratio, the bank now has another $883.60 in excess of resources which can be loaned to someone else.

How much additional currency can be created from the perpetual loaning of the excess reserves? It appears an awful lot of people are using the same currency at the same time. A multidimensional currency for the New World Order. Since the reserve was created out of nothing and

Is in reality nothing, you have currency backed by nothing to back the deposits of more nothing.

I ran the calculation to its ultimate end myself to see hoe much currency can be created with 6% Fractional Reserve Banking. The initial $1,000 borrowed into existence and used as a reserve to its ultimate end creates about $15,549.88. I will not show the entire calculation as it ran out to one hundred fifty-one places. This is what the first ten places of the calculation look like.

Amount to be loaned	Reserve Required
1. 1000	60
2. 940	56.40
3. 883.60	53
4. 830.60	49.84
5. 780.76	46.85
6. 733.91	44.03
7. 689.88	41.39
8. 648.49	38.91
9. 609.58	36.57
10. 573.01	34.38

In the end the Reserve Required adds up to $1,000 and the amount able to be loaned is about $15,549.88, for a total of $16,549.88 created out of nothing and made to look as if it were backed by reserves. Reserves of nothing? They must think we're stupid. Oh, wait a minute, we must be stupid, because we are like sheep, smilingly being led to slaughter.

Again, I ask the question, if it takes money to make money, where did the money to make the first money come from? A friend of mine said they borrowed it. You can borrow fiat debt currency into existence.

We have a currency, but there is no money!

Money in the bank is like sex, if you keep taking out what you put in, you lose interest.

I have a fractional reserve pay check

CHAPTER 13

THE MATHEMATICS OF MONEY

What exactly is mathematics? Most of us think we know what it is, but we truly don't. Math is one of the least favorite subjects taught in school an yet its importance is eclipsed only by the ability to read. If you can read, you can learn any other subject that has been written about.

Our teachers told us math was important to us, but no teacher I ever encountered could make a good argument for me to believe them. I had to discover for myself how important it is. We truly do use math every day.

Mathematics can probably best be summed up as the science of numbers. I never really thought of math as a science but it is, and it is important to note that it is an exact science with absolutes. Remember this because it is important, mathematics is an exact science.

When I was a freshman in high school, my algebra teacher was a man named Mr. Frank. He was a portly man with a rather large head and thick glasses, but more that anything else, he was a brilliant mathematician. In all his years of schooling from first grade through graduating college, he had only gotten one math problem wrong!

That is a truly incredible feat! He once told us what the odds were of this accomplishment, but I don't remember how big the number was. We had to take his word for it because none of his students were ever smart enough to figure it out to challenge him. I was either blessed or cursed to have Mr. Frank as a teacher for three years of advanced math in high school.

Back to that freshman year in algebra now, Mr. Frank asked, "What is the square root of 49?" The he called my name.

I calculated the answer in my head as Mr. Frank maintained eye contact with me. "It's about 7." I answered.

"Wrong." Mr. Frank barked.

I could feel my face got hot as it turned red with embarrassment. I was sure the answer was 7. Everyone was in shock.

"Anyone else?" Mr. Frank asked.

One brave student spoke up and said, "Mr. Frank, that is exactly the same answer I got, seven."

"That is correct." Mr. Frank said, still glaring at me.

"Then why did you say I was wrong?" I asked.

"Because you said about 7, the answer is exactly 7." Mr. Frank walked up to me, leaned over and put his face only inches from mine. "There is no guessing in math, it is an exact science and the answers are either exactly correct or they are wrong."

His voice deepened and his face was somber. "Do you understand that boy."

"To the nth degree." I said through clinched teeth.

"I certainly hope so, or you will get a zero in this class," said Mr. Frank. "Do you want a zero in this class?"

I said, "I want exactly two zeros with one one in front of them." (100)

Mr. Frank said, "That will never happen, I have never given a 100 to anyone. You would have to be perfect to get 100% an nobody is perfect." He said.

He kept his promise and learned that math is an exact science. Nothing brands that into your brain like being embarrassed in front of every nerd and geek in advanced math class the first day of high school.

Most of us only remember a fraction of what we learned in math class. We were happy to be done with it so we could put t out of our minds, Therefore, before we can get into the mathematics of money, we need to review briefly what math is.

Mathematics is an abstract science related to logic and based on a fundamental process. It proceeds from a body of explicitly stated assumptions (axiom or postulates) and deduces from them statements (theorems) of relationship. There are several branched of mathematics.

Elementary mathematics is normally directed to the study of number and space, and the statements are in terms of physical experience, but theoretical mathematics may deal with assumptions that are not drawn from the physical world. The distinction between the various branches of mathematics is made according to the nature of the assumptions on which each is based.

Algebra: The assumptions of algebra have to do with operations on sets of numbers. The basic operations are addition, and multiplication, and in elementary algebra the numbers are "real numbers." Algebraic operations are said to have "properties," which are the ways in which numbers are assumed to behave. These properties are utilized in arriving at other relationships. Records as far back as the 16th century B.C. show that the Egyptians solved problems requiring the use of algebra.

Geometry: The basic assumptions of geometry concern the study of space and involve the use of the accepted but undefined terms, "point, line, and plane." Around 300 B.C. Euclid was the first person to organize geometry into a coordinated body of deductive knowledge with his "self-evidence truths."

Euclidian geometry has a great number of applications in the everyday world. Plan geometry denotes the study of figures (such as circle and the square), that lie entirely in one plane. Solid geometry denotes the study of figures (such as the sphere and the cube) that are three-dimensional and therefore not in one plane.

The projections you wanted for your meeting will be waiting for you on the plane.

These are other geometries such as descriptive geometry, the study of projection of solid figure upon a plane. This is important in an architecture and engineering. There is also differential geometry, the theory of those properties of figures describable in calculus. Analytical geometry introduced by Rene Descartes in the 17th century, may be described as the study of space by means of algebraic equations.

Trigonometry: The study of one set of functions is often signaled out for separate study as trigonometry. Historically, trigonometry developed as a method for determining unknown measures of a triangle when certain measures were known.

Calculus: The assumptions of calculus are those of mathematical analysis with the addition of the concept of limit. This leads to the concept of two basic definitions, the derivative and the integral. Differentiation is concerned with computing the rate at which a function is changing. Integration is the opposite and is a method for determining the function by using a given derivative.

Together the differential calculus and the integral calculus are called the infinitesimal calculus. Before the development of calculus,

Mathematics dealt with more or less static situations. Calculus, with its study of limit, can be applied to determining instant rates of change and can even be said to be "grasping the fleeting instant." The uses of calculus are so numerous and so fundamental that advanced mathematics and modern science would be impossible without it.

Arithmetic: In the broad scope of mathematics, arithmetic is a part of algebra. It deals with purely numerical, ungeneralized instances. Conventionally, arithmetic has been most widely applied to simple teaching of the skills of dealing with numbers for practical purposes, computation of areas, proportions, costs, percentages, interest, merchandising and logistics. There are four fundamental operations of arithmetic. They deal with the manipulation, and divisions pf whole numbers and fractions.

After Midnight Math, I had truth Theorium.

We concern ourselves really in our every day lives mostly with basic arithmetic. Arithmetic has certain concepts that when learned will allow you to do most any calculation. A concept is an abstract or generic.

Idea generalized from particular instances. A concept is also something conceived in the mind.

I would like to use as an example the English language. One of the concepts of English is that it has an alphabet consisting of 26 letters. The concept of letters which are represented by a different symbol for each one is another concept. The concept that of the 26 letters in the alphabet, some are consonants and some are vowels. The concept that the letters can be combined in endless combinations to form an endless number of words. The concept that each word must have at least one vowel. The concept that words can be strung together in a coherent order to form sentences. The concept that sentences can be strung together to form paragraphs.

If you understand these basic concepts of the English language, you can read or write and communicate with other people using writing.

Mathematics also has some basic concepts. The concept of the base numbers 0 through 9. The very concept of zero as a number. The Romans had no number for zero and no concept for it. There is no logic in measuring something that does not exist. Zero is a measure of no value and that is zero's only value. You can't measure nothing, so zero has no value and had no value for the Romans. The concept that each of the ten base numbers is presented by a different symbol called numerals. The concept that numerals can be strung together in endless combinations to form an endless number of numbers, or sets of numbers. The concept of place value, is that the value assigned is based on its position in a set, such as in 2, or, 20, or 200.

On the abstract end is the concept of perceived value, in that we only know what the value of numbers are because someone taught us that it had that value is. The concept of the decimal system and the use of a period or comma to separate the parts of a number set that are larger or smaller than one, such as 1.3 or just 0.3.

Without a pip, the decimal system would be pointless

Then there is the concept that numbers and sets of numbers can be added to, subtracted from, multiplied by, and divided by other numbers and sets of numbers. Now, let's take a closer look at each of these concepts.

NUMBERS: In arithmetic, numbers are either the count, or sum, of objects in a group, or the position in an ordered list of objects. The term refers also to the symbol that represents the count or the position of cardinal numbers. Numbers used to indicate position in an ordered list are ordinal numbers.

The Cardinal ordained the count to his position.

The system of cardinal numbers, which consists of the natural numbers, that is, positive whole numbers only, has been extended from time to time to include new types of numbers and zero were added, forming with the natural numbers a group referred to as the integers.

Throughout the ages, people have attributed certain characteristics to certain numbers, such as the association of the number 13 with bad luck. The use of numbers as having metaphysical properties has given rise to numerology. Numerology bears the same relation to arithmetic, the science of numbers, that astrology bears to astronomy.

The theory of numbers is a branch of mathematics concerned

with higher arithmetic in which the properties of integers only are suited. A prime number is one has no factors other than itself and the number 1. The first few prime numbers are 2, 3, 5, 7, 11, 13, 17, and 19.

Of the many observations made regarding primes, some are trivial. Such as the fact that 2 is the only even prime number. Euclid proved that there are an infinite number of primes.

You should not find it odd that I will get even.

Divisibility is another topic in the theory of numbers, and is closely connected with the concept of prime numbers. Another important part of number theory, known as the theory of congruences, consists of a generalization of the idea of classification of numbers into odd and even.

NUMERALS: Numerals are the symbols used to represent or denote the number. The decimal system is believed to have originated in counting on the fingers, using the to hands as the most convenient abacus. We use Arabic numerals. The Arabic numerals are, 0. 1, 2, 3, 4, 5, 6, 7, 8, 9. You will notice there are ten numbers.

Roman numerals are I, II, III, IV, V, VI, VII, VIII, IX, X. These were the first ten. The Romans used many more numerals to include C for one hundred. This is why hundred-dollar bills were called c-notes. Again, the Romans had no number for zero.

It is widely believed that both Arabic and Roman numerals are based on counting on the hands. 1 or I is one finger, 2 or II is two fingers, and 3 or III is three fingers. The word "digit" is from Latin "digitus," which means "fingers." The Roman V seems to be the open hand, and X seems to be two open hands.

The symbols called Arabic were learned from the Arabs y Europeans, but they apparently originated in India. Numeral symbols are ideograms, or picture symbols. The meaning of numerals is clear no matter what language you speak.

NUMERATION: In mathematics, numeration is the process of designating numbers according to any particular system. The number designations are in turn called numerals.

In any system of numeration, base number must be specified, and groupings are then made by powers of the base number. The most widely used system of numeration is the "Decimal System." The decimal system we use is truly a decadecimal system using 10 as the base number. Thus, in the decimal system, the number 234 means (2×10^2) + ($3 \times 10\^1$) + ($4 \times 10 \^ 0$), or 200 + 30 + 4.

The binary system uses 2 as the base number. The binary system is important because of its application to modern computers. In the binary system, the numeral 111, for example, means (1×2^2) + ($1 \times 2 \^ 1$) + ($1 \times 2 \^ 0$), or 4 + 2 + 1, which is 7 in the decimal system.

The decimal numeral 7 and the binary numeral 111 are thus designations for the same number. Whereas the decimal system uses the ten digits 0, 1, 2, 3, 4, 5, 6, 7, 8, 9, the binary system uses only the two digits 0, 1.

You are number one, you are No. 1, you are no one, 0, 1.

The Sumarian culture used a hexadecimal system using the number 6 as the base. It is believed by some that this was passed on to the Sumarians by their fore bearers the Ananaki, which are believed to have been Polydactyl, or having six fingers on each hand, and six on each foot.

The decimal system we use is merely an easy way of writing the values of the numbers in the real number system in terms of our decadecimal familiarity. Leonardo da Pisa introduced the decimal system to the Europeans. He found the Arabians using the system, and they in turn told him they adapted it from the Hindus in India.

NUMBER SETS: When stringing together numbers, a standardized method known as standard form is used. Numbers are grouped together in sets of three. Each of these sets is called a "period." Each period is separated by a comma. Example: 6,392. In this example, 392 is a period.

She told me our date was off because she got her period.

PLACE VALUE: In the decimal system, the system could not work without place value. In place value, the value of the number depends on its position in a number set, such as 2, or 20, or 200. Each digit is a different place value. In the example of 6,392, the 2 is in the "ones" place. The 9 is in the tens place.

It should be noted that the use of place value in our decimal system would not work without the number zero. In "Place Value," when no other number goes in a position, the number zero is placed there to hold the place for a given value. For example, in the number set 103, reads one hundred three, which means one hundred, no tens, and one three. Without the zero to hold open the tens place, the number set would look like 13. In place value, zeros are but a pip.

She asked if I would hold her place. I said, "What do you think I am, a zero?"

PERCEIVED VALUE: All values ultimately are perceived values. We believe each number has a different value because we are taught that they do. We are taught that the number 3 has more value than the number 1, so when we see the number 3, we perceive it as more valuable than the number 1. Its value is perceived in our mind.

I will share a couple of stories with you to illustrate this point. When I was a young man, I accepted a job at a large hospital as a janitor. At each break time and lunch break, all the janitors sat together. We laughed and joked each time we took breaks. Each break became a quarter of a comedy hour and each lunch was a half of a comedy hour.

I soon noticed other groups within the hospital positioning themselves close to the janitors' tables so they could hear what was so funny so they could laugh too. The X-ray technicians, the maintenance men, emergency nurses and lab techs swarmed around and sat silently listening to us yack and laughing when we laughed.

Finally, one day, one of the lab techs came up to our table as break was about to end. She said, "We have been watching and listening to you guys for weeks. We discussed it among ourselves and we just don't understand how you can be so happy all the time."

"Well why shouldn't we be happy?" I asked.

"You guys are janitors." She said as she stared coldly at us. "You people earn less money than anyone else in this facility. You perform the absolute worst menial duties cleaning up after everyone. You even clean up behind the kitchen workers."

"I don't understand what difference that makes." I said.

"Don't you get it?" She huffed. "You're poor!"

We looked around the table at each other and burst into laughter.

"What's so damn funny?" she demanded.

I spoke up, "We just didn't realize that we were poor, so it never bothered us."

We didn't have the same perception that the lab techs did. They perceived us poor and we perceived them as dull. We never perceived that being poor was a reason to be unhappy! We also never thought of ourselves as poor.

Why would you or me or anyone choose to be poor? We wouldn't! Some of us have been taught to believe we are poor by bankers and other people who want us to believe they are rich and therefore better than us. They are not better than us.

Don't let them control your mind. You take control of your mind and you take control of your own life. You take the power away from the brain washers. Wake up! Value yourself and never anyone devalue you ever again.

Only bankers and cowards find strength in numbers. The truly brave find strength in not needing nothing!

The other story I want to share with you is the story of the twenty dollars. A marketing company had assembled a focus group to examine perceive value. They asked the group a hypothetical situation. You are in a store about to buy a toaster oven for $50. Someone in line tells you they just saw the same toaster oven at another store two blocks away for $20 less.

Would you go two blocks away to save $20? Overwhelmingly the focus group said. "Heck yes, that's twenty dollars!"

Now the same group was asked another hypothetical situation. You are on a car lot looking to buy an automobile for $20,000. Someone walks up and tells you they just saw the same automobile at another car dealer two blocks away for $20 less.

Would you go two blocks away to save $20 on an automobile? Overwhelmingly the focus group said, "Heck no, it's only twenty dollars!"

What? These were the same people that said they would go two blocks to save $20 on a toaster oven just two minutes earlier. In two minutes did $20 suddenly lose its value? That's ridiculous, $20 is $20!

Did the $20 change in value? NO, but the perception of the value of the savings changed. On a $50 toaster oven, saving $20 in a savings of 40%. On a $20,000 automobile, saving $20 is a savings of one hundredth of one percent, or .001%.

One hundredth of one percent savings on a $50 toaster oven would be five cents. When asked if they would go two blocks to save 5 cents on a $50 toaster oven, the focus group said no.

40% savings on a $20,000 automobile would be a savings of $8,000. When asked if they would go two blocks to save $8,000 on a $20,000 automobile, the focus group said absolutely, that's a huge savings.

The perceived value of $20 seemed to changed on a dime. The value does not change on the piece of paper, the value changes in our minds. We perceived or understand a change has occurred, and then we assign it a new value. Matter of perspective changes the perception and the value changes.

The perception of any change in values occurs only in our minds. We cannot change the Federal Reserve Notes, and we cannot change other people's perception of what value they place on Federal Reserve Notes.

What we can do is change our own perspective and perception and the value changes for us. This is like in the movie, "The Matrix," where there is no spoon, don't try to bend the spoon, bend only yourself. The bending of yourself is called "inflection."

Again, it is important to understand that all value, even place value, is perceived value. The value only changes in our minds. If we understand the concept of place value in our mind, then our mind makes it real.

I said I wanted to kiss her 288 times. She said that would be two gross, so I got a different girl.

ADDING, SUBTRACTING, MULTIPLYING, and DIVIDING: Let's take the concept of adding first. We understand that we can ass numbers to other numbers or sets of numbers to get numbers that are larger in value once combined. $1 + 1 = 2 . 2 + 10 = 12$.

Subtraction is the opposite of adding. We understand that we can subtract numbers from other numbers or sets of numbers to get numbers that are lesser in value once taken away. $10 - 2 = 8$. $8 - 7 = 1$.

Multiplication of numbers is another concept we understand. $3 \times 4 = 12$ is really $4 + 4 + 4 = 12$. It is 4, three times. $4 \times 3 = 12$ is really $3 + 3 + 3 = 12$. It is 3, four times. We understand that we can multiply numbers or sets of numbers to get numbers in a long string of addition. Division is the opposite of multiplication. We understand that we can take a large value number set and divide another number or set of numbers into it to get numbers or sets of numbers of groups of lesser value, $12 \div 4 = 3$ is really dividing 12 into four equal groups with three in each group, $12 \div 3 = 4$ is really dividing 12 into three equal groups of four in each group.

If you can add, subtract, multiply, and divide, you can figure out most calculations you will encounter in everyday life. The invention of the modern hand-held calculator has all but replaced needing to do these calculations at all. Still, it is rudimentary and good to know.

ZERO: Zero is a magic number. It has a value of absolutely nothing. Its main value is in that it has no value. The decimal number system we use could not work without the number zero or 0.

The Romans did not have a number for zero in their number system. It had no value and so there was no sense in using something that meant nothing. If there is nothing to count, it doesn't count, so why count it?

Zero is like the color black. Black is the absence of color and zero is the absence of anything. Zero is the absence of all magnitude of quantity. Zero, like any other number has no mass and no energy, it is only a number, or a concept in our mind. A number can be neither good nor bad, it is only a number, a figure, a symbol.

When you add zero to anything, or anything to zero, it is no greater that it was. Zero equals nothing. $0 + 2 = 2$, or nothing added to 2 gives you 2, since nothing was added to it. $2 + 0 = 2$, or 2 added to nothing gives you 2, since there is nothing to add it to, you have only what you started with.

Anything minus itself will give you zero. $3 - 3 = 0$. You started with three, you took three away and you are left with nothing or zero.

Anything minus zero will not change the value of the number you started with. $3 - 0 = 3$. You started with three, you took nothing away from it so you still have three.

Zero minus anything will give you a negative number. $0 - 3 = -3$. I call negative numbers ridiculous because in reality they do not exist. The Romans did not use negative numbers for very good reason, in reality they do not exist.

Negative numbers are conceptual in nature only, meaning they only exist in your mind. If I have three cans of beer in my refrigerator. I know I can take one, two, or three cans of beer out of the refrigerator. Once the last beer is out of the fridge there are none left and I can see and comprehend that.

I cannot go to my fridge when there are zero beers left and take out more beer and call it negative beer. I would have had to costume a lot more beer and call it negative beer. I would have had to costume a lot more beer to believe that one! Negative beer is better for you because it contains no calories and no alcohol because it doesn't exist.

In reality there is nothing less than zero. If it isn't there, it isn't there. Yet our number system uses negative numbers for a very good reason. Out entire financial system is based on negative numbers in our debt-based currency.

Again, if it takes money to make money where did the money to make the first money in the beginning, so they started with zero, or nothing, and worked backwards into the negative debt currency we use today. There was no money, and there still is no money.

Now, on to multiplication of zero. We are taught that anything multiplied be zero equals zero, and that zero multiplied by anything equals zero. Zero equals nothing. 3 x zero is really zero three times, or nothing plus nothing, which equals nothing, or zero. 0 x 3 is again zero three times, or nothing + nothing + nothing, or zero. You simply cannot multiply something that isn't there.

Now on to division and zero. Any number divided by zero leaves you the same number you started with. Since zero equals nothing anything divided by nothing means that no division has taken place, 4 divided by 0 = 4, or four divided by nothing equals four.

Zero divided by any number is also zero. Since zero equals nothing, you cannot divide the nothing that isn't there. 0 divided by 4 = 0, or nothing divided four times equals nothing. Like the negative beers I cannot take out of my refrigerator, I cannot slice up and divide a pie I don't have.

Now let's recap. Zero added to anything does not increase its value, it adds nothing. Anything minus zero does not decrease its value, it takes nothing away. Zero multiplied by anything is zero, since zero equals nothing, you can't multiply something that isn't there. Zero divided by anything is zero for the same reason, zero equals nothing and you can't divide something that isn't there.

Place value and zero. Zero has no value of its own. In place value we are taught that without the number zero, our decimal number system could not work. In place value, zero holds the place for a value when no other numeral goes there. For example, the number "10" means one ten and no ones. The number "200" means two hundreds, no tens, and no ones.

In place value we are asked to believe that although zero has no value of its own, when placed behind of any other number it increases the number in front of it ten times its original value. The number "10" is ten times the value of the number "1."

By placing a second zero behind the number ten it again increases ten times its original value to one hundred. "100". This is truly amazing considering that we just learned that zero added to anything does not increase its value. Yet in place value we are asked to believe that by adding a zero behind another numeral it is ten times as valuable. This is truly amazing again because we just learned that zero cannot multiply anything, let alone multiply its value ten times.

In our currency system we are asked to believe that a ten dollar Federal Reserve Note has a value ten times a one dollar Federal Reserve Note because it has a zero behind the one on it. We are also asked to believe that a one hundred dollar Federal Reserve Note is one hundred times the value of a one dollar Federal Reserve Note because it has two zeros behind the one on it.

A number is neither good nor bad, it is only a number. A number has no mass and occupies no space, it is only a number. A ten dollar Federal Reserve note costs no more to make than a one dollar Federal Reserve Note, and a one hundred dollar Federal Reserve Note costs so more to make than either a one or ten dollar Federal Reserve Note.

So what makes a ten dollar Federal Reserve Note more valuable than a one dollar Federal Reserve Note? It is the "zero." The zero adds the value! Zero equals nothing. The nothing added the value because nothing can! The number "1,000,000" or one million, is really one with a whole lot of nothing behind it.

Your house cost $1,000,000, wow, nice place.

It's kind of funny discussing why a ten dollar Federal Reserve Notes is worth more than a one dollar Federal Reserve Note when we already know that Federal Reserve Notes, no matter what denomination they have on them, are worth nothing.

Zero is often called a goose egg. Which came first, the chicken or the egg! I'll settle this old argument right now. The chicken came first. You have to have something before you can add to it, subtract from it, multiply it, or divide it. Nothing to begin with you couldn't get an egg. The chicken came first.

I choked my chicken until it came first.

Math is an exact science. Zero is worth nothing. In an exact science where something has no value, you cannot assign a value to it by placing it behind another number. That is illogical in a logical science and that cannot happen. Zero cannot have positional value because that would give it value.

Now we know why the Romans did not use zero. It has no value so there is no value in using it, anywhere! Federal Reserve Notes have no value so why use them?

The human mind is limited only by itself. It is truly limitless, zero to infinity. The values of numbers do not change on the paper, the value only changes in our minds. It's not the money, it's the thought that counts. Your brain thought the value changed, and it only changed in your mind and thoughts. Perceived value is what you believe in your mind to be the value whether it truly is or not.

The volume of my imaginary money is greater than the volume of your imaginary money.

The Money Matrix is a number game where even the numbers in the black are in the red. It is like a carnival ride where you sit stationary while the scenery moves by either forward or backward. In reality you are going nowhere.

You can divide the word nowhere to get, you are nowhere or you are now-here. Are you nowhere or now here? You don't know do you? That's all right, neither do you.

Mathematics is an exact science and it proves exactly that money cannot exist. Anything less than zero has no value, like our debt based currency.

Rest in peace Mr. Frank, I finally get that zero you offered me so long ago, and nothing makes me happier.

They said my numbers won the lottery. Dang, I wanted to win. Beaten by my own numbers, I threw them away!

The sum of the parts must equal the whole, or hole.

Phillip Tilley

Chapter 14

The Mechanics of Money

"The threatened collapse of our Western Civilization has nothing to do with the political issues between capitalism and communism, but is the consequence of its false money system." – Frederick Soddy

"No discussion of the "Money Matrix" would be complete without discussing the mechanics of money, or how money would work if there were real money. For this I drew inspiration from one of the most brilliant scientists of the 20th century, Frederick Soddy.

Frederick Soddy was an English chemist that won the Nobel Prize in Chemistry in 1921 for his work on radioactive isotopes. Soddy wrote a total of eight books, five of them concerning matter and energy, and three of them concerning money. Most of the books have been out of print for years. Soddy was an advocate of technocracy and believed that money behaved according to the Laws of Thermodynamics.

It is important to understand that Soddy lived at a time when real money existed and was in use. It was difficult to locate any information of Soddy's views on the connection of money and thermodynamics. This caused me to think long and hard about what connection there could be, and like particle of physics itself the answer permeated my mind.

After all, real science is discovery, not invention. The truths are already there, it is a matter of seeing them or not.

What are the Laws of Thermodynamics and how do they relate to money? The First Law of Thermodynamics states that no energy is ever lost or gained, it cannot be created or destroyed, it only changes from one form to another.

I wanted to make more money, so I joined an alchemy class.

An example of this might be the burning of a candle. Some of the energy of the candle is released as light as we see the flame on the candle. Some energy is released as heat as the candle burns. The potential energy of the candle becomes kinetic as it burned and the energy changed from a candle to light and heat. The energy was not lost, it changed form. If you cannot destroy energy it must always exist and you can always use it.

The Second Law of Thermodynamics states that when energy changes form, some of the potential energy will escape into the surrounding environment. This energy becomes absolute and cannot be converted to anything useful again.

In the example of the candle, some of the candle escaped as smoke into the surrounding environment. The burning of the candle yielded light, which is useful, heat, which is useful, and smoke, which is not useful. This unusable energy is called entropy.

The Third Law of Thermodynamics states that every substance known to man undergoes entropy, that is, a measure of the availability of energy to perform work that approaches zero as the temperature approaches absolute zero. The temperature absolute zero is minus 273 degrees centigrade, or minus 459.69 degrees Fahrenheit.

Reaching absolute zero has proven to be impossible for scientists. It is hypothesized that at absolute zero, all molecular activity stops and no heat exists.

What does this third law mean? It means that as energy is changed from one form to another and back again, less and less of the energy is useful and more and more is converted to entropy. Perhaps entropy is the dark matter that makes up most of the universe and we just don't know how to use it.

It should be noted that the Law of Conservation of mass states that mass of an isolated system will remain constant. Matter cannot be created or destroyed, it only changes form. This is so similar to the first law of thermodynamics that in modern times they have been combined to form the law of conservation of mass and energy.

It should also be noted that the second law of thermodynamics can also be called the law of diminishing returns. This is simply that never get more energy out than you put in, and in fact you will get back less usable energy than you put in, thus the diminished return.

In science, everything is either a particle or a wavelength. With wavelengths you have frequency, volume, amplitude and modulation. Frequency is the number of repetitions of a period's process in a unit of time. Volume involves quantities. Amplitude is the quality or state of being ample or fullness. Modulation is the process of varying the amplitude or frequency.

Frederick Soddy said money could be compared to the laws of thermodynamics, so what was he thinking? If money were a wavelength, frequency would be how often you get paid, whether it was weekly, every two weeks, monthly or, at the end of each day. Volume would be how much money you received. Amplitude would be whether the volume of the money you received was enough for your needs or not. Modulation would be varying whether the money was ample and how often you would get more. If you didn't have enough, perhaps you would sell something or pawn something before your next payday, or moonlight a side job for additional income.

Remember, Soddy lived at a time when real money, that is gold, silver, or paper money backed by gold and silver, were in use. With the first law of thermodynamics, money could not be created or destroyed, it would only change form.

All the gold and silver on Earth has always been here. No more can be created and it can't be destroyed. It is here, it always was here, and always will be here. It can be changed by exchanging gold coins for silver coins or vise versa. Gold could be exchanged for paper money backed by gold or silver, and paper money backed by gold or silver could be exchanged for gold or silver. You can write a check and the check can be cashed. You could also exchange it for goods and services.

If you had money in your house and your house burnt down, the gold or silver would still be here among the ashes. If it had of been paper money, the gold and silver that backed it is still at the Treasury, so it could not be destroyed.

Hey, my VISA gold card isn't even gold, it's plast

On the other hand, although Federal Reserve Notes can be exchanged for the token coins we use and the coins can be exchanged for Federal Reserve Notes, in the case of a fire, the Federal Reserve Notes would be gone. Because they can be destroyed completely, they are not money.

With the second law of thermodynamics, as the money changes form, some value is lost to entropy. When you get your paycheck, if you are paid ten dollars an hour and worked forty hours, you would expect to get $400. However, taxes and other deductions would leave you with maybe $264. The rest is converted to entropy, lost to the tax man never to be seen again.

Similarly, the interest on any loan is the entropy. With real money, interest was less because there was a finite amount of money. With a debt based currency the amount is infinite, so interest is higher.

With a debt based currency you can create more from nothing. You could not create real money. The entropy of Federal Reserve Notes is inflation. It becomes worth less and less. An ounce of silver is still worth an ounce of silver.

With the third law of thermodynamics, as the money changes form, its purchasing power would have less value. In a society where population increases but the amount of money stays the same, there is less of it to go around. This creates the effect of where it works or circulates less and less until in theory there wouldn't be an ample amount to go around.

With Federal Reserve Notes, as we the common people circulate the fake money, the Federal Reserve gets paid in gold. When our Government runs out of gold to pay the Federal Reserve, our economic activity will hit absolute zero. The time of absolute zero is almost upon us my friends.

People ask me where the money goes when the stock market goes down. They say the money simply disappears. That could not happen with real money as it cannot be destroyed or lost for good.

The "money" they paid for the stock was spent by the company who issued the stock. It went for utilities, production costs, wages, and most likely excessive executive salaries. That "money" is still around somewhere, even if it was Federal Reserve Notes.

When someone loses money in the stock market, someone else made money. It only changes form or changes hands. If the electricity goes out and you have real money, then you still have money. If you have electronic money that is just numbers in a computer and the electricity goes our, it's gone! If it were real money it could not be so easily destroyed. Perhaps the "E" in E-Money stands for entropy!

If money were a particle it would have to have mass and occupy space. We know that gold, silver, and platinum are very heavy metals, so they certainly have mass and occupy space. The numbers in a computer occupy a tiny amount of space on a hard drive, but have no mass and are therefore not money. The numbers are easily created and easily destroyed. Gold, silver, and platinum cannot be created or destroyed.

Debt is man made and not subject to the laws of nature such as thermodynamics and deterioration. The Laws of Thermodynamics prove that Federal Reserve Notes are not money, and since that's all we have to use, there is no money.

CHAPTER 15

WHAT IS TRUE WEALTH?

True wealth, what is it? Some people would say there is a difference between being rich and being wealthy. In their definition, there are only three ways to get rich. First, you are born into a family that is already rich, so by virtue of inheritance of some or all the riches your family has, you are rich. Second, if you were not born rich, you can marry someone who is, and as their spouse, you are then also rich. Lastly, you could get lucky and win the lottery.

My friend Rocco says that the odds of being struck by lightning are greater than the odds of winning the lottery. I bet him fifty bucks he doesn't get struck by lightning before he wins the lottery. Even if he wins he loses.

These people believe that wealth is different because you generate it in your lifetime with your own efforts. Nobody gives it to you, you don't marry into it, and you don't win wealth. You have to earn wealth in their view.

They say nobody gets wealthy by working a job for someone else. In their view you should start your own business and by your own hand you will reap what you sow and become wealthy.

I have run several small businesses and I never got rich or wealthy. I got tired of working sixteen hour days seven "daze" a week. It seems that when it comes to running a business I'm best at running them out of business.

Anyway, these people believe that riches are owned by people already rich that did nothing to earn the riches and that wealth is created by creative business people in their own creative lifetimes by their own creative hands. They are of course wrong. I have already shown that no one is rich, and unless they are God, they are not creating wealth.

The Government in fact encourages this view that you should start a business. This is one of the reasons the Small Business Administration, (SBA) exists, it to help people to get loans from banks to start a business. Why would the Government care? I'll tell you why.

Each time I ran a business it looked like I was actually going to make a profit. Then tax day arrived and I found out the Government was going to get my profit. I had learned in Business School that most small businesses and individuals earn enough income, until taxes.

If you think you pay a lot in taxes as an individual you haven't seen anything. Small business pay double the taxes of an individual, especially if you are the sole proprietor, or a one person business. The Government of course knows this, and that is why they encourage you to first go into debt to start the business so they can tax you out of business.

If you go out of business you lose everything and the Government and the Banks gain everything. It's all part of how the "Money Matrix" was set up to keep the so called rich, rich and the so called poor, poor.

Even if you beat the odds, 90% of all small businesses fall within the first two years, you still will not be wealthy. If you generate large amounts of profit in the form of Federal Reserve Notes you have generated a large amount of debt currency which is a large amount of debt. Debt is a negative and wealth is supposed to be a positive, so you went the opposite direction of your intention and you are not wealthy or rich if you have accumulated a huge amount of debt!

All the wealth that is on this planet now has always been here, and it will be here long after we are gone. We cannot create what is already here. We can only use it and hopefully show good stewardship of it so future generations may also use it as did our ancestors.

The dictionary says wealth is: much money or property, a great amount of wordly possessions, affluence/ a large amount or abundance of something/valuable products, contents, or derivatives/everything having economic value measurable in price/any useful material thing capable of being bought, sold, or stocked for future disposition.

Another definition is ownership of labor or anything upon which labor has been expended, whether material or immaterial, which directly satisfies the needs or wants of people. In that view a field of wheat that is not yet harvested is not wealth. Labor must be exerted in order to benefit from the wheat.

It could be largely agreed upon that all forms of wealth are positive quantities subject to the laws of nature and subject at some point to deterioration. It could be largely agreed that debt and debt based currency are negative quantities not subject to the laws of nature or deterioration. Wealth really exists in our three dimensional world while debt exists only in our minds.

So in the dictionary definition of wealth, "much money", is absurd since we don't have any money, only debt based Federal Reserve Note currency. Our currency is not backed by any physical wealth. "Money" as we know it has no value of its own, it is only a measure of valuable things. True wealth is the valuable things.

Frederick Soddy believed that wealth is a physical phenomenon, and debt is a mathematical phenomenon. From his scientific view of the production process, Soddy replaced Adam Smith's traditional factors of production, "Land, Labor, and Capitol," with "Discovery, Natural Energy, and Human Diligence."

He believed that before you could create wealth, you have to first discover the means to make your efforts valuable. The natural energy Soddy spoke of is solar energy that our planet continually gets from our Sun, which is the root from which all the energy our planet receives. He pointed out that people work less and less in the physical sense by using machines. We direct with Human Diligence an inanimate source of power to do what, left alone, it could not do. Machines extend the range of human efforts but never replace it completely. Like the "Matrix," machines do more and more.

Currency is not wealth, it is debt. You can't own land, so expensive property holdings is not wealth. It labor or production wealth? Not if you are producing something useless. Producing a snake catching device to be sold in Ireland would be useless.

There are no snakes in Ireland since St. Patrick crushed them under 1 shamrock. Sorry, St. Patrick drove the snakes from Ireland, which was no easy task since most of them were not automatics, they were four speeds with clutches. Anyone who has been in the clutches of a Python knows it is a constricted space and they are difficult to drive anywhere.

Is laughter wealth? Maybe. In many ways laughter is better than sex. I can laugh with people of the same gender and no one thinks it's wrong. I can laugh with children and not be sent to prison. It's alright to laugh in public and with groups of people. If you get paid for making people laugh it's not a crime.

When I went to the comedy show I was charged with laughter.

One time while rounding up some donkeys, which are also called asses, we started making ass jokes. We laughed so much the donkeys ran away. When we realized we laughed our asses off we laughed even more.

It feels good to laugh, and everyone can use a good laugh, so laughter has value to society and must be some form of wealth.

Even a man in prison is free to laugh.

Is freedom wealth? Wealth gives people the freedom to do as they wish when they wish and go where they want without worry. My brother traveled the country hitch-hiking and riding trains and did many interesting things all without any "money." You don't need wealth to be free, if you are free, you are already wealthy.

Is power wealth? Power is the main reason people want "money." They don't really want all the little green pieces of paper, they want the power over other people that having those Federal Reserve Notes gives them. But power over people is a form of Greed, and greed is not wealth. You can't share greed. You must share wealth. If there is nobody to share the wealth with then it is not worth having. Perhaps that is why it's lonely at the top. Wealth has no value if there is no one to share it with.

He was the wealthiest person in the world but had no one to share it with, poor man.

Are friends wealth? A friend in need is a friend indeed. In my will, when I die, my friends are to be deeded to someone else in need.

Is knowledge wealth? If it were, instead of pennies we would use cognizants. The United States has a huge untapped wealth of knowledge. Lots of people know lots of things, but nobody listens to them or wants to believe them. We are like machines, moved in whatever direction we are directed to. Any deviation makes you a deviate.

Having knowledge is like potential power. It only becomes useful when it is used, like kinetic power. To go to college and learn how to market products and then work as a pipe fitter is ridiculous. All that marketing knowledge goes untapped.

Perhaps action is wealth. To act on the things we know, to bring some value to society is noble indeed. To know how to fix something or help somehow and do nothing is rather cowardly.

Are our talents wealth? Perhaps. Like knowledge, and financial resources, talents are only valuable if you use them in a way that adds

Value to society. If you use the talents you were born with or learned along your way in life you will likely never be poor. Talents, used wisely, can add wealth to your life.

If you were to say that wealth is natural resources. I would not argue with that. I would say that if they are natural resources they occur naturally and cannot be owned by anyone. You can't own the wind, but you can make use of it.

I had a chance to own a wind farm, but I blew it.

I would say water is our most valuable natural resource. Without water, no life would exist on this planet. We know that we are 90% water ourselves. Even food broken down to its base compounds is mostly water with a little bit of nutrients. That is why a multi-vitamin-multi-mineral pill is small in comparison to eating three meals.

I had my frozen assets in the snow bank, but when the economy heated up, they were liquidated.

What about man-made resources? It was discovered years ago that crystals pick up radio frequencies. As a child, I built several crystal radios. These same crystals are useful in all electronic devices, especially computers. The problem was, finding natural crystals of a uniform size and purity was difficult and expensive.

Scientists devised a way to grow silicon crystals in the lab that were of uniform size and quality and purity. Chips from these man-made crystals are in all electronic devices we enjoy today. Some people would say that the man-made resources created an abundance of useful products.

I would ask the obvious question of where did the raw material to make the man-made crystals come from. They came from natural resources that pre-existed on this planet. The scientists did not make those crystals out of nothing, and they did not make the raw materials to use in making the crystals. We only manipulate the natural resources available. My definition of Artificial: Natural Resources manipulated by humans.

> To believe currency is money is as absurd as believing cubic zirconia is a diamond.

Some people would say that intellectual property is not a natural resource since we are glad to conceive the thoughts in our town mind as humans. I would say that it is natural for humans to conceive ideas so they too are essentially natural resources.

Everything that is useful or can be made useful is valuable and therefore wealth., and truly, that is everything. Everything on this planet is or can be made useful whether we have discovered a use for it yet or not. Nothing was put here by accident. God doesn't make any junk!

Gold for instance has a multitude of valuable uses, only a fraction of which we have discovered. Remember that science is discovery, not invention.

Wealth is a state of mind. On a hot day in the desert, the man with an unopened bottle of water when everyone else has none is the wealthiest man there at the time.

In a recent survey of "rich people", only seven percent of them thought of themselves as rich. This group earned over half a million Federal Reserve Notes a year before they personally felt they were rich.

Half a million as a yearly income, think about that.

The Government, as of this writing, considers anyone with an income of $125,000 a year to be rich. That is nearly triple the national median income. Thirty-nine percent of those earning more than $125,000 considered themselves to be middle class. Over 70% were embarrassed to be called well off. I know several of these people personally and none of them think they are rich. There is a very good reason for that. Their sub-conscious mind knows that their whole lot of nothing is equal to your little bit of nothing. Nothing at any magnitude, is still nothing.

It seems that the value of wealth is purely subjective to each individual. To each their own and wealth is like beauty, it is in the eye of the beholder. It is perceived value.

Frederick Soddy called this economic paradox of poverty in a world technically capable of creating sufficiency for everyone.

Soddy said, "Never was there an age in history so dowered as ours with all that could have sufficed for a noble and enduring civilization, whereas it is still to ancient civilizations we must go if we wish to find evidence of human effort and imagination being squandered on a national scale on something not strictly utilitarian in purpose. The most gigantic powers await our commands to provide us with all that we require, but we lead a harried, driven life, concerned for the most part with the immediate necessity of keeping the wolf from the door."

It should be a crime that people on this planet starve, not for the lack of food for it is plenty, but for the lack of money to pay for the food. In the United States alone, we throw away enough food every year to feed the starving people on this planet.

There are those in the New World Order that say we are over populated and that is why we have a tragedy of starvation in poor countries. The truth is that these same individuals of the New World Order are overly greedy.

Frederick Soddy said virtual wealth is the well know phenomenon where the rich to get richer while the poor get poorer.

Soddy said, "It is the virtual wealth which measures the value of the purchasing power of money, and not money which measures the volume of wealth, The important thing is that this 'virtual wealth' does not exist. It is an imaginary negative quantity, deficit or debt of wealth."

Wealth truly is a state of mind, so whether you think you ate or think you aren't, you're right. In that case, why not believe from now on that you are wealthy. Don't let anyone else who wants to think you're poor, bully you around. You only have to take their abuse if you want to, and that my friend is ridiculous.

He who has nothing has everything. If you lack for nothing, you are truly wealthy.

CHAPTER 16

WHAT WOULD AN ALIEN THINK OF OUR MONEY

Since the concept of money and its cousin currency are inventions of humans and do not occur in nature, I wondered what aliens from another planet would think of our "money." This chapter is dedicated to observing money from an alien point of view.

Message to the United Federation of Civilized Planets from Captain Kronus of the Star Cruiser Veracon. We have discovered the inhabitants of this small blue planet have a very strange religion and religious worship. They call this religion "Money."

It seems that nearly all the inhabitants are taught from the earliest age of understanding about "Money." They are told how important "Money" is to their lives. This religion worships a group of Gods. Each of these Gods in some way in the past history did great deeds which ate of great importance. Without these deeds, these human as they call themselves would be enduring much suffering.

Each God has a story of their deeds, and are honored and worshipped by having their likeness engraved on metal medallions or printed on pieces of green paper. Everyone carries these medallions and pieces of green paper with them everywhere they go. They are inscribed with hieroglyphics that say "In God We Trust."

The medallions   are called coins and change, while the green pieces or paper are called dollars. The more highly regarded a god is, the higher the dollar that bears their image is valued Sometimes these dollars are referred to by their pre-designated numerical value, such as five, ten, or twenty. Collectively, the medallions and dollars are called "Money" and are a major tool in the money religion.

When someone does not have the proper medallions or dollars when they are stopped at one of the many checkpoints, a great amount of distress is observed. It appears to be a disgrace to be found without any medallions or dollars to show you honor the Gods and the religion of money.

There are six metal medallions and seven pieces of green paper in the Money religion for a total of 13. Each bears an image of one of the Gods, although some of the Gods are so highly regarded that their image is on a medallion and a piece of green paper.

On the other side of the medallions and dollars is an image of a temple built to honor the greatest of those Gods, and the city bears his name he is so highly regarded. Washington.

Some of the medallions have an image of a fierce bird known as an eagle. This seems to indicate these particular gods were gods of war. Each medallion has a hieroglyphic that says, "Liberty." We believe this to be the name of this planet. When we interrogated some of the humans, they informed us that this was the land of liberty.

The children attend educational centers where a prayer is recited every morning which refers to the Gods and Liberty. The children show homage to the Gods by presenting medallions or dollars at one of the check points at mid-day before they eat. If a child does not have the medallions or dollars to honor the gods, they are not fed with the other children and must fend or forage themselves.

It seems they are taught from an early age that if you would dishonor the gods, you will become a social outcast. In the "Money" religion, if you work hard and do a good job, you will be rewarded with a good quantity of medallions and dollars.

Each city has one or more branch temples known as Banks, where humans regularly go to pick up and drop off medallions and dollars. We observed humans arriving at these Banks after they had closed their doors. The humans were distressed that they were unable to get medallions or dollars to properly worship in the "Money" religion. Some where they held up the center digit on their hands. This gave them a small measure of forgiveness.

We gathered a large amount of medallions and dollars from a heavily armored transport as it moved between temples. This allowed us to do scientific analysis of the medallions and dollars and to conduct a number of very interesting experiments involving human reactors and interactions involving "Money."

The medallions are an amalgamation of common base metals, mostly copper, nickel, and zinc. They are not rare and seem to have little value other than as a tool in the "Money" religion. All the medallions conduct electricity, yet none are subject to magnetism. We felt that was important because many of the humans we interrogated spoke of the power of "Money" and the "Almighty" is also another term for "God."

It was also noted that the amalgamation of the metals in the medallions does not occur naturally. They were combined by humans in the amalgam for some reason we cannot yet determine. Some of the medallions have cogged edges for use as gears in some machine that dispenses food and drink. One human we interrogated referred to this machine as the "Economy," which would grind to halt without "Money."

When we examined the paper dollars are made of, we discovered it too is an amalgamation of many things that do not occur in this combination naturally. The fibers are in acid free high quality of cotton and wood pulp which is durable and strong. A phosphorescent metallic strip ran the length of most of the dollars, but not the one referred as "One." The "One" is also another term for "God."

Many of the inks used were metallic in composition. In spite of this we did not find them to be good conductors of electricity, and were also not subject to magnetism. Inscriptions in hieroglyphics say "Federal Reserve Notes." It may be possible that these notes are a frequency at which the power of "Money" is transmitted.

Several of the humans we interrogated referred to these notes as currency, even though we measured no current. One of the humans, who was a low-level religious leader, informed us that the dollars had to be circulated or passed from one human to another for the power of "Money" to work. That led us to conduct experiments involving humans and their actions and interactions involving "Money."

We set up every type of measuring instrument that we could think of to measure any effect or energy transfer from the power of "Money" when humans touched or worship it.

We placed medallions on busy pathways that humans walked regularly. The smaller medallions were walked past by most of the humans. It seemed the larger the medallion the sooner a human picked it up.

When we placed dollars on the busy pathways, they were picked up by humans almost immediately. When we placed dollars with the more highly regarded gods' images on them, humans knocked each other over trying to get to them first. This resulted in a few minor scuffles between some of the humans.

Our delicate instruments never detected any energy transfer from the "Money" itself. However, we detected activities in the brains of humans that were remarkable. When a human found the "Money" on the pathway they became excited, Blood pressure and respiration increased, pupils of the eyes dilated, heart rate increased, and as the human touched the dollars when they picked them up a state of euphoria overcame them as their brains excreted chemicals that caused signals in the humans' brains. The reactions and effects on the humans were real and measurable even though no energy transfer was detected from the "Money" to the humans. The same effects were measured each time this experiment was repeated.

When more than one human detected the "Money" at the same time and only one of them got to pick it up, the human that did not pick it up showed no measure of euphoria. Different chemicals were emitted by their brains, and they became violent and tensed their muscles. Euphoria only occurred for the humans that got to keep the dollars we placed on the pathways.

Anybody for a little money madness?

This led us to conduct an experiment where a large quantity of dollars was placed on the busy pathway. There was enough for many of the humans to take one, get the feeling of euphoria, and leave the other dollars for other humans to also worship and get the euphoria.

That is not what we observed. The first human to find the "Money" picked up as much of it as they could carry. A measurement of extreme euphoria overcame them much like a drug overdose. In almost every instance where we repeated this experiment, riots broke out. The humans who did not get to share in the euphoria attacked the euphoric human so they could have euphoria as well. If it was not shared, the humans would take it forcefully in nearly every instance.

This led us to conduct an experiment where a large amount of "Money" would be given to one individual to worship and get the euphoria. Then we would take the "Money" away from the human.

When we took the dollars away from the humans in these experiments, different chemicals were emitted by their brains and a solemn sadness overcame them. In a few instances we measured the anger response and the same solute was given with the center digit o the hands thrust upwards at us. Again, this seemed to give a small measure of forgiveness for losing control of the "Money" to worship.

In several instances we destroyed the dollars by burning them in front of the humans. Much sadness was measured and some of the humans wept for the gods as the power of that "Money" would never be enjoyed. Again, the effects were real and measured each time this equipment was conducted.

These dollars do not have any food value, yet in one experiment, a human was told he could have as many of the dollars as he could eat. He picked out only certain dollars with particular Gods on them and consumed more than we could have thought possible. The most popular Gods chosen in this instance were the one with the bald head and the fat one with a beard.

In another experiment we placed a large quantity of dollars in a room with two male humans. We told them that only one of them would be allowed to keep the dollars to worship and the other would get nothing. They were told to decide between them which would keep the dollars and which would get none.

To our shock and amazement, they attacked each other and battled with such ferocity to be the sole human to worship the Gods on the dollars that both of them perished. It must be a great honor to worship these Gods. We were told by a human we interrogated later that the death of those two humans was not considered a great loss because they were Lawyers.

In another experiment, we gave a male human a large quantity of dollars and told him he could share it with any of the other human captives we had. He shared different quantities of it with female human if they would help him worship. We then observed them engage in several strange breeding rituals thrashing about and calling out to those gods. "Oh God, Oh God. I'm coming." Even though they never went anywhere, a euphoric feeling was experienced and measured in all who were partaking in this worship of the Gods.

In another experiment, we told a female human she was going to be returned home and she could have as much of the "Money" to worship as she could carry. She removed her clothes, tied off the sleeves on her shirt and pants, and stuffed them to enormous proportions and used them as carrying bags. She was quite clever and resourceful in her duty to worship as many of the Gods as she could.

This led us to conduct an experiment where a male human was told the same thing, he was to be released and could have as many of the dollars to worship as he could carry. With the male though, we took his clothes so he could not stuff them as the female human had.

Again, a great deal of cleverness and resourcefulness as demonstrated. The male human, meticulously rolled the dollars into a tight bundle and inserted as many as he could into every orifice. Then he stacked dollars into such a manner that with his hands and arms he could carry a large quantity.

In many instances the "Money" acted as a drug, giving a short lived euphoric feeling which dissipated as the humans parted with it. Then they crave the euphoric feeling again.

The power of "Money" to give humans as euphoric sensation is passed on with the dollars as other humans receive them. Although we could not measure it, the current in the currency must be real.

It also did not seem to matter where on the planet we picked up humans and did our experiments. Universally, no matter where they were from, they recognized the Gods on the dollars and the euphoria was measured in their brains.

One of our scientists believes that "Money" is not a religion, but some form of mental disease. The more of it you have the crazier you become, and it is highly contagious.

Most of us believe though that "Money" is only a religious tool. We could find no other useful purpose for "Money." Captain Kronus of the Star cruiser Veracon signing off.

CHAPTER 17

THE CASHLESS SOCIETY OF THE NEW WORLD ORDER

"The invisible Money Power is working to control and enslave mankind. It financed Communism, Fascism, Marxism, Zionism, and Socialism. All of these are directed to making the United States a member of World Government." – American Mercury Magazine

"Three groups spend other people's money: children, thieves, politicians. All three need supervision." – Dick Armey

"Everyone wants to live at the expense of the state. They forget that the state lives at the expense of everyone." – Frederic Bastiat

"When a government takes over a people's economic life it becomes absolute, and when it has become absolute it destroys the arts, the minds, the liberties and the meaning of the people it governs." – Maxwell Anderson

"But how is this legal plunder to be identified? Quite simply. See if the law takes from some persons what belongs to them, and gives it to other persons to whom it does not belong. See if the law benefits one citizen at the expense of another by doing what the citizen himself cannot do without committing a crime." – Frederic Bastiat

"A power has risen up in the government greater than the people

themselves, consisting of many and various powerful interests, combined in one mass, and held together by the cohesive power of the vast surplus in banks." – John C. Calhoun

"When through a process of law the common people have lost their homes, they will be more tractable and more easily governed." – Civil Servants' Year Book

"If you put the federal government in charge of the Sahara Desert, in 5 years there'd be a shortage of sand." – Milton Friedman

"The collection of taxes which are not absolutely required, which do not beyond reasonable doubt contribute to the public welfare, is only a species of legalized larceny. The wise and correct course to follow in taxation is not to destroy those who have already secured success, but to create conditions under which everyone will have a better chance to be successful." – Calvin Coolidge

"Whoever controls the volume of money in any country is absolute master of all industry and commerce." – James A. Garfield

"Here I close my opinion. I could not say less in view of questions of such gravity that go down to the very foundations of the government. If the provisions of the Constitution can be set aside by an Act of Congress, where is the course of usurpation to end? The present assault upon the capital is but the beginning. It will be but the stepping stone to others, larger and more sweeping till our political contests will become a war of the poor against the rich; a war growing in intensity and bitterness." – Justive Stephen J. Field

"The Trilateralist Commission is international... (and)... is intended to be the vehicle for multinational consolidation of the commercial and

banking interests by seizing control of the political government of the United States. The Trilateralist Commission represents a skillful, coordinated effort to seize control and consolidate the four centers of power – political, monetary, intellectual, and ecclesiastical." – Barry Goldwater

"Gold still represents the ultimate form of payment in the world." – Alan Greenspan

"It is to be regretted that the rich and powerful too often bend the acts of government to their selfish purposes." – Andrew Jackson

"The real menace of our Republic is the invisible government, which like a giant octopus sprawls its slimy legs over our cities, states, and nation. At the head is a small group of banking houses generally referred to as "international bankers." This little coterie...run our government for their own selfish ends. It operates under cover of a self-created screen...and seizes...our executive officers...legislative bodies...schools...courts...newspapers and every agency created for the public protection." – John F. Hylan

"The system of banking is a blot left in all our Constitutions, which, if not covered, will end in their destruction...I sincerely believe that banking institutions are more dangerous than standing armies: and that the principle of spending money to be paid by posterity... is but swindling futurity on a large scale." – Thomas Jefferson

It seems an awful lot of very intelligent people have warned us for a very long time that the money matrix could occur. It seems most of us were to poor to pay attention, trying to keep the wolf away from the door. We are busily working to put food on the table a roof over our

24111111111

heads, too busy to care what the Government is doing.

My reality check bounced because I was too poor to pay attention.

I first learned of "Maslow's Heirarchy of Needs" when I was in business school. Quite simply, it is a five-level pyramid that describes human behavior. It explains why different classes or economically different people behave different from each other and value different things.

The pyramid looks like this.

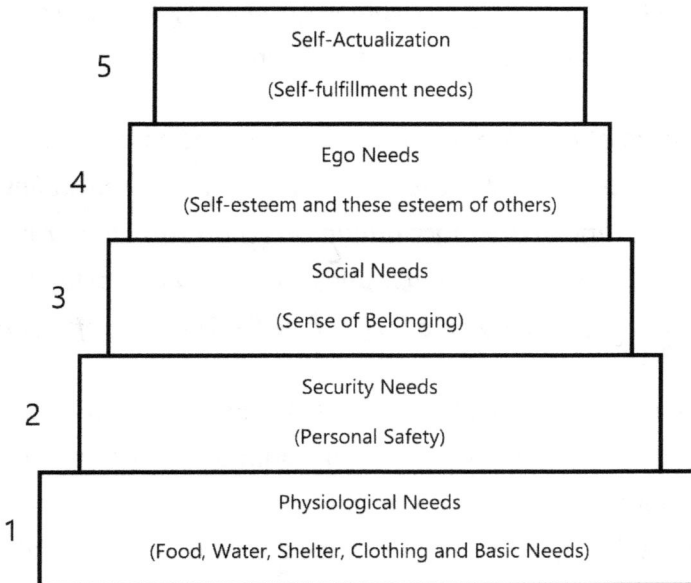

5 — Self-Actualization (Self-fulfillment needs)

4 — Ego Needs (Self-esteem and these esteem of others)

3 — Social Needs (Sense of Belonging)

2 — Security Needs (Personal Safety)

1 — Physiological Needs (Food, Water, Shelter, Clothing and Basic Needs)

The very first of the humans' needs are the physiological needs. If you were dropped on a strange planet by aliens, these are the needs you would have to fulfill first or you would surely die. You would need food, shelter, clothing, water etc... You would concentrate on fulfilling these needs until they are sufficiently satisfied to ensure your survival.

Once these needs are met, you would move on the next level of needs be filled, which are your security needs. However, if you were not able to fulfill the basic needs, you would continue trying to meet those needs until your eventual death.

If the basic needs were met, security would take the forefront of your thoughts. Keeping yourself from being attacked by predators, having a dwelling to keep out the elements, etc... You would keep working on those needs until they were fulfilled.

Assuming your basic needs and security needs could be fulfilled, you would move on to the social needs. You would try to find other people nearby that the aliens might have also dropped off on this planet. You would want someone to talk to and listen to. If there were others you would want to be accepted into their group.

This is a good place to note that sadly, most of us never make it past the first three levels. Also, if you lose your job, which could cause you to lose your house, you immediately, regress to trying to fulfill your basic and security needs. Downsizing, outsourcing, plant closings, rising unemployment, or over-employment if you have to work two jobs to make ends meet, rising inflation and rising interest rates all exacerbate the problem of not raising above the first three levels of Maslow's Hierarchy of Needs!

If you make it beyond the first three, you will have an ego, and rightly so, because you got somewhere few people do. Pat yourself on the back and grow big head. Now you can root your own horn and strut like the cock of the walk.

If you should become financially independent, you will probably make it to the fifth level, self-actualization or self-fulfillment. Now you get to be eccentric and do whatever you want and say whatever you want, and if people and government do not like, they can go to hell. You're so rich, you don't care what anyone else thinks, so you get to be yourself.

Reaching this level though make you a threat to other people on this level and governments. A person out of control, or rather their own control, is a dangerous person.

We think we are too intelligent to be manipulated by the government and big business interests. Yet, here we are, enslaved in money system I call the "Money Matrix." It is a system where seemingly the rich get richer, the poor get poorer, and the middle class disappears. In reality it is money which has vanished. Like Pavlov's dogs, we respond an expected every time they ring the bell.

To solve a problem, you have to first know you have a problem. Most of us fail to recognize that in fact there is a problem, and there lies the problem. The problem is: we actually believe we are a free people living in a free country with robust free market economy. We think we elect the officials that run this country. This is what the new world order wants you to believe.

It's closer to the truth to say that at the turn of the twentieth century; a group of monied elite overthrew the government. It has been said we have the best congress money can buy, and certainly bribery blackmail, and betrayal are not new to American Government.

Our "Founding Fathers" that freed this nation were notorious fat protesters that fought against seemingly insurmountable odds against a tyrannical King. Europe had been ruled for hundreds of years by a monied elite called royalty. Subjects, or servants, or citizens, were really nothing more than worker bee slaves to the royal rulers. The common man subjugated themselves to service of the royal monied elite.

Once America was freed from this tyranny, the Founding father sought to set up a form of government that would ensure we were never subjugated again. The Great Seal of the United States was created. This can be seen on the black of the one-dollar Federal Reserve Note. Symbolically, the seal reflects the beliefs and values of the Founding Fathers, which they wished to pass on their descendants.

On the front side of the seal, is an eagle clinching a banner that says "E Pluribus Unum." It is Latin and translates, "Out of many, one" or roughly "many united as one." This refers to the uniting of the 13 states to form this Nation.

On the back of the seal, sometimes referred to as the spiritual side, is the unfinished pyramid. At the top of the pyramid is the "Eye of Providence." Above it appears the motto, "Annuit Coeptis," or "He (God) has favored out undertakings." On a banner under the pyramid is the motto, "Novus Ordo Seclorum," or "A new order of the ages."

This heralded the beginning of the new American era, or a New World Order. The tables were turned on the privileged few and empowered every American to become the privileged many. What had been exclusive to the monied elite was now the norm of every American.

Free to be themselves and do as they pleased instead of doing what pleased someone else, an explosion of prosperity spread through the new nation of the United States. It is human nature that people will work harder for themselves than they will for an ungrateful boss, and the results were obvious.

This "New World Order", called democracy was dangerous because it made everyone eccentric. With the success of the American Revolution, the French, who had been allies to the Americans, had their own Revolution beginning 1789. They beheaded the King and Queen and revoked the special privileges of nobles, clergy, and cities.

As you could well imagine, the monied elite of Europe were terrified by this spreading democracy. This led other European countries to attack France to squelch the spread of freedom. They failed. Other nobles were thrown down in other countries as in domino effect.

To kill a snake, you have to cut off its head and since America was at the head of this revolutionary movement, it had to be beaten down and subjugated. The monied elite thought they had order when they were in control. The Americans had unleashed chaos, not order.

After the French Revolution, Napoleon grabbed control of France and made himself Emperor, as well as the King of Italy. He needed money to finance his ambitions in Europe, so he sold the United States what became known as the Louisiana Purchase. This was in 1803. President Jefferson authorized Congress to pay 22.5 million dollars for the Louisiana Territory, effectively doubling the size of the U.S.

Napoleon fully intended to take it back by military means after he was done conquering Europe. His plans didn't work out and we were spared. The British defeated Napoleon.

All the while, American and European shipping were under attack by pirates along the Barbary Coast of North Africa. Those pirates were not part of the powerful Ottoman Empire. Instead, they were a loose confederation of Sheiks and warlords.

At the request of American shippers who had put up with all they were going to, President Jefferson dispatched a small Navy and Marine contingent to handle the problem. A handful of Marines captured a major city, and a peace was negotiated in favor of the Americans were more dangerous than previously thought. They had shown the ability to project power beyond their borders. If Americans could attack Africa, they could attack Europe.

America was again at war with England by 1812, as the monied elite tried again unsuccessfully to defeat the young democracy. War is chaos, and everyday life in America is chaotic, so Americans are very good at winning wars. With independent thinking and de-centralized judgement calls, democracy has not one person in charge, but everyone in charge at once.

In 1821 Mexico gained its independence from Spain. In 1823 President Monroe issues the Monroe issues the Monroe Doctrine. Essentially, it is said that America would not tolerate Europeans meddling in the affairs overthrow any governments would be considered an act of war on the United States itself, and the U.S. would bring all forces to bear against the intruders.

In return, the Monroe Doctrine promised that the United States would stay out of the affairs of Europe. In a nutshell, it was a "you leave us alone and we'll leave you alone policy."

In 1823 the Mexican province of Texas was settled by Americans that began colonizing. These were mostly southerners with slaves. In 1824 Mexico abolished against Mexico, winning their independence and establishing The Republic of Texas.

Texas tried to gain official recognition as an independent country from Mexico, but Mexico never gave them recognition. Texas was having continuing skirmishes with Mexico and realized they would not stye independent long.

In 1845 Texas asked the United States to annex them in as a state and the U.S. government agreed. Mexico felt that U.S. was messing with its internal affairs and has unjustly taken away the province of Texas.

It is likely that the U.S. Government meant all along to grab Texas. It is no accident that essentially Jim Bowie and Davy Crockett had led a Special Forces unit to the Alamo to aid in the fight for Texas independence. Crockett had been both a Colonel in the army, and a U.S. Congressman.

In April 1846 Mexican Calvary attacked American troops near the Rio Grande. U.S. Congress declared war on May 13, 1846. Mexico declared war on May 23, 1846. California declared its independence from Mexico and joined the U.S. in the war on Mexico.

U.S. forces defeated Mexico. The Treaty of Cahuenga in 1847 ended fighting in California. The Treaty of Guadalupe Hidalgo was signed February 2, 1848, ending the war. It also gave the United States control of Texas, California, Nevada, Utah, Colorado, Arizona, New Mexico, and Wyoming. Mexico was given $18,250,000. This was the Mexican American war.

The monied elite realized that America could not be beaten in war. An elaborate plan was set into motion to divide the United States against itself. After it was weakened by a civil war, the monied elite could swoop in and take over.

In 1864, the Civil War did indeed break out in America. British troops were stationed in Canada. The hope was that we would wear ourselves down and they would attack us from the North. They would not be alone in this attack.

Nepoleon III of France had stationed troops in Mexico to attack from the South. He intended to install Archduke Maximilian of Austria as a Ruler of Mexico. The Mexicans surprised the French troops by attacking them. The French were defeated on May 5th, 1862. This is the Mexican holiday Cinco De Mayo, which celebrates their victory over the French invaders.

President Lincoln assisted the Mexicans by sending them modern weapon and having the Navy blockade the port of Vera Cruz to prevent French reinforcements from landing. It was in the best interests of the unio and backed by the Monroe Doctrine.

Lincoln knew the preservation of the Union was the most important thing. Without it, all would be lost. The British knew that without the help of the French to invade from the south, their plan would fail.

The Civil War ended in 1865 and the United States remained united. The war did bankrupt the Nation and destroyed many of the resources. However, the democracy showed a never-before-seen resiliency and came back to prosperity quickly.

War was also raging in Europe at this time. Austria was defeated by Prussia. In 1867 Austria-Hungary was created and it was agreed the Habsburg family would be emperors of the Austria Empire. This same year the U.S. purchased Alaska from Russia and the Romanovs.

The monied elite realized that things would never return to the old order. However, by using the new system of democracy, a New World Order could be established. An ambitious plan was devised and set into motion at the beginning of the twentieth century.

To gain control of America, they would have to work from the inside and first gain control of the finances. All great nations are vulnerable from within. Tyrants are masters at mind control and financial control. Every tyranny in history has been energized and financed by the oppressed people themselves, tricked into paying the cost of having themselves violated, abused, plundered, and enslaved.

The monied elite decided to get some of their own people elected to the democratic governments of the world. The only way to change things is to be one of the powers that be. Congress makes new laws all the time, if they didn't, they would go out of business. If laws were static and unchanged, why would you need a congress to make laws?

In 1894, Congress passed an income tax law. One year later, in 1895, the Supreme Court ruled the income tax to be unconstitutional. (Article

I section 9 Clause 4)

The aristocratic leaders of Spain were losing control of their Empire. By the mid 1890's they were left with a few scattered possessions in the Pacific, like Guam and the Philippines, Cuba and other islands in the West Indies, and some in Africa. Much of the Empire had gained its independence, with the remaining ones struggling to get Independent, Guerilla forces had gained control of most of Cuba and the Philippines.

Also, in the 1890's in America, the monied elite had gained control of the press. They used the power of the press to influence American opinion in favor of war with Spain. With often fabricated stories, the newspapers of the time stirred up the American public to intervene in Cuba.

Tomas Estrada Palma was given a $150 million loan from U.S. bankers to purchase Cuba's independence from Spain. Spain refused. He then asked the U.S. Congress for help. Much of Cuba's economy was already run by Americans.

The monied elite had used its media propaganda to make Americans believe it was their manifest destiny to colonize and make the nation grow larger. History books from this time make dear the motivations of material gain for the U.S. government and financial interests. The monied elite were taking control.

With the end of the Indian wars of the 1870's and 1880's the Army had nothing to do. Senator John M. Thurston of Nebraska said. "War with Spain would increase the business and earnings of every American railroad, it would increase the output of every American factory, it would stimulate every branch of industry and domestic commerce."

The monied elite were trying to convince everyone that war was good for business, a practice that continues to this day. The U.S Congress passed a bill for intervention.

On February 15, 1898, the American battleship USS Maine exploded in Havana harbor in Cuba. The American press run by the monied elite proclaimed this sinking of the USS Maine was an act of sabotage by the Spaniards. Public opinion was now in favor of war.

On April 19, 1898, Congress proclaimed Cuba independent from Spain. On April 25, 1898, Congress declared was in Spain. Within a month Cuba was in American control. On December 10, 1898, the Treat Paris was signed.

The U.S. gained most of Spain's colonies to include Guam, the Philippines, and Puerto Rico. Cuba was granted independence. The Spanish-American War saw the Pacifist America Nation emerges as an imperial global power.

The United States entered a lengthy and prosperous period of high economic growth, population growth, and technological innovation which would last until the stock market crash of 1929.

The U.S annexed Puerto Rico, Guam, and the Philippines, William Randolph Hearst became a media tycoon. He had more influence than most politicians. The war cemented relations between the American North and South. It gave them a common enemy for the first time since the Civil War.

For Spain, the Monday would soon fall. For the U.S., a length war on the Philippines began. War raged from 1899 to 1915 when President Wilson introduced a plan to give the Philippines full independence over

204

a transitional period of time.

At the turn of the 20th century, half of Europe was still ruled by Kings and Queens, and half were ruled by some form of democracy. The four ruling families of the remaining Old-World Order were the Hohenzollerns which ruled Germany. The Habsburgs ruled Austria-Hungary. The Romanovs ruled Russia, and the Ottomans ruled the Ottoman Empire in present day Turkey and the Middle East. The U.S. had just beat down the Spanish.

It was in the best interests of the monied elite to pit the remaining kingdoms of the Old-World Order against the fledgling democracies in Europe. There could be only two outcomes. If the royals won, the monied elite also won. If the democracies won, the monied elite were already solidly among the governments, so they would still win. It was more to their interest if the democracies won, as they could then emerge with a plan for a New World Order with them solidly in charge.

They set about moving most of their wealth to the United States to use as a safe haven and power base. On April 14, 1912, the Luxury liner Titanic Sank, taking with it some of the monied lite and the fortunes they were moving to America.

In 1913, with more of their people in Congress, the 16th amendment to the Constitution of the United States of America was pushed through. It was an income tax law. It was to go into force February 12th, 1913, and was declared ratified on February 25, 1913, and became the law of the land.

The Constitution Article I Section 9 Clause 4, forbids any direct tax unless it is apportioned. The 16th Amendment did not repeal this clause.

It was certain to be ruled upon by the Federal Supreme Court within a year and would likely be found unconstitutional.

On December 23, 1913, during Christmas break, with most of the Congressmen home with their families, the monied elite in congress that stayed in Washington D.C. passed the Federal Reserve Act. It was quickly signed into law before the other members of congress could get back to Washington D.C. to do anything about it.

With Federal Reserve Notes the new currency backed by nothing, the monied elite would have used the same argument I use today had the Income Tax Law been challenged in the Supreme Court. They would have said that since the Federal Reserve, they are not really "paying" any "money" in the form of a tax anyway, so what difference does it make? It's really no big deal. Give them back some of their nothing for the use of their nothing.

Only two things are sure in life, debt and taxes.

These arguments never had to play themselves out in the public arena. If they had of, the whole plan would have come undone, as the American people would have realized immediately what was happening. The monied elite needed a diversion. As part of their plan, events were put into motion which ultimately led to the outbreak of World War I.

There is probably no single concise or conclusive assessment of the exact cause of World War I. This much we do know. On June 28, 1914 Franz Ferdinand, Archduke of Austria and heir the Austra-Hungarian throne, was assassinated in Sarajevo. The assassin was part of the group of fifteen that were assisted by the secret society known as the "Black Hand."

The group was pro-Serbian nationals with links to the Serbian military. Austria-Hungary sent an ultimatum to the Serbs. Serbia agreed to all demands except one, and Austria-Hungary declared war July 28, 1914, The Russian government had pledged in 1909 to protect Serbian independence. Russian mobilized its forces by order of Tsar Nicholas II.

Kaiser Wilhelm of Germany declared war on Russia on August 1, 1914 and two days later against France, which was an ally of Russia. Britain declared war on Germany on August 4, 1914. On October 29, 1914, the Ottoman Empire entered the war on the side of Austria-Hungary and Germany. With this, he monied elite had all the principals involved in the conflict that they wanted there.

The United States was a neutral country, and the monied elite continued to move their fortunes and themselves to America. Like the Titanic, the Luxury liner Lusitania was used frequently by the monied elite for moving themselves and their fortunes to America.

On May 7, 1915, the Lusitania was sunk by a torpedo from a German U-Boat. A secret warning had been given to the monied elite before the ship set sail. They were advised not to travel because U-Boats would be gunning for Lusitania.

The German Embassy even sent a public warning to the United

States. It read: NOTICE TRAVELERS intending to embark on the Atlantic voyage are reminded that a state of war exists between Germany and her allies and Great Britain and her allies; that the zone of war includes the waters adjacent to the British Isles; that, in accordance with formed notice given by the Imperial German Government, vessels flying, the flag of Great Britain, or any of her allies, are liable to destruction in these waters and that travelers sailing in the war zone on the ships of Great Britain or her allies do so at their own risk.

IMPERIAL GERMAN EMBASSY

Washington, D.C. April 22, 1915

Lusitania continued in its role as a luxury liner built to convey people and property between England and the United States. On May 7, 1915, six days after it left New York, Lusitania took a torpedo from German submarine U-20. This triggered a second explosion in the ship.

The Germans claimed secretly carried munitions on board ignited causing the second explosion. Indeed, part of the cargo was riffle bullets, shrapnel shells, and fuses. By international law, the military cargo made a passenger ship a legitimate target. German spies in New York knew ammo had been loaded onto the ship. This is the reason the German gave for stacking Lusitania. This is ridiculous due to the fact that the cargo was quite small.

It makes more sense, coupled with the warning to the U.S. Government from the German Embassy, that truly the intended target of the attack was the monied elite themselves that were on the ship.

Some of the well-known people that died on the Lusitania included:

The daughters of H. Montagu Allan

American author and playwright, Justus Miles Forman

American theatrical producer, Charles Frohman

American philosopher and writer, Elbert Hubbard

Irish art collector, Hugh Lane

American Engineer, entrepreneur. Fredne Stark Pearson

Vanderbilt family member, Alfred Gwyne Vanderbik

Genealogist, Lothrop Withington

Of course, the American press, run by monied elite, went ballistic trying to whip up a public outcry that would now send the United States into war. The Germans countered that the British conspired with deliberately have Lusitania sank to draw the U.S. into the war.

This is of course, absurd. The Germans intended to kill the monied elite that had instigated the war in the first place. They knew full well what they were doing. They failed to get them all, and angered the monied elite even more. The United States stayed out of the war for another year, but sinking of Lusitania played a big role in the final decision.

Most historians will agree that it was the "Zimmermann Telegram" that was the final straw that broke the camels' back and pulled the United States into WWI. The telegram was dispatched from Arthur Zimmerman, Foreign Secretary of the German Empire to the

Germans ambassador in Mexico, Heinrich von Eckardt. This was on January 16, 1917 at the height of the war.

The telegram was interpreted by British Naval code breakers and decrypted. This was possible because the code the Foreign Office used had been partially crypt-analyzed using a captured codebook for an earlier version of the cypher. The United States did not at that time have any code-breaking capabilities like the British had.

The British government had a dilemma, if they exposed the explosive nature of the telegram, the United States would be drawn into the war for sure. On the other hand, the Germans would know their code was broken and would stop using it. Depriving the British of valuable intelligence.

The message in the telegram proposed an alliance between Germany and Mexico. Mexico would attack the U.S. and German would supply funding and make sure Mexico would get Texas, New Mexico, and Arizona. Making this proposal would of course violate the Monroe Doctrine and draw America into the war against Germany.

The British waited over a month and in fact stole a copy of the telegram from a telegraph office in Mexico City. It turned out that in fact the German used the exact older code the British had captured when they sent the message from their Embassy in Washington D.C. to the Embassy in Mexico.

On February 23, 1917. The British gave a copy of the telegram to the U.S. ambassador in Britain, and it was relayed to President Wilson. Sentiment in the U.S. at that time was anti-Mexican as well as anti-German. U.S. troops had been chasing the bandits revolutionary

Poncho Villa all over Northern Mexico. Villa had carried out several raids across the border. News of the telegram angered the Americans even more.

The U.S. government gave a copy of the telegram to the press on March 1, 1917. Most people thought it was a ploy by the British to bring America into the war on the Allied side. The German and Mexican diplomas denounced t5he telegram as fraud.

Then on March 3, 1917, Arthur Zimmermann confirmed that the telegram was indeed real and he did indeed send it. He reiterated this in a speech on March 29, 1917. Then Zimmermann blamed President Wilson for breaking off relations with Germany after the telegram was made public.

Confirming that Germany was getting hostile to the Americans enraged the public. On April 2, 1917, President Wilson asked Congress to declare war on Germany, which four days later they did. The United States was now at war with Germany and its allies.

For Germany to anger the U.S. into war at this time makes no sense Germany was winning. Seven months later, the Bolshevik Russian Revolution overthrew the Romanovs, installed a communist form of government and five months later made peace with Germany and withdrew from the war.

With this in mind, it would have allowed Germany to concentrate on the western front where they would have certainly beat down the French and British and ended the war. With America in the war on the western front, this would not be possible.

So why would Germany do this? The answer is they didn't. even a year and a half after Americans entered the war. Germany was still winning. In September of 1918 factions inside Germany overthrew the Kaiser and formed a demonic government. Germany was declared a Republic on November 9, 1918. Imperial Germany had died, and a new Germany had been born: The Weisner Republic. The Kaiser fled the country.

Two days later on November 11, 1918, at 1100 hours the Armistice was signed ending World War One. On June 28, 1917, the Treaty of Versailles was signed.

At the end of the war Germany was still winning. To be sure, with the American in the war, it was only a matter of time before the Germans were beat down and their country and industry destroyed. Many Germans felt they were betrayed from within, and they were.

The monied elite did not want Germany destroyed, they wanted Germany's wealth. And the Treaty of Versailles forced Germany to pay reparations for the war to the Allies. This helped to bankrupt Germany.

With this in mind, it becomes obvious that Zimmermann was an agent on the payroll of the monied elite. The Germans didn't need the U.S. to enter the war. Britain needed America to enter the war, but the monied elite desperately needed America in the war. They were moving their people and assets to America as a safe place to operate from because no military power had shown the ability to beat the United States.

Also, it was imperative for the Monarchies of the old-world order to be replaced with democracies before the new world order the monied elite envisioned could come about.

Zimmermann sent that telegram using a code he knew full well the British had already broken. He knew the British would show the telegram to the U.S. which could bring America to war. When it was made public, other German officials denied its authenticity. Yet Zimmermann fully and publicly admitted to it! Then to ensure it would draw the U.S into the war, he publicly insulted President Wilson! Obviously, he was working for the monied elite.

The monied elite had positioned enough of their people in the U.S. government and media to, if when necessary, bring the American war machine and warriors into the conflict to swiftly bring and end to it. As I have said before, nobody is better at winning wars than the Americans.

Then with Germany still winning the war, the monied elite activated agents inside Germany (remember, all great nations are vulnerable from within), to overthrow the Kaiser and surrender. This is the only conclusion that makes sense. Otherwise, Zimmermann's actions and the overthrow of the Kaiser and surrender make no logical sense. You don't entice a powerful nation into a fight you don't need and you don't throw up your hands and quit when you're winning!

I have just suggested that the monied elite both started and ended WWI. Before you think I've gone off the deep end it should be noted that I am not the first person to say this. Back in June 16, 1918, Eugene V. Debs, a Presidential candidate said the same thing in a speech.

If it's obvious to me ninety years after the fact, imagine how obvious it must have been to a politically savvy Presidential candidate at the time it was happening? Debs essentially said don't register for the draft, let the monied elite that started the war die for their cause.

In 1917 President Wilson pushed the Espionage Act through Congress, and in 1918 the Sedition Act (essentially the Patriot Act of its time.) President Wilson had Debs arrested imprisoned and his citizenship stripped, because Debs attributed World War I to financial interests.

Eugene Debs for his part had exercised his constitutional right to free speech, and as a Presidential Candidate, he attacked the war effort, and obvious target for political debate. Debs called an ace an ace, a spade a spade, and an asshole an asshole! For his honesty for calling, it as he saw it firsthand with a ringside seat from a position of authority, he was sent to prison.

This would be like sending Jessy Jackson to Prison for talking out about the Iraq War today. Unbelievable yet true. President Wilson was not only part of the monied elite and a bigot, he was married to the monied elite.

With the end of World War I, the four remaining Monarchies of the old-world order were destroyed. The Hohenzollerns of Germany, the Habsburgs of Austria-Hungarian, the Romanovs of Russia, and the Ottomans of North Africa were no longer world powers. The old-world order would never recover from the shock.

At the end of the war, President Wilson introduced the idea of a "League of Nations." The proposed League of Nations was incorporated into the Paris Peace Conference at the Treaty of Versailles in 1919 The League of Nations was the first real attempt t the "New World Order."

It was an international organization with goals of disarmament, preventing war through collective security, settling disputes between nations through negotiation and diplomacy, and improving global welfare. The diplomatic philosophy of the League of Nations presented a dramatic shift in thought from the Old-World Order.

The philosophy of The Old-World Order saw Europe as a shifting map of alliances among nation-series, creating a balance of power by maintaining strong armies and secret agreements.

With the new philosophy, the League of Nations was President Wilson's idea, the United States never joined. Nationalism, sovereignty, and a feeling of, nobody is going to tell us what to do, were stronger than the monied elite realized.

Ultimately, the League of Nations lacked an army of its own, or any real way to enforce resolution. Japan withdrew in 1932 because they saw it as Euro-centric. Hitler pulled Germany out in 1933. 1933, remember that year, it's important. World War II doomed the League of Nations.

The Treaty of Versailles was signed June 28, 1919. It was imposed on the defeated German Empire by the Allies. Germany had to give up economically important territory in Europe along with its colonies. Germany had to admit to sole responsibility for the war, and pay huge reparations totaling 32 billion marks.

Most Germans resented these terms with bitterness. They lost wealth, power, status, and dignity. It led to economic devastation in Germany that in turn led to under consumption that in turn led to the Great Depression. This was a bitter pill for the Germans to swallow, after all, they had been winning the war when politicians overthrew the government and surrendered.

It was however exactly what the monied elite wanted. There were also things that did not work out as well as the monied elite had hoped for. The Romanovs were gone from Russia, but Russia chose to members that run a communist politburo become the monied elite of that country. It is easy to get you monied elite people elected to office communist government from within.

The United States refused to join the League of Nations. No New World Order could be brought about with a major nation as communists or with the Americas not a part of it. This meant that something would have to be done.

The monied elite decided that they needed to create a crisis. A financial crisis would be best. Once people are instantly reduced to seeking food and shelter as per Maslow's hierarchy of needs, they would be easier to control. Like Pavlov's dogs, the conditioned response when you ring the dinner bell puts you in control of the masses. Thus, the monied elite could lead them to slaughter (financial slaughter that is.)

Throughout the 1920's they cast a wide net. Using the media they controlled, people were led to believe they should all be wealthy and party like the rich people did. They should invest their savings in the stock market where fortunes were being made by common men every day. Rags to riches stories were heavily publicized.

The monied elite also controlled the banks, so if you didn't have any money to invest, they would loan it to you. Everyone was doing it, and on paper everyone was getting rich. Only the monied elite at the top knew the profits were over inflated. Once they had snared as many as they could, the trap was sprung. From 1920 to 1929 stock prices had quadrupled in value. Most of the capital in the United States was represented by stocks at the time.

Millions of Americans borrowed money to buy more stock. Banks lent heavily to fund the stock buying spree. The investment drove stock prices rising farther. This fueled further rises, and created an economic bubble.

At the same time that stock prices were reaching record highs, congress was passing the Smoot --- Hawley Tariff Act. This would impose a heavy tax rate of 60% on more than 3,200 products and raw materials imported into America. This would quadruple the U.S. tariff rates. Other countries responded by raising their tariffs on American products in retaliation. These tariffs would certainly raise prices for American manufacturers and ultimately consumers. This would reduce business profits.

On October 21,1929, an amendment to impose4 tariffs only on imported agricultural products was defeated. Stock prices anticipated future profits. Since it was obvious future profits would be smaller, millions of investors began selling off their stock before the price came down. Three days later on October 24,1929, the stock market suffered its first one day crash. By noon on this "Black Thursday," there were eleven suicides of prominent investors. Without money they had nothing, and so, nothing to live for.

At 1:00 P.M., leading Wall Street bankers had a meeting to find a solution. They purchased large blocks of shares in "blue chip" stocks above the market value. This action stabilized the stock market temporarily. Over the weekend, newspapers controlled by the monied elite ran stories to dramatize the danger of losing money in the stock market. On Monday, many investors sold out and the market dropped a record 13% for the day.

On Thursday, October 29,1929 a rumor hit the media that President Herbert Hoover was not going to veto the Smoot-Hawley tariff bill, the prices of stocks sank even further. Over the next several days stock prices collapsed, ruining many investors. The banks became saddled with debt the broke investors couldn't repay. This caused many banks to fail. Business lost their lines of credit and went out of business.

The business closings caused massive unemployment as people lost their jobs. Demand for goods declined because people were poor. New investment in business comes from the sale of stock. Since nobody could afford to buy any new stock, business stagnated. The "Great Depression" was under way.

There was chaos in the banking system. The banks couldn't collect from broke investors, and banks had themselves invested depositors' money in the stock market, which were now worth little or nothing. By July 1932, the stock market had lost 89% of its value. People went to the banks to draw their money out. The Federal Reserve System would not give more finds to the banks, so the banks began to fail and close their doors by the hundreds in 1932 and 1933.

People were afraid the government would print worthless paper money to fill the withdrawals, so the customers demanded their money in gold. A good number of the people had gold certificates. Each gold certificate said it was redeemable of gold payable to the barer on demand. The people wanted gold and redeemed their certificates demanding gold. They wanted gold.

By March 1933 the banking system of the Great United States ceased to function. The people had elected a new president. Franklin D. Roosevelt closed all the banks in the United States for three days, March 6 through March 9,1933 declaring a "Bank Holiday." The monied elite had succeeded in creating the financial crisis they wanted.

The government didn't want to honor their promise to pay in gold. President Roosevelt proclaimed a "National Emergency" was caused by "heavy and unwarranted withdrawals of gold and currency," for the purpose of "hoarding." "Hoarding" just means a person holding o to their own money instead of gold. The people's fear of worthless money was coming true.

Banks were slowly reopened with strict limits on withdrawals. To prevent future disasters, the federal government set up the Federal Deposit Insurance Corporation, or FDIC for short. Backed by FDIC, even if a bank went out of business, the government would reimburse depositors. This effectively eliminated the fear of bank runs, where depositors line up to withdrawal their money before the bank runs out.

Also, in 1933 Congress passed the Glass-Steagall Act. This mandated a separation between commercial banks, whose activities involve the taking of deposits and making loans, and investment banks, whose role is to underwrite, issue, and distribute stocks, and bonds. Also, commercial banks were banned from investing depositor's money in stocks.

On March 10,1933, President Roosevelts issued Executive Order #6073 which forbids people sending gold out of the United States, and forbidding banks to pay in gold. On April 15,1933, President Roosevelt issued Executive Order #6102. This was the order to confiscate everyone's gold. Everyone was to deliver their gold certificates to a Federal Reserve Bank, where they would be paid paper money.

You might ask yourself, why weren't there any riots? Why didn't the people revolt? You have to realize that the majority of the people at the time trusted the Government. Furthermore, the Government assured them this was a temporary measure until the crisis was over. There was them this was a temporary measure until the crises was over. There was grumbling to be sure, and some called it bank robbery in reverse, where the bank steals your money, and they were right.

On May 12,1933, congress passed the Gold Reserve Act, making all gold holdings illegal. On April 19,1933, President Roosevelts announced the United States was off the gold standard. On August 28,1933, President Roosevelt issued Executive Order # 6260 forbidding the export of gold in any form, the export of currency from the United States. In section 4, Acquisition of Gold Coin And Gold Bullion - No person other than a Federal Reserve Bank shall after the date of this order acquire in the United States any gold coin, gold bullion, gold certificates except under license therefore issued pursuant to this Executive Order.

At this point the monied elite had effectively stolen the money of the American people. Since this was not widely publicized by the monied elite's media outlets, it went mostly unnoticed y the majority of the American public, which still believed it was temporary.

Fact: Cash is paper money. Fact: Paper money is order to be money must be backed by something of value. Fact: Federal Reserve

Note are not money because they are backed by nothing at all, so they are not cash!

Fact: People were forced to turn in their real money for Federal Reserve Notes. Facts: In 1933 cash was replaced by Federal Reserve Notes which means that in fact we have been a cashless society since 1933!

President Lincoln once asked his Cabinet, "If I call my dog's tail a leg, how many legs does my doge have now?" The Cabinet members agreed the dog would now have five legs. Lincoln said "NO, my dog has four legs, calling a tail a leg does not change the fact it is only a tail." Calling Federal Reserve Notes cash does not make them cash.

On March 7,1933 the game of "Monopoly" was invented. It used fake money. It is no accident that the monied elite stole the real money and replaced it with fake money at the same time with little fuss.

Also, at this point, the United States effectively became a socialist republic, which again went mostly unnoticed by the majority of Americans. It did not however, go unnoticed by everyone. The taken over American government and stolen the Americans money. That such a powerful country could be so easily taken over and its people enslaved without a fuss was unbelievable.

So why is it important to mention Adolph Hitler? Hitler has always been villainized by historians, but since we only learn in school what the government propagandists want us to think, it is important to examine Hitler, as he is likely misunderstood. Let's examine Hitler then.

Adolph Hitler was not German; he was born in Austria and did not become a German citizen until 1932. Hitler served in the German Army during world War I. After that war, Hitler stayed in the army, which was mostly concerned with suppressing the socialist uprisings breaking out across Germany. Hitler was sent to March in 1919 and was art of an army group that tried to create a scapegoat for the outbreak of WWI and the defeat of Germany. The blame was on "international Jewry" which really was the monied elite, communists, and the Weimar Coalition government that had surrendered.

In July 1919, Hitler was appointed a V-Mann, which was a spy or intelligence commando. He was to infiltrate a small nationalist party, the German workers party. Hitler was impressed with the fact that they in fact thought pretty much the same way he did. He was discharged from the army in March 1920 and joined what became the Nazi party as member 555.

Hitler had been shocked when Germany in 1918, since as a soldier he knew the army remained undefeated. In speechless against the Treaty of Versailles, Hitler blamed civilian politicians and the Jews. In a speech at a beer hall, he attacked Jews, socialists, liberals, capitalists, and communists.

In November 1923, the Nazis and Hitler tried to overthrow the government. While in prison, Hitler wrote his political book "Mein Kampf (My Struggle). He detailed how he would make a political comeback when he got out of prison.

Hitler blamed the social democracy and the Jews for Germany's economic problems. Hitler stated in Mein Kampf, that if twelve fifteen thousand Jews (monied elite), had been killed before or shortly after WWI had started, millions of other people would not have suffered.

The needs of the many outweigh the needs of the few or the one. Twenty million people died as a result of WWI. If you could get in a time machine and go back and kill 15,000 key individuals to prevent all this, would you? Hitler would have.

Hitler was correct in identifying the monied elite as the root cause of WWWI and the sad state of the German economy after the war. German people, he could kill those 15,000 now. They only problem was that like Pavlov's conditioned response and Maslow's Hierarchy of needs, human behavior also has the pecking order.

15,000 replaced the 15,000 he eliminated. This happened again and agree with his tactics. Often those who have been oppressed become the oppressors. It is a vicious cycle.

The things about the pecking order is that the one at the top is always the biggest pecker.

Perhaps it is best not to do as the Russian did on their revolutions, killing the monied elite, or Hitler attempting to kill those he feared would take their money and enslave his people. Perhaps instead we should eliminate money, but in the United States, that has already been done.

Let's examine a time line of significant events in 1933. On January 30, 1933, Adolph Hitler is worth in as Chancellor of Germany, and pledges to pull Germany out of the depression. February 15,1933,

President-elect Franklin Roosevelt survives an assassination attempt, troops out of China. March 3, Franklin D. Roosevelt is inaugurated as the 32nd President and pledges to pull America out of the "Depression." In his speech, he said, "We have nothing to fear but fear itself." March 6,1933, President Roosevelt proclaims a bank holiday.

March 7, 1933, Germany's Nazi Party won a majority in the German Parliament. On March 9, 1933, the U.S. Congress passed the "Emergency Banking Act." On March 10, 1933, President Roosevelt and forbidding banks to pay in gold.

On March 13, 1933, Josef Gobbels became the German minister of "Information and Propaganda." On March 16,1933, Hitler named Hjalmar Shaft as president of the Bank of Germany. On March 21, 1933, the German Reichstag passed the "Enabling Act" granting Hitler dictational power.

March 23,1933, Hitler tried to incorporate churches into his government calling them, "most important factors," for the maintenance of German well-being, March 27, 1933, Japan withdrew from the League of Nations. March 31, 1933, U.S. Congress authorizes Civilian Conversation Corps.

April 1, 1933, Nazi Germany begins persecuting the Jews by boycotting Jewish businesses April 7, 1933, the first Nazi anti-Jewish laws were passed barring Jews from public office and legal offices. April 8,1933, in England, the Manchester Guardian newspaper warned of an unknown Nazi terror.

April 15, 1933, President Roosevelt issued Executive Order # 6102 to confiscate Americans' Gold. April 19, 1933, President Roosevelt announced the United State drop the Gold Standard.

May 5, 1933, Nellie Ross became the first woman as director of the U.S. Mint. May 12, 1933, The Federal Emergency Relief Administration and the Agricultural Adjustment Administration were formed to help farmers and the needy. May 18, 1993, President Roosevelt signed the Tennessee Valley Act to build dams. May 27, 1933, the Federal Securities Act was signed into law.

June 5, 1933, the U.S. officially abolished the gold standard. June 6, 1933, the United States Employment Services was created to co-ordinate putting people back to work. June 12, 1993, the Financial and Economy World conference opened with 66 countries in attendance. June 13, 1933, the Federal Home Owners Loan Corporation was established. June 13, 1933, the National Industrial Recovery Act 1933, the United States Deposit Insurance Corporation (FDIC) was created, June 30, 1933, the United States Assay offices in Boise Idaho, Helena Montana, and Salt Lake City Utah were closed.

July 1, 1933, Nazi Germany decided married women shouldn't work, Hitler believed women's priorities were in house work and raising children. July 8, 1933, the Public Works Administration is started in the United States. July 12, 1933. Congress passed the first minimum wage law, with the minimum at 33 cents per hour. July 4, 1933, in Germany, the Nazi party becomes the only party. July 20, 1933, Pope Pius XII sent Vatican Secretary of state Pocelli to sign an accord with Hitler.

August 1, 1933, Germany sets the death penalty for anti-fascists. August 28, 1933, President Roosevelt issues Executive Order # 6260 forbidding the exporting of all gold.

October 14, 1933, Nazi Germany announced its withdrawal from the League of Nations. October 17, 1933, Albert Einstein arrived in the United States as he fled Nazi Germany.

November 8, 1933, President Roosevelt created the Civil Works Administration. November 16, 1933, President Roosevelt established diplomatic relations with Russia. November 21, 1933, W.C. Bullitt became the first U.S. ambassador to the Soviet Union.

You might be wondering what my point is. My point is this, it is clear that Hitler was watching what was happening in the United States very closely. Each time Roosevelt did something, Hitler would make a move in Germany a few days or weeks later.

What we have here are two men, each the leader of a world power, with the same goal of pulling their country out of the worst financial depression known to men. Although their stated goal was the same, their methods were near opposites. President Roosevelt, a member of the monied elite or at least working on their behalf after his near assassination attempt, was enslaving his people to the monied elite. Hitler on the other hand, a poor person himself, was attempting to free his people of the tyranny the monied elite had imposed on them.

To the untrained eye, what Roosevelt was doing looked like a good thing. To Hitler, it looked like the American people were robbed of their money by the government, which was taking control of every corner of people's lives, from employment, housing, banking, and a mediocre wage that enslaved them to the monied elite. Americans were not allowed to own money, mine money, or ship money out of the country.

Hitler recognized the United Stated had in reality become a Social Republic. Hitler feared democracy, and why shouldn't he? He had observed the monied elite infiltrate and take over every democracy in existence. Hitler had himself been a spy. He recognized what was happening. Where Hitler feared democracy, he hated communists even more, and in his eyes, the United States was the next thing to communists, even opening diplomatic relations with communist Russia.

In Germany, Hitler had taken the necessary precautions to get the monied elite out of government and keep them out. He put a trusted German in control of the Bank of Germany. He bared the monied elite from government office. If they opposed him, they would get the death penalty. It was better they should leave Germany quickly, as they were not welcome and it would not be safe for them.

Hitler also did not like lazy people. If you were not going to help rebuild Germany, he had no use for you. Lazy people were killed. He also had psychiatric patient, mentally retarded, and Jehovah's Witnesses killed. He did not tolerate lazy people, crazy people, stupid people, and religious fanatics. Who among us has not at one time thought about killing someone that was in one of these categories? Hitler went beyond thinking about it and did the unthinkable, he actually had them killed.

Hitler had persuaded the Germany people that he was their savior from the Treaty of Versailles, the Communists, the Great Depression, and the Jews, which were seen by him as the monied elite. He oversaw the greatest expansion of industrial production and civil improvement in German history. The unemployment rate was near zero, mostly because of arms production, the fact that women were sent home so that men could have their jobs, and lazy people were killed. Hitler was largely responsible for the design of the Volkswagen Beetle car. Volkswagen means, "People's car."

Hitler the opportunities of the Jews that remained in Germany. Most of the Jews had their citizenship revoked. They lost their jobs, their businesses, their property and churches. The smart ones left the country, many of them moved to the United States.

By 1938, Hitler was Time magazines Man of the year. There were many people in the United States supported Hitler and the Nazis, morally and financially. About half the population of America was of German ancestry, and they were sympathetic to Germany and its causes.

Hitler did not like women to wear cosmetics, he was an avid non-smoker and promoted aggressive anti-smoking campaigns not unlike the ones in use in the United States today. Hitler improved the economic, political standing, and general conditions of the German people, just as he promised he would. Then, World War Two broke out.

The monied elite could not allow Hitler so successfully oppose them. It would mess up the "New World Order" they wished and had worked so hard to establish with them in control. Hitler was the one person, having opposed them in Germany and expelled them, that could expose them to the world. Anyone who really listened to his speeches knew they were more than propaganda, there was an eagle of truth in them.

The Italian occupation of Ethiopia for seven months from 1935-1936 was the actual start of WWII. On July 7, 1937 Japan attacked China, starting the war in Asia. China was already in a civil war with communities and the Democracy. In Europe, Germany annexed Austria and Czechoslovakia. Then on September 1, 1939, Germany invaded Poland.

Britain and France had a defense pact with Poland and declared war on Germany. On September 17, 1939, Russia invaded Poland from the East. Poland was defeated by October 6, 1939, Russia, which had a treaty with Nazi Germany, did not fight the fascists. Stalin believed his enemies were the capitalist West and Nazi Germany, and it was to his liking they should fight each other and leave Russia alone.

The United States remained neutral as they had at the start of WWI. Americans were reluctant to fight someone else's war again. Also, a lot of people in America supported Germany financially and with moral support.

On September 27, 1940, Japan, Germany, and Italy signed the "Tripartite Pact," which split the Earth into three spheres of influence with each member of this "Axis Powers" vowing to defend one another against aggression. Germany and Russia as part of their treaty were to divide Eastern Europe into regions of influence.

It should be pointed out that Italy still had a king, even though he didn't run the fascist government there. Hitler was working closely with Prince Ruprecht, and Japan still had an emperor. It would appear they were the weak reflection of the "Old World Order" attempting to resurrect itself. This also meant they would eventually have to deal with the communists, for there is no room for communism in the old order of things. Hitler's main enemy was the monied elite in the United States which for the time remained neutral, but ultimately would have to be dealt with.

On November 30, 1939, Russia invaded Finland. By March of 1940, Finland surrendered territory to Russia.

On April 9, 1940, Germany invaded Denmark and Norway. Norway surrendered in June. On May 10, 1940, Germany invaded the Netherlands, Belgium, Luxembourg, and France. Belgium, Luxembourg, and the Netherlands were quickly conquered. France surrendered on June 22, 1940. British forces had been cornered in the French costal town of Dunkirk. They made a hasty retreat across the English Channel.

In June of 1940, Russia invaded Estonia, Latvia, Lithuania, and Northern Romania.

Hitler was unable to secure peace with England, and Germany began to prepare for invasion of the British Isles. A battle for air superiority began, with the Royal Air Force defeating the larger German Luftwaffe by the end of October 1940. German U-Boats tried to keep "Lend Lease" cargo from the United States from reaching England. Prime Minister Winston Churchill said the British would never surrender and President Roosevelt moved America from neutral to "non-belligerent."

Hitler made no serious attempt to destroy the British fleet. His eventual plan was to use the ships of the captured British fleet to launch coast and Japan attacking the west coast. Spies for the monied elite thus depriving the Nazis of the free navy they needed. News of the plan also prompted the monied elite in America to prepare for an eventual showdown with Hitler.

The British had no real means of re-invading the European mainland, so Hitler did not have to fear them even if peace was not quick in coming. Italy had already attacked British forces in North Africa trying to take the Suez Canal. Hitler continued night time bombing of London. This was a resource better spent on his next move, against Russia.

On June 22, 1941. German troops invaded Russia. Hitler was smart enough to sign a treaty with them in August 1939 making them think he would divide Eastern Europe with them. This was a brilliant plan that made the Russians feel safe and spread the Russian forces out to the areas they were told they could have. This made it easier for the German forces to catch them off guard and divided.

The plan was to crush the Russians before the winter hit. The Germans pushed the Russian army all the way to Moscow and Leningrad before the Russian winter stopped them. The Germans may well have succeeded were it not for the American "Lend Lease" plan which gave weapons and ammunition for the Russians to fight the Germans.

Even though America was not yet in the fight, they were supplying weapons and ammo to both Russian and Britain. Also in May of 1940, President Roosevelt signed a secret executive order allowing U.S. Military personnel to resign from service to participate in the covert operation in China. It was called the American Volunteer Group, which became known as the Flying Tigers.

Flying Army Surplus P-40 fighter planes, over a seven-month period, with less than 100 planes, the Flying Tigers down over 600 Japanese planes, sunk numerous Japanese ships, and stalled the Japanese invasion of Burma. President Roosevelt and the monied elite knew that they had to get America into actual fight.

Wow, The Flying Tigers shot down over 600 zeros!

Hitler was too smart to take the bait. American weapons and ammo from the lend lease program had prevented him from taking either England or all of Russia. He was plenty busy now fighting two fronts, Hitler did not want to take on the United States until England and Russia could be defeated. Taking on America before that would lead to German defeat.

The Japanese however did not have the advantage of patience, President Roosevelt cut off oil supplies to Japan. Japan only had a two-week supply of oil to run their industry and war effort in China. Their hand had been forced. The invasion plan they had with Germany to strike America had to go ahead without the Germans.

On December 7, 1941, Japanese warplanes attacked Pearl Harbor, the largest U.S. naval base in the Pacific. Japan also attacked U.S. air bases in the Philippines and the British Colonies of Hong Kong, Burma, Borneo, and Malaysia.

On December 8, 1941, the United States declared war on Japan. On December 11, 1941, Germany had to declare war on the United States due to its treaty with Japan. The monied elite had succeeded in getting America into the war. This gave President Roosevelt the pretext he needed for America to join the war in Europe with full commitment.

What happened next was a very strange thing. After being attacked by Japan, it would be reasonable to think that immediate vengeance would be sought by America. All available military resources should have been brought to bear against the Japanese Imperial Army and Navy.

In fact, military planners had suspected for years that a confrontation with Japan was not a matter of if, but when. A complete battle plan had been drawn up. It was expected the Japanese would hit the Philippines first. America had only granted the Philippines independence several years earlier after 20 years of fighting that continued after the Spanish-American War. America still had air and naval basses there. The strategy was to hold off the Japanese until reinforcements arrived.

The Japanese of course did not hit the Philippines first, they hit Pearl Harbor. The U.S. Military mush have known the attack was coming Pearl Harbor, in fact decoded messages foretold of it, days earlier. The day before the attack, all American aircrafts, carriers, and other modern warship were sent to open ocean away from the incoming Japanese fleet. The only remaining ships at Pearl Harbor were older WWI type ships that would have soon been mothballed anyway.

On December 22, 1942, a couple weeks after the attack on Pearl Harbor, Winston Churchill and his top military planners arrived in Washington D.C for high level meetings with President Roosevelt and his top military planners. This was called the "Arcadia Conference." This consisted of twelve meetings on the British and American chief of staff. These meetings, oddly enough, were held in the Federal Reserve

Building!

In spite of the vicious attack on Pearl Harbor, it was agreed that to win the war, it would be necessary to defeat Nazi Germany first. American leaders agreed the bulk of Allied ground forces should confront the German threat as soon as possible. This became known as the "Europe First" strategy.

This does not make sense to the untrained observer. Japan attacked American interests in the Pacific, a battle plan for such a scenario was already drawn up. If the United States committed all military resource most likely have been beaten down. The Japanese were already so burdened with dighting in China that they couldn't help Germany invade Russia.

Beating down the Japanese in a year did not suit the needs of the monied elite. With Japan defeated quickly, it might be easy for America to make peace with Germany without going to war in Europe. After all, Hitler was too smart to want a fight with America just yet. Hitler was a threat to the monied elite because he was on to them who they were, and what their plans were. That is why it was absolutely necessary to defeat Hitler first.

At the ARCADIA Conference, with meetings held at the federal Reserve Building, the monied elite were able to impose their strategy on Roosevelt and the Chief of Staff. A total of twenty meetings were held with the combined Chiefs of Staff of the Allies from January 23 to May 19, 1942. All the materials of these conferences were classified "Top Secret." All the materials were declassified in 1973 with the exception of the ARCADIA Conference. The secret that is so secret that it remains top secret to this day is that ARCADIA Conference was orchestrated by the monied elite toward their arms. It was not in the best interest of America; it was in their best interests.

In August 1942, the British led an unsuccessful attack on the French port of Dieppe. This demonstrated that only a massive, coordinated Allied invasion of Europe would be successful. In fact, the U.S. military planners already knew that too. Three months before the attack on Pearl Harbor, General Albert Wedemeyer had drawn up what he called the "Victory Program." It called for a massive invasion of northwest Europe and a decisive confrontation with the German military.

Besides the "Germany First" strategy, the other significant thing that came out of the ARCADIA Conference was the establishment of the "United Nations." Twenty-six nations joined immediately and pledged to employ their full resources, both military and economic, to defeat Germany and the Axis powers. By the end of WWII, 45 Nations were members of the U.N.

Although a defensive only strategy against Japan was good for the monied elite, it was not good for the American public in general. They demanded retribution. President Roosevelt ordered military to come up with a plan to hit Japan back on their home turf. The Japanese continued attacking American and British interests in the Pacific with impunity, believing their homeland was safe from attack. The Americans had believed Pearl Harbor safe from attack until it was hit.

In the military there is a saying, "If you can see the enemy, they can probably see you, and if the enemy is within range of your weapons, you are probably within range of theirs." The Japanese seemed to forget that. On April 18, 1942, Jimmy Doolittle and his raiders, using modified

B-25 medium range bombers launched from the deck of America's largest and most modern air craft carrier, a feat which had never before been done, bombed Tokyo in a daring daylight raid. Doolittle and his raiders used special incendiary bombs on military targets.

Although Doolittle's raid did little physical damage, it did huge psychological damage. The Japanese realized they were indeed vulnerable to the crafty Americans. This caused them to pull back much of their invading forces to protect Japan, thus buying time for the Americans.

On June 20, 1942, a second conference was held in Washington D.C. with Winston Churchill and resident Roosevelt and the combined Chiefs of Staff. The Germans were attacking North Africa in an attempt to seize the Suez Canal. It was decided American forces should not sit idle during the buildup on Europe invasion. First priority now was to stop the Germans in North Africa.

On November 8, 1942, American forces led by General Dwight Eisenhower attacked North Africa. The British navy did an excellent job of cutting the German supply lines across the Mediterranean. By May 13, 1943, the German African Corps were defeated and 250,000 soldiers surrendered to the Americans.

In the mean time in the Pacific, American, and Australian forces thwarted a Japanese invasion of Port Morosely, New Guinea in May of 1942. A month later, June 1942 the Japanese invasion of Midway Island was prevented. American pilots sunk four Japanese aircraft carriers.

With these victories, about one third of America's military was devoted to fighting the Japanese, the other two thirds were devoted to the priority of defeating Nazi Germany. After the North Africa victory, another conference was held in Washington D.C.

May 12, 1943, the "TRIDENT Conference" was held in Washington D.C. with Winston Churchill and President Roosevelt ad the combined Chiefs of Staff. For two weeks, strategic issues were discussed, with six meetings between Roosevelt and Churchill at the White House. The combined Chiefs of Staff daily at the Board of Governors room at the Federal Reserve Building, where the monied elite imposed their plans on them.

It was decided at the TRIDENT Conference, to attack Italy from North Africa while continuing to build up an invasion force in England for the eventual invasion of Western Europe. Over next year, the largest buildup of men and material ever seen assembled in England.

On July 10, 1943, Italy was invaded. On July 25, 143, the King of Italy fired Mussolini and appointed a new government. On September 8, 1943, Italy surrendered.

In the Pacific during 1943-44, America and Australia pounded the Japanese out of Solomon Islands, New Guinea, and the Dutch East Indies, New Britain and New Ireland. The Philippines was retaken at the end of 1944 with the Battle of Leyte Gulf, the largest naval battle in history.

On June 6, 1944 the Allies invaded Germany held Normandy from the air and sea. Realists in the German military knew defeat was inevitable. The Americans had begun the beat down of Nazi Germany. By the end of 1944, the Russian forces had reached Berlin.

On April 30, 1945, Adolf Hitler committed suicide, Karl Donitz became the new German leader and quickly sent the German High Command to Reims, France, and surrendered unconditionally ending the war in Europe. Hitler's attempt to improve the economic conditions of his people ended in failure.

Unlike the German surrender of the First World War which left Germany intact. The monied elite made sure Germany was completely destroyed, even fire-bombing the cultural central of Dresden.

On April 12, 1945, President Roosevelt died and his Vice-President. Harry S. Truman, became President of the United States. Truman was not a member of, or under the control of the monied elite. With Hitler's Suicide and Germany's defeat within a month of Truman becoming President, it didn't matter. The agenda of the monied elite was fulfilled for now.

With the defeat of Germany, America was able to turn its full attention to bearing down Japan. With the capture of Iwo Jima and Okinawa, the Japanese homeland was now in range of air and naval attack. Fire bombing of Japan began with 90,000 people dying in Tokyo alone. Within a few months Japan would have surrendered anyway due to cold and hunger.

President Truman wanted the Japanese punished big time. He ordered the dropping of the atomic bombs on Hiroshima and Nagasaki on August 6 and 9, 1945. Japan surrendered unconditionally on August 15, 1945.

By the end of the war, the European economy had collapsed with 70% of the industrial infrastructure destroyed. Although Russia demanded 660 million dollars in reparations, the Western Allies did not demand compensation from defeated nations.

President Truman could see the interests of the communists and the capitalist west were polls apart and introduced the Truman. Doctrine to contain communism. This made the monied elite happy because for them to be in control, communism must be wiped out. Because communism flourishes in deprived areas, Congress went along with the Marshall Plan to allocate billions of dollars for the reconstruction of Europe.

In July 1944, representatives of the 44 nations that were the United Nations up to then had met at the Bretton Woods Conference. It established the International Monetary Fund and International Bank and provided for reconstruction and development at the end of the war. The Bretton Woods system was put into effect to rebuild global capitalism and linked all currencies to the U.S. dollar.

Since the League of Nations had failed, Truman gave full support to the United Nations to construct a new international order. A New World Order! In the nations occupied by the Western Allies, new democratic governments were created. In the nations occupied by Russia, communist governments were established.

President Truman implemented Operation Paperclip to get as many former Nazi scientists moved to the United States. Truman was

instrumental in getting Britain to leave Palestine so the nation of Israel could be established. Truman also established the CIA.

On November 1, 1950, two men tried to assassinate President Truman. The monied elite were firmly in control of all currencies in the free world, the U.N., the CIA, and the American government. Senator

McCarthy was pushing the anti-communist agenda and a showdown was inevitable.

With the communists taking over China in 1949 and invading Korea in 1950, America was at war again. American forces quickly drove the communist invaders back to the Chinese border. General Douglas McArthur recommended that President Truman let him use atomic bombs on China to quickly bear them down, Truman refused and fired McArthur.

Three years later the Korean Conflict ended in a stalemate with half the country free and the other half I communist hands as it remains to this day.

The Cold War began, with the interests of the communists and the capitalists monied elite at odds with each other. By the early 1960's the monied elite in control tried using the powerful American military machine to squash communism wherever it grew. Cuba, in 1962, nearly brought Russia and America to nuclear war. Vietnam poised China communists backing North Vietnam and America backing capitalist South Vietnam. The building of the "Berlin Wall" separating communist held East Berlin in Russian hands, and West Berlin in the hands of the U.S., Britain, France, and West Germany, saw more tension between the Russians and Americans.

It was President Kennedy who was at the focal point during this crisis. President Kennedy's father was after all, one of the bankers in league with the monied elite. His father was close personal friends with Senator McCarthy, the lead communist hunter the monied elite had rounding up and imprisoning American who were communists, and leading the fight against global communism.

Global communism is of course diametrically opposed to Globalist monied elitists. Both try to extinguish the other so that only one prevails in a "New World Order."

When President Kennedy was inaugurated, his speech asked Americans to be active citizens. "Asked not what your country can do for you, ask what you can do for your country." He also asked the nations of the world to join together to fight what he called the "common enemies of man: tyranny, poverty, disease, and war itself." President Kennedy created the "Peace Corps," in an attempt to improve the world without the use of military might.

President Kennedy knew full well who the monied elite were, they are supper at his father's table when he was growing up. He knew full well their plan for a "New World Order." He knew two things drive up debt, war, and a privately run central banking system. He knew the tyranny in our government, and he opposed them.

President Kennedy intended to pull U.S. troops out of the Vietnam conflict. If communism kept the monied elite from completing their plan, then it wasn't all bad. In addition, President Kennedy issued Executive Order # 11110, ordering the U.S. Treasury to issue silver certificates backed by the silver in the treasury. That would have put the Treasury Department back in the money business. It would have put the Federal Reserve Bank of New York out of business. It would have put 4.3 billion real dollars into the U.S. economy that wasn't controlled by the Federal Reserve.

The monied elite of course could not allow that to happen. Kennedy was assassinated before it could be carried out. In 1965, the U.S. Mint stopped using silver in our coinage. All silver certificates had to be turned in before 1968. At that point, all real money was gone from the economy. It is worth noting here that Executive Order # 11110 remains in effect to this day. No other President has issued an Executive Order to repeal it!

So the Vietnam War took place as the monied elite tried to beat communism using the U.S. military. The communists eventually ended up controlling all of south-east Asia. Then something strange happened.

In 1989, the Russian government switched to a capitalist form of government and disbanded the Soviet Union, freeing many countries that had been held hostage to communism. These countries became capitalists. After nearly seventy years, communism was crumbling.

China was now the largest remaining communist country in the world and with one fifth of the world's population, the "New World Order" the monied elite envision still could not come about. That is the main reason the Chinese are now being turned into the manufacturing hub of the monied elite. It should take only twenty years or less before China switches to a capitalist form of government. After making and using all the good things that go along with the good capitalist life, the Chinese people will naturally move in that direction. I look for this to happen before the year 2016.

Them on September 11, 2001, terrorists flew airplanes into the World Trade Center in New York City. The group that claimed responsibility was the Al-Qaida network, a group of Muslims with headquarters in Afghanistan. This is really a remnant of the old Ottoman Empire trying to re-establish itself.

Some people say the terrorists attacked America. Yet, their target was very specific. It was the World Trade Center, the power base and headquarters of the monied elite trying to establish a "New World Order." They knew exactly who their real enemy was, and like the German u-boats of WWI, they hit their enemy where it really counted. The World Trade Center went down like the Lusitania. The World Trade Center became "ground zero." Zero is nothing!

My friend was a zero, but I knew him none the less.

The monied elite acted predictably, dispatching the fierce American military to Afghanistan to beat down the Al-Qaida terrorists. What the Russian military failed to do in nine years, the American military did in a few short months, Afghanistan fell quickly and the Al-Qaida dispersed and their leader vanished.

The American military then invaded Iraq. I suspect Syria and Iran are next to be beaten down. These remnants of the old Ottoman Empire cannot be allowed to challenge the monied elite.

Have you ever wondered why the United States has such a close military alliance with Israel? Israel is a small nation without oil reserves on an insignificant chunk of desert. It makes no sense. The only thing that makes sense out of it is the monied elite want the United States to protect Israel.

In America, the "Patriot Act" usurped the Constitutional rights of its citizens. It seems there has been a steady, yet slow process to dwindle, the rights of Americans for a long time. Another case of cooking the frog slowly, which heated up with the Patriot Act.

Americans know something is wrong. Disintegration of families neighborhoods, cities, states and the nation proliferates.

Governments are instituted among men, deriving their just power from the consent of the governed. We are taught in school that we are a free country with a free market economy. These are the same schools that our government controls, public schools. We cannot blame the teachers, they have been through the same mind control institutions as the rest of us.

Federal Reserve Notes are the currency we are forced to use today. Liberty is the ability to choose. We are not given the liberty we are entitled to as to whether or not we want to use this pseudo dollar. Federal Reserve Notes are backed by nothing. The government tells us that our Federal Reserve Note currency is backed by all the goods and services of the American people.

That sounds like communism to me! My goods and services are not the governments to give! All humans have an absolute right to their property. Modern currency has become a means for the total confiscation of private property by our government. This remains obscured from the majority of Americans until soon an economic crisis will shock this increasingly impoverished and enslaved public from its slumber. Wake up people, the "Money Matrix" has you!

Ben Franklin was America's first self made millionaire. He was able to accomplish this task by his mid-forties because he ran his own printing business. Were Ben Franklin alive today, he would be told he couldn't operate his business unless he had a license. The principles of Liberty remain the same as they were when this nation was founded. You are entitled to carry on your private business in your own way without owing any duty to the government or your neighbors to divulge your business or open yourself to any investigation, as it may incriminate you.

In an altruistic society, the government's prime function has become the redistribution of property. It has assumed ownership and control of everything, including you and me and the rest of the citizens. What would make the government think they could get away with confiscating our rights?

Almost all Americans have bank accounts. When you open an account, you are actually creating a contract between yourself and the bank. The government claims that this contract makes citizens private merchants and dealers in the national commerce. As a private merchant, the government claims you have waived your Fifth Amendment right to your financial records.

Bank spelled backwards is knab!

The Supreme Court found that records you make voluntarily are not protected under the Fifth Amendment, especially when those records are held by someone else, like your bank. Your bank records belong to the bank, which is an institution created with permission from the government. The monied elite run our government anyway.

You have the right to give up your rights. You have the right to remain silent. You also have the right to freedom of speech. If you speak up, you give up your right to remain silent. If you have a contract with a bank, your records are now public property.

As a private merchant dealing in the nation's commerce, you are doing business every time you buy something, using the privately issued Federal Reserve Notes. Private rights became business rights. Your private home and private automobile are used to get to the store to buy food (engage in commerce), which you transport back to your home for storage, and use. If you have a telephone, cable TV, or the internet in your house, you are engaged in interstate commerce.

The government claims they now have a legitimate interest in your home and car, and they are subject to taxes and regulation. Private property becomes an oxymoron. A free society has a collective right to know your business.

The government, acting under its police powers to protect the health, safety and welfare of the citizens, can and does pass laws to make things a crime that otherwise would have been your natural right. They put themselves in command of every aspect of our lives.

Now we have government issued privileges instead of rights. These privileges are granted with licenses and permits: driving, occupations, professions, marriage, business, dog tags, needing a permit to protest. It's ridiculous. I have the right to gather and protest.

But if I don't go to city hall to get a permit for permissions, I could be arrested. In a truly free country. I don't need the government's permission to protest!

I took a test in political correctness and I scored an FU!

We become guilty of these victimless crimes, like driving a car without a license, license plates, insurance and such. The cop pulls you over because your car had no license plate to indicate you have government permission to drive it on public streets and of course a record of registration so they can pry into your private business.

"Are your papers in order?" Driver's license, registration, proof of insurance. Sounds like a Nazi Gestapo tactic. No proof? Well, the cops will have to impound (confiscated), your private property. This is when you pull your pistol from under the seat, which you also don't have a permit for, and inform the officer you're not going to allow him to arrest you or take your property. After all, you have the right so self defense and to defend your private property. Poor bastard, you'll probably be shot by the cop.

It is illegal to steal another man's property, unless you are the government. Through taxation, the government redistributes wealth. This is known as communism! Politicians are parasites that live off currency confiscated from working people. Free enterprises should function without government stealing profits.

Karl Max, the father of modern communism, designed his manifesto to destroy the middle class. America became the greatest nation in history due largely to a middle class that made the free enterprise system work very well. The first plank of communism is a property tax to destroy your right to own property. You become little more than a tenant on what you thought was your property. If you fail to pay your property taxes, you will be removed and someone else that will pay the taxes takes possession of the property. The government owns all the land and is your landlord. In America, no one "owns" land or private property anymore.

The number two plank of communism is a progressive income tax. This is designed to destroy incentive, profits, initiative and the production of wealth. The harder you work, the more you are taxed, so why would you work harder?

The third plank of communism is an inheritance tax, or the death tax as it is called in America. Proverbs 13:22 says, "A good man leaveth an inheritance to his children." The government would much prefer you let them have it when you die, and if you don't, they tax it so heavy that you might as well have just given it to them.

The fifth plank of communism favors a private control banking system, like our Federal Reserve Bank System. This places an impossible debt on future generations. It will lead to the collapse of our economy.

The tenth plank of the communist manifesto is free education for all children in public schools. This allows the government to brain wash each generation to believe what they want them to believe.

The first amendment to the Constitution of the United States of America secures the right to a free press and freedom of religion. In fact we hear all the time about the separation of church and sate. This is why you can't pray in public schools, or put the Ten Commandments on the courthouse lawn. Why then, does the government require churches to form a 501 corporation to be permitted the privilege of calling themselves a church? If we have freedom of religion, we do not need the government's permission! That's ridiculous!

We are taught that America has the best free market economy in the world. That did indeed used to be the case, but not anymore. Now we have the Federal Reserve Board that manipulates the economy to prevent any big booms or any large busts in the economy. They prefer slow growth and low inflation. In a true free market economy there would be busts and booms, inflation and deflation, recessions and rapid growth.

My uncle manufactures size 44DD bras. The bust business is booming.

I would be remiss in my duties if I failed to mention the farmers and ranchers in the New World Order. As most of us know, the family farms are going out of business, replaced by corporate farms. It didn't used to be that way. In 1900, 90% of all Americans were farmers and ranchers. Farmers and ranchers are anarchists by their very nature.

They can be self sufficient in prodiving their own needs, and they all have guns.

The first thing the monied elite did was create the manufacturing sector of the economy to lure the farmers' children to the cities. Few of them ever went back to take over the farm after their father died. Manufacturing also created better farm implements. Tractors and combines were faster and more efficient than horse drawn plows.

Then, after WWII, the use of animal dung for fertilizer was replaced by nitrogen. Nitrogen made the plants green and grow well, but supplied none of the minerals the soil needed from animal dung. The result is a depleted soil that puts no minerals in the food grown on it. Today, if it's not an organic farm, the top soil isn't.

Charlie Daniels did a song called "Long Haired Country Boy."

In the song lyrics, he said, "I ain't got no money, but I damn sure got it made, cause I ain't asking nobody for nothing." He understood no money, and currency is nothing and he had no use for it.

The government has many programs to subsidize farmers. They pay them not to plant on half their land. They pay them not to grow certain crops, and pay them to grow other crops at a loss. Tobacco is heavily subsidized and then the manufacturers of cigarettes are damned for producing a hazardous product.

It is my opinion that in a capitalist society, the government should not subsidize anyone. If you can't earn a profit in your business you should go out of business or go into a business you can earn a profit in. The monied elite want the farmers to be in collusion with the government so they are easily controlled.

Also, plenty of farmers and ranchers are in debt to the bankers for the expensive farm equipment they must have. One bad crop and without a government bail out, the farm is gone! Bankers and government subsidies keep them in line.

Left to run their farms and ranches as they know they can, they could feed the world twice over. The monied elite would have you think we can't feed the population we have now. That's bullshit! We can feed them, they just can't pay for it.

In a true free market economy, success and failure is determined by competition and innovation. We live in an era of government subsidies for farm products and industries which should either make it on their own or go out of business. The citizens of a free market economy should not have their tax dollars paying to prop up these unprofitable private businesses. Why does the government have such an interest in businesses that are none of their business?

At the turn of the twentieth century, the monied elite gained enough control to argue that the rewards of a free enterprise economy are unfair. They wanted the government to take from the rich and give to the poor. At the same time, the same thing was going on in Russia. We called it communism.

The Federal Reserve Act of 1913 and the income tax of 1913 helped to advance their agenda. The Great Depression shook the public's faith in the free enterprise system. After WWII, Congress became generous with the publics money and began to get involved in regulating business and the economy. Now the regulations that are in place make it near impossible for small businesses to compete with big businesses. The government then subsidizes the small businesses that its regulations made unprofitable so they don't go out of business. In a free market economy the government wouldn't tell businesses how to run their business, they would leave that to businessmen.

In medieval times, surfs were not considered free because they owed a third of their labor to the feudal lords. In 1993, American citizens worked from January through July 13 to pay the cost of local, state, and the federal government. That is more than half your labor before you begin worked for yourself. Productive taxpaying people never regain what they pay out in taxes. I'd be upset if I were paying with real money, but since we pay the taxes with Federal Reserve Notes, which are worthless you can't lose what you never had!

Still, depriving the citizens of their unnatural resource of hard earned worthless Federal Reserve Notes is taxing the resources of society. During WWII, the government instituted the "Victory Tax." A withholding of 5% worker's earnings. This was an unlawful tax, but during a time of war, no patriotic American would challenge it. Congress promptly repealed the Victory Tax in 1944.

In 1943 that same Congress passed the "Tax Payment Act," which is the current method of the government with holding our earnings as an income tax. Although an income tax is unconstitutional. Article 1, sub section 2, clause 3 of the Constitution, the government said the Sixteenth Amendment made it legal.

Authors Bill Benson and Red Beckman researched government records on the ratification of the Sixteenth Amendment. They concluded the records were falsified and showed their evidence in their book "The Law That Never Was." The federal courts and U.S. Attorneys said it was a political question and besides, it's too late to do anything about it now. They've been taking the tax for so long and there is no way to give any of that money back. That's the same as a murderer saying, "Well, what good does it do to try me for killing someone? They're dead now and there is no bringing them back." That's ridiculous!

In England in 1815, with a high national debt and a declining standard of living, parliament stunned the world by eliminating the nation's income tax. The result was an unprecedented sixty year period of growth that became the "Industrial Revolution." Shortly after their government reinstated the income tax, they began to decline again.

President Reagan did a similar thing when he lowered the tax brackets in the mid 1980s. The top tax went from 70% to 35%. The results of Reaganomics were not seen until President Clinton, with a total of 13 years of record growth in the American economy.

This brings me back to the Federal Reserve. The Federal Reserve makes use of several tools when setting our monetary policy. Since 1980, the Fed establishes the reserve requirements of not just its member banks, but all banks. The Fed sets the discount rate, this is the interest they change member banks to borrow additional reserves. In addition the Fed buys and sells government securities through its open-maker operations.

Congress established the Federal Reserve originally as an independent agency to stabilize the nation's money supply, avoid inflation, avoid deflation, and prevent another banking crisis. Through the years these goals have been changed. In 1978, Congress passed the "Full Employment and Balanced Growth Act." This directed the Federal Reserve to maintain long run growth of the economy, increase production, promote maximum employment, stable prices, and moderate interest rates with low inflation.

"Federal Reserve Act, Section 2A – Monetary Policy Objectives. The Board of Governors of the Federal Reserve System and the Federal Open market Committee shall maintain long run growth of the monetary and credit aggregates commensurate with the economy's long run potential to increase production, so as to promote effectively the goals of maximum employment, stable prices, and moderate long-term interest rate, Amended October 27, 1978."

In afree market economy in a free country, why does the government feel the need to regulate the economy so it isn't a free market? The Federal Reserve Act says nothing about life, liberty, or the pursuit of happiness!

We use a debt based currency system. Currency doesn't exist until it is borrowed into existence. This brings up the question. "If everyone repaid all loans off at once, would all the currency vanish?" I say yes! It's worth nothing and if it's gone you have nothing left, but when it's here, you still have nothing. There already is no money!

At this point I should mention "Virtual Wealth." Virtual Wealth is assumed to currently exist for accounting purposes. Essentially it is wealth that could be created if all the requirements for its creation existed. It is potential wealth to be created at some point in the future through production. This is the reason banks extend credit to you, based on your potential for future production of income to pay them back.

Let us not be confused by the goals of the monied elite. Maximum employment is not the same as low unemployment. Low unemployment is defined as most everyone that wants to work is able to find a suitable job and work. Maximum employment means everyone who is able to work is working, even people that should be retired who now find themselves having to work to make ends meet. Some people work two jobs. It's not that everyone would have a good paying job. It's that everyone is working as hard and as often as they can, even if it is low paying jobs, which most of them are.

The idea is to keep everyone in debt to the monied elite with car payments, college tuition loans, a 40 year mortgage and a second mortgage. You must be kept borrowing currency into existence so it can never all be paid back, in which case all currency would indeed cease to exist.

We are quickly reaching critical mass. The people are working almost as full and hard as they can. Debt continues to grow. Real wealth is gobbled up by the monied elite as we accept worthless Federal Reserve Notes for all our efforts. At a point very soon, we will not be able to continue building debt. Wake up people, the Money Matrix has you. Debt based currency systems and incompetent congressmen are both subject to change by popular vote!

This should serve as a fair warning to those who advocate a one world currency system. Full enslavement is required before the monied elite can have their New World Order. And I do mean enslavement. If you are being paid with a currency that is worth nothing then you are working for nothing, which is slavery!

So why don't we just return to a Gold standard? The biggest problem with restoring the "Gold Standard" is re-entry. With the universal So why don't we just return to a Gold standard? The biggest problem

evolution to fiat currency systems world wide, no currency is supported by convertibility to intrinsically valued commodities like platinum, gold, and silver. After WWII with the Bretten Woods agreement to link all currencies to the U.S. Federal Reserve Note, and the creation of the International Monetary Fund, government has become the problem, not the solution, to a stable currency.

The dollarization of Eastern Europe and Latin America shows that a foreign currency can and does become a substitute for a less valuable domestic currency. Governments can finance their spending in three ways: Taxes, borrowing from the public, and printing currency. The cost of printing currency is negligible in comparison to any control it has over the public purchasing of goods and services. When a government does this, they are stealing resources from their people.

The European Union created a currency to be used freely in Europe called the "Euro." The Euro is partially backed by gold, which makes it a more desirable currency. Now, other commodities that have traditionally been tied to the U.S. Federal Reserve Note are looking to switch to the Euro. One such commodity is oil, on which the American economy depends heavily.

With the fact that the total outstanding currency supply of Federal Reserve Notes is at least four trillion, complete convertibility to the 264 million ounces of gold the U.S. Treasury says it has, would dive the price of an ounce of gold to $15,000. If silver and platinum were added as a tri-metallic monetary system, the prices of all three metals would skyrocket, with gold closer to $13,000 an ounce.

In a panic, the government might declare a banking emergency and confiscate everyone's gold like they did in 1933. In 1933 the majority of the American public trusted the government. Today, most of the public has reason to distrust the government. In 1933, the majority of Americans got their news and information from the radio. Today we have a well informed society gathering news and information from TV, radio, newspapers, and the internet.

In 1933 when the government stole all the gold, they told the public it was temporary and the public believed it. Then, a few months later when they made it permanent, it went largely unnoticed. The government would never get away with that today. Add to that the fact that we have learned from history, reminds me of the old saying, "Fool me once, shame on me, fool me twice, shame on you!" The public would revolt this time, unlike in 1933. Returning to the Gold standard would be expensive and risky. Besides, the Golden Rule is, he who has the gold rules, and the monied elite already has the gold and are not likely to give it up. That is why they prefer we continue to play their game and go along with the idea of E-Currency or E-Cash.

It is estimated that 90% of modern currency is electronic currency. It is ones and zeros in the banks computer. It has given a whole new meaning to "computer banks." The old term for this currency was "checkbook money." They are simply book keeping entries from one account at one bank to another account at another bank. Just as well. Paper currency makes a visible representation of the invisible money that is already not there!

We're more familiar with E-Currency in the form of credit cards, and more recently debit cards. No cash changes hands. It's all done electronically. The commercials pushing the use of debit cards say they can be used just like cash. So can cash! But since cash is paper money backed by something of value, which we do not have anymore, we don't have any real cash to use anyway.

Just as fiat currency replaced specie and specie-backed paper money, electronically initiated debits and credits are becoming the most used method of payment. The banks argue in favor of E-Currency as being a secure form of small value transactions. E-Currency could help cyber markets grow on the internet.

E-Currency could be kept on a so called "smart card" similar to a credit card, or it could be encrypted onto your personal computer hard drive which could be transferred to your P.D.A People could buy products on the internet and pay electronically. Products capable of being transmitted electronically, such as movies, music, E-Books, or information would be shipped instantly.

Of course, what is secure today may become vulnerable to a brilliant hacker tomorrow. With regular Federal Reserve Notes, you have privacy and anonymity in your purchases. If you buy or sell drugs for instance, there is no way for the government to track it. With E-Currency that would not be the case. Complete knowledge and control of your purchases could be at the government's discretion. Federal Reserve Regulation "E" does currently give consumers some specific rights. Another drawback of E-Currency is that when you go out to a bar, ladies would not know if you were loaded with currency or not. With Federal Reserve Notes, if you pull out a roll of cash the ladies know to flock to you because you have a big wad.

Money. The most powerful female attraction pharamone known to man.

Another reason banks favor E-Currency is traced to the terror attacks on 9-11. All airplanes were grounded after the attacks. Check processing centers normally used air cargo to ship and process checks. For several days no currency moved through the system because checks written were not getting processed. This led the Federal Reserve and Congress to pass the "Check Clearing for the 21" century Act." also known as "Check 21."

Check processing centers have been processing fewer checks each year. More Americans are using electronic funds transfers to pay bills. Utilities offer something called "Auto Pay," where the currency you owe for your utility bill is automatically transferred from your account to their account on an agreed upon day. Assuming the funds are available in your account, it saves time and if you forget, you don't have to worry about a late fee, and the utility gets a steady currency flow.

With Check 21, an ARC, accounts receivable conversion, turns your check into a debit transaction. A trade group known as "NACHA or The Electronic Payments Association," claims it is the fastest growing payment application. They call it automated checks.

People use credit cards to pay a lot of bills, but write a check to pay the credit card bill. Imagine getting a bill from your credit card company and paying it with your credit card. You can't do that! The total of mortgages, credit cards, insurance premiums, and gasoline purchases that are converted to ARC payments has now exceeded two billion a year.

NACHA says that most consumers seem comfortable with the electronic system. Only 4% of check writers have questioned or complained about it. Those are of course the vocal minority or as I like to call them, those who are awake!

NACHA thinks the service it provides creates a win-win situation. "It's good for consumers and gets more paper out of the check clearing system," they said. They did not explain how it was good for consumers oddly enough.

Here's how the system works. Credit card companies or other businesses receive the checks at the post office. Scanners read the data on the checks, and use the information to clear them electronically through the Federal Reserve System. The transaction shows up on the consumer's bank statement as an electronic debit. The check is than destroyed.

Banks and savings banks must allow consumers to opt out of the ARC processing. So far, less than a quarter of a percent of consumers have chosen to do so, probably because they were not aware that they could.

Banks also point out that when all currency is electronic currency, it will be impossible for someone to walk in and rob a bank or liquor store, or a seven-eleven, because there won't be any cash. There already is no money. Willy Sutton robbed banks because that's where the money was. The key word here is "was." Anyone who steals worthless Federal Reserve Notes deserves to go to jail for stupidity! It's centsless,

The Federal Reserve likes electronic-currency because it is so far impossible to counterfeit. Counterfeit currency is making a fake of their fake money. It's a double negative. I believe it is also impossible to counterfeit gold, so what's wrong with using that? A smart twelve year old with a good computer might be able to create all the E-Currency you could imagine, they can't do that with gold. If we had the electronic grid go down and the nation lost power, all the E-Currency would vanish forever!

In the mean time ARC has created another consumer problem while solving all the banks problems. When you write a check, your funds are transferred instantly. But when you deposit a check, even though the bank electronically received those funds instantly, they sit on it for up to five days before they make it available to you! That's ridiculous! If they want everyone to buy into an instant E-Currency system, then it better be instant for all parties involved!

That's not what the monied elite want. They want one more way to pur their hand in your wallet. If you deposit a $600 check in your account, then your auto-pay extracts your phone payment and electric payment, your car payment, and you pick up a few groceries on your home, you may be hit with boo coo overdrafts. Your deposited check won't become available for use until up to five days later.

Another problem is account pinging. This is where a creditor, or one of the auto-pay systems, checks your account to see if funds are available for them to do an ARC or authorized funds transfer. If the funds aren't there, they will ping the account again in a few days to see if funds are available yet. Some bank computers count a ping to check for available funds as an overdraft, even though no funds were transferred.

Data from regulators shows that banks, credit unions, and thrifts collected a record $37.8 billion in service charges in 2004 alone. That's double the amount from ten years earlier. About 45% of those fees came from customers overdrawing their accounts. That's no accident; Banks are using service charges as a steady source of income. It's bank robbery in reserves and it's unconstitutional. Permanent debt is the oldest form of slavery.

Another thing that has come to light in this globalizing one world order is the buying up of America. Increasingly, foreign investors, and foreign central banks, are buying American assets and financing American debt. An Arab company trying to buy U.S. port operations focused attention on this otherwise unnoticed economic fact of life. Hotel chains and fast food chains, real estate, home mortgages, stocks, bonds, and U.S. Treasury securities. 70% of home mortgages are foreign owned, as is half the U.S. government's publicly traded debt. $2.2 Trillion in Treasury securities are in the hands of central banks including China, Japan, and Britain.

China has pegged its currency tightly to the U.S. Federal Reserve Note dollars. We as a nation, borrow over two billion dollars a day from foreigners to finance our trade deficits. If those foreigners were to pull out of the U.S. markets all at once, it would bankrupt America, which technically was and has been bankrupt since 1933 when the monied elite stole our money!

If the foreigners bought our debt with Federal Reserve Notes, which are worth nothing, then they don't really own anything. For wealth to change hands, something of value must be traded for something else of value. Since Federal Reserve Notes have no value, nothing ventured nothing gained.

It has been brought to my attention that some people believe the New World Order is putting radio frequency identification tags (RFID), in our existing Federal Reserve Note currency. One example of this is the fact that when you microwave one of the new $20 bills, they explode always on the right eye of Andrew Jackson. This can be seen at Alex Jones' website, PrisonPlanet.com.

I know a lot about how our currency is produced, and my personal take on it isn't that an RFID tag was in Jackson's right eye. Our currency is printed using metallic inks, and the ink of Jackson's right eye is particularly heavy. Metal and microwaves don't mix well, that is why we have none metal microwave cookware. The high concentration of metallic ink in Jackson's right eye does react violently when microwaved.

Two other things that come to mind are Social Security and the National Debt. Social Security is in the headlines a lot, so I'll deal briefly with that first. The Social Security Act was signed into law in 1935 by President Roosevelt. That is fully two years after he stole all the gold in 1933. People complain that by the time they retire, Social Security will run out of money. The problem with Social Security isn't that it's going to run out of money, it's that it never had any money in the first place. It was created after the money was gone. It's been a giant "Ponzi" scheme the whole time!

As of this writing, the National debt is $8.4 Trillion. That's 28 thousand dollars for every man, woman, and child in America. It is 64% of the GDP. So who do we owe the National Debt to? As a government of, by, and for the people it seems to me that we owe it to ourselves. When I owe myself money I just say screw it, I'm not paying myself back.

The Treasury department says we owe 6.5% to pension funds that bought Treasury securities. 22.7% is owed to Foreigners that have done the same thing. 40.6% is owed to the Federal Reserve for lending currency to the government that wasn't created in the open market with private debt currency creation. The rest is owed to banks and other institutions, as interest on the debt. any.

We can't owe it to the banks, they didn't lend anyone, not even the government any money because they don't and didn't have When a nation goes into debt using a debt based currency, it can never pay the debt off because all new currency must be borrowed into existence which creates new debt to pay the old debt which leads to debt paying debt which is ridiculous!

It's like digging one hole to fill in another hole; you still have, and always will have a hole.

Two thirds of the Federal budget goes to pay just the interest on the National debt. That's very interesting. The imaginary interest on the imaginary debt of the imaginary loan of imaginary money is a drag on real productivity. Any thinking human can't see it for what it isn't! National debt! Debt supported by ever increasing debt. With everybody digging more holes to fill in the other holes, it's only a matter of time before we run out of places to dig. The time of reckoning will soon be before us all. It's easy to ignore a barking dog, but when it bites you in the ass, you can't ignore it any longer.

Only by complete control of the currency system can the monied elite completely enslave us all. You can stop worrying about the cashless society of the New World Order. The cash has been gone for a long time. Now I know what the sign on president Truman's desk meant when it said, "The Buck Stops Here." It really did.

Recently there has been talk about combining the economies of Canada, Mexico, and the United states in a union similar to the European Union. Instead of the Canadian Dollar, the Peso, and the U.S. Federal Reserve Note, the currency would be a new unit called the "Amero." It is suggested that the economies of Canada and Mexico would be made stronger by a single currency with the U.S. It would be implemented in 2010. Calling it the Amero would not sting their pride as much as Dollarizing their economies with the U.S. Federal Reserve Note, which would economically achieve the same goal.

Calling it the Amero, the Amigo, the Greengo, the Québec buck. or a Dollar makes no difference. By wanting to implement it by 2010 shows the monied elite are getting desperate. The gold at For Knox runs out of backing the Federal Reserve Note in 2012. By combining with Canada and Mexico, the monied elite would gain access to Canada's gold reserves and Mexico's silver reserves. This could also extend their run perhaps another 20 years.

See if for what it is, not for what it is not. Any currency backed by nothing is still in itself nothing. A further extension of the illusion that we have money so the public will sleep longer while being robbed even further. Wake up people, The Money Matrix has you.

I deposited "money" into my memory banks.

CONCLUSION

"There is a certain enthusiasm in liberty, that makes human nature rise above itself in acts of bravery and heroism."-Alexander Hamilton

"A mind stretched by a new idea can never go back to its original dimensions."- Oliver Wendell Holmes, Jr.

"If the government is big enough to give you everything you want, it is big enough to take away everything you have."-President Gerald Ford

"Injustice anywhere is a threat to justice everywhere."-Martin Luther King, Jr.

"I reflected that I have as yet done but little, very little indeed, to further the happiness of the human race, or to advance the information of the succeeding generation. I dash from me the gloomy thought and resolved in future, to double my exertions and at least indeavor to promote these two primary objects of human existence, by giving them the aid of that portion of talents which nature and fortune have bestoed on me; or in future to live for mankind, as I have heretofore lived for myself."- Captain Meriwether Lewis.

"Knowledge will forever govern ignorance, and a people who mean to be their own Governors, must arm themselves with the power knowledge gives."- James Madison

A conclusion is what you get when you are tired of thinking.

Follow the money. That's what good investigative journalists are told to do. As I did the research for this book that was a very short trail. The "American Dream" is just a dream. Money really is the elusive pot of gold at the end of the rainbow. When you get there, it isn't what you thought it would be.

The insomniac's nightmare is when they fall asleep they dream they are awake. The Money matrix nightmare is to wake up to find that you have been asleep while you were awake. A good question is. "If there is no money, why do we pursue it so hard?" We are taught to pursue money.

We've been brain washed from childhood to believe we're supposed to want two big SUV's, a big house, all the latest gadgets, and one and a half jobs to pay for it all. We're taught that if you're smart you'll make a lot of money, and nobody wants to think they are stupid. We are taught that if you want to be successful and happy, you have to be rich.

Do you really believe money and riches have anything to do with happiness? You need only open your eyes and look around you at allthe miserable rich people to see that isn't true. 90% of the big lottery winners are broke again within five years.

In June of 2005, John T. Walton, son of Wal-Mart founder Sam Walton, listed by Forbes magazine as the 11 richest man in America with an estimated net worth of $18 billion, died when he crashed his experimental lightweight aircraft in the Rocky Mountains in Wyoming. Some people asked why the hell would a senart rich man try to fly a paper airplane over the Rocky Mountaine? I guess being rich doesn't automatically make you smart.

But that wasn't it at all, because he really was smart. He knew the true nature of money and didn't want to spend his life chasing after nothing. He was a Vietnam veteran, a US army Green Beret and was awarded the Silver Star for bravery. He worked as a crop duster and a boat builder, was a member of the Wal-Mart Board of Directors, was active nationwide in efforts to improve education, and was a huge philanthropist, giving away as much money as he could to good causes. He is sorely missed. He died doing what really matters, living life.

We live in a culture that stresses money instead of money management. We should not be preoccupied with money, nor should we worry about it. Schools don't teach financial competence and neither do most parents, who never learned the true nature of money from their parents. Money it seems, is a necessary evil, the Bible tells us that much. And since there is no money anymore, why stress about it?

Lots of books have been written lately about money. They all make you think the party line, that you too can be a millionaire if you read their book. Hog wash! There is no money. The concept is only in your mind. If you want to enjoy life, don't obsess over money. Do what y want, not what you've been brainwashed to believe you should do. Make a difference, live in the moment and with passion doing what you love. Invest in yourself, because that's the only sure thing.

The Commerce Department recently reported that Americans' personal savings rate had dropped to zero. As a society, no one is willing to save for the future. This is scary for the Bankers. Either Americans are addicted to immediate gratification, or the low savings rate is partly a statistical mirage. Nobody wants to save worthless Federal Reserve Notes. The whole currency is a mirage, that's the real problem. The fact that people are discovering it is a problem for the monied elite.

Why would you want to save something that's worthless? Bankers say that if your money is in their banks, as savings, you will get more money earned as interest. Money equals nothing because there is no money, only worthless Federal Reserve Note currency. To say that if I save some of my nothing. I'll be rewarded with more nothing is like saying if I save some free air I'll be given more free air as a reward. People aren't stupid and they are not addicted to immediate gratification, they spend all their Federal Reserve Notes so they can get full value for their nothing!

I used my left over Federal Reserve Notes as toilet paper. Maybe that's why it's called disposable income.

The Commerce Department calculates the personal savings rate by subtracting total consumption spending from your total after tax income. The leftover amount, if you have any, is called "disposable income." Perhaps the Commerce Department should think the problem over differently. The real problem is that it takes everything we earn. to live. We don't have any disposable income to save if we wanted to!

Additionally, if we must spend everything we have left after taxes, perhaps we are paying too much tax!

This savings rate has gone from a high of 10.8% in 1984, to 4.6% in 1995, to 1.8% in 2004, and in June 2005 hit zero. We know from math that it cannot go any lower than this. You can't save less than nothing of the nothing you didn't have left. The sum of the parts must equal the hole, um, whole.

The Federal Reserve Chairman Alan Greenspan in 2005 expressed his concerns over the "wealth effect." Huge increases in home values and stock prices make the people who think they actually own them, feel richer, which causes them to go deeper into debt. The Federal Reserve was concerned because "homeowners" were converting higher real-estate values into cash.

This was accomplished in three ways. First, let's say they bought a home for $100,000 five years ago. Prices were estimated to have risen by 53% over that same period. The real-estate value of that home is now $153,000. If the owner sells, they get $53,000 minus any broker's fees This capital gain can be offset by purchasing another home within a certain period of time.

The first problem I see with this logic is that over five years the "homeowner" probably paid that much in interest. If they really did own the house, which we know from an earlier chapter in this book has been proven impossible, and if there really were money, which we know from earlier chapters in this book has been proven to no longer exist, they would only have broken even. It's like the peanut butter and jelly sandwich we were going to have if we had some peanut butter, and if we had some jelly, and of course, some bread. The illusion of the "wealth effect," like the illusion of money itself and the illusion of homeownership exist only in your convoluted minds. Greenspan knew this and that's why he was concerned.

The second way "homeowners" were converting higher real-estate values into cash was by refinancing their existing mortgage for a higher amount and pocketing the extra money. This is called a "cash out" refinancing. Again we will use the example of the $100,000 home bought five years ago. The real-estate value of that home is now $153,000. The bank gives you $53,000 minus closing costs and refinances your home for 30 years at $153,000.

The "homeowner gets $50,000 or so right now to spend anyway "homeowner" likes it because they get cash now. The Bank likes it they want. It's like giving yourself a pre-approved long term loan. Th because they know the interest they make on a loan of $153.000 is more than the interest on $100,000. Over 30 years, they will make their investment back five fold, about $250,000 in interest more, just for $53,000.

This concerned Greenspan because we have a debt based currency, for currency to be created it must be borrowed into existence. Cash out refinancing creates more currency than the Federal Reserve was projecting, screwing up their calculations. They didn't expect additional currency creation on the perceived value of that home until it was paid off twenty-five years later.

The third way "homeowners" were converting higher real estate values into cash is to take out a home equity loan against the higher home value. In all of these cases the Bank wins. The "homeowner" is now further enslaved and will have to work more years of their life away to pay back the loan.

In 2004 alone, this put over $600 billion more in the hands of consumers than the Federal Reserve wanted. The Federal Reserve claims they don't know how much was spent and how much was saved. The Commerce Department figures show that it was all spent because savings have dropped to zero. The net results were a marathon shopping spree that pumped up the economy.

Greenspan and the Federal Reserve were upset because ordinary people had found a way to do what the Federal Reserve does all the time, make money out of nothing. Counterfeiting Federal Reserve Notes is making a fake of their fake money, and that's not legal. Borrowing up in more currency into existence against the "virtual wealth" built your home is perfectly legal. And since you don't really own the house anyway, if you can get yourself some extra Federal Reserve Notes to help make your life easier for now, why not go for it?

This is where the Federal Reserve said the housing market was creating a bubble of false value that would burst at some point plunging home prices lower. This scare tactic is meant to keep people from enriching themselves. The government warned that higher interest rates. higher energy costs, higher debt payments, higher inflation, and falling wealth gains individually don't matter much. The combination of all factors means higher risk for the consumers.

This is of course a part of the master plan of the monied elite. They got away with stealing all the gold in 1933. Now the plan is to steal the only wealth most people have left, their homes.

Don't be fooled by the threat of falling home values, they won't. First of all, the only real value of your house is as shelter. That's all! Second, with the population rising, more people will need more shelter. Demand for housing will only go up, continually.

In the 1950's, a home loan was for a ten year period at 4%. In the 1960's, it was for fifteen years at 5%. In the 1970's it went to 20 years at 6%. In the 1980's, it was a 30 year loan at 10%. Now Fanty Mar, one of the government home loan plans, is talking about 40 year loans. This cannot go on forever. A crash is immanent!

Don't think the monied elite can't take what you think is your house because they can. If you miss three consecutive payments, you are in default and they can seize your property. Losing your job to a foreigner because it was outsourced could cause you to lose your home as well. If the banks get into trouble, they can call in all outstanding loans. That means if you still owe $70,000 on your $100,000 homr they can demand you pay the $70,000 or they take your house, which really isn't yours anyway.

property You either pay rent to the government in the form of taxes, and/ or you pay a government sanctioned bank in the form of a mortgage. The banks and the government don't deny they are in collusion. They openly admit the govemment licenses banks, so banks are an agent of the government, or ultimately the monied clite.

The government and the bankers want you to think that in a cashless society, your money is safer in the bank's computer. I was told by a seventeen year old, that not only could hackers break into the computers, they could as casily program the computer to think they have money they don't. After all, it is only ones and zeros in a computer anyway, it doesn't physically exist!

And what if the power grid went down nationwide? My good friend

Bob was trying to use his ATM card to draw out some cash. ATM is an Automated Teller Machine. Bob couldn't get any money through because the bank's main computer in Minneapolis was down. I bet this has happened to some of you as well.

It was announced in the mid 1970's, that if a one megaton nude warhead were detonated 200 miles above the ground, directly over Omaha Nebraska, the exact center of the United States, an electromagnetic Pulse (EMP), would wipe out the entire power grid of the US. With few technological advances, we now have 95% of all currency in bask computers. In an instant, all hard drives would be wiped clean, cdl phones would go dead, and most of our satellites in space would be rendered useless.

In John Carpenter's "Escape from L.A." Snake Plisken decorates such a device at the end of the movie in what would be the year 2013. Remember that year because it could be important. In the Fox Network Television series "Dark Angel," such a device shut down the entire west coast of America, which was trying to rebound many years later. In the movie "Fight Club," the ultimate goal was to blow up all the banking computers to wipe everyone' slate clean. You can see it has been conceived of before, and it could happen.

If all the money and bills owed suddenly disappeared at once, the nation would find itself in a financial crisis such as the world has never seen before. There are those in the monied elite that wish to do just that. whether thy use a third party to blame it on or not, they ultimately are behind it all.

Now it might interest you to know that the Federal Reserve was created in December 1913. The Federal Reserve gets paid a small percentage for controlling our currency. The Federal Reserve is paid in "Gold Certificates" which are redeemable for only one thing, gold! At one percent a year, it would take 100 years before they could slowly steal all the gold. If you're doing your math, you know the gold rus out in 2013. The Mayan calendar runs out in December of 2012. A coincidence? I don't believe in coincidence.

It seems like it takes a crisis to get Americans to do anything. The monied elite first get as many people as possible to start buying a house. Then, they make the payment plan for as long as your productive years of your life last. This way they enslave you for your lifetime trying to pay for a house that's not even yours. Lastly, they create a crisis, a financial crisis, and steal the only wealth you feel you have, your home.

Now, I'd like to share a story with you. A long time ago in a desert far away, a young boy and an old man were walking along together. Suddenly an earthquake hit the area. The ground heaved and rumbled for about twenty seconds. When it stopped, they noticed a hole had opened in the ground ahead of them.

The old man and the boy peered down into the hole and saw something shiny and sparkly reflecting the sunlight that was able to make it down the narrow shaft. Curiosity overcame them, and the old man and the boy climbed down about thirty feet to the bottom of the hole.

To their amazement they were now standing in a cavern filled nearly to the ceiling with treasure of every imaginable kind. Geld and silver coins and statues, jewelry and gemstones filled the cavern. They both gasped at the sight of it all.

Then, a loud thunderclap snapped them out of it as a seven foot tall genic appeared before them. The genie informed therm that the treasure was his, but they would be allowed to take whatever they wanted. The old man and the boy wandered through the cavern to see what was all there that they might have.

In the middle of the cavern stood a six foot tall bull made completely of solid gold. The old man reshed up to it and proclaimed that it was what he wanted. He climbed on top of it, hugged it, and ran his hands up and down its magnificent horns and calling out that it was his.

The boy poked around, trying on different sized rings, some with jewels and some with ornate carvings. When the boy had found a ring that fit each of his fingers and thumbs, be returned to the genie and proclaimed that he wanted the rings on his fingers.

The genie told them their choices were final. The genie slammed his hands together, mumbled some magic words and everything else in the cavern disappeared except the large gold bull with the old man on it, and the ten rings on the boy's hands.

The old man started laughing. He called out to the boy, selling him what a fool he was. He pointed out to the boy how large his gold bull was and how much it must weigh being solid gold.

The old man said. "You could have had so much more you young fool!"

The boy said, "Oh, I wanted more, but what good is it if you can't take it with you?" He then turned and climbed up out of the hole, leaving the old man with a lot of bull behind him.

Really, what good is it if you can't take it with you?

Do you sell a gold bull in a gold bull market?

Now I have a scenario for you. Let's say you have a dog and you are taking your dog for a walk at three o'clock in the morning. On this walk you notice an apartment building on fire. It's a four story building and flames are coming out a third floor window. What would you do?

You have several options. You can do nothing, stand there with your dog and watch the building burn. If you do nothing, some or maybe most of the people in the building will die. Certainly all their possessions will be lost to the fire.

If you have a cell phone you could call 911. In the absence of a cell phone, you could run to a pay phone, or run home and call it in to 911. If you do that, much precious time is lost and again, most if not all of the people in the building will die and of course the property will be lost.

Or you could run into that burning building, pound on all the doors and ting door bells to wake everyone up, all the while yelling "Fire." Some of the people will still probably die, in fact somebody is probably already dead because of the fire you saw in the first place. Also, most of everyone's possessions will be destroyed, but at least if they were awakened, they have a fighting chance.

If I were asleep in the burning building, I would want somebody to wake me up. I believe if you see something like that, it is your duty to wake them up! That's what I am doing with this book, I can see what's happening. I can see most people are asleep to the money matrix, and it is my duty at least to try to wake you up.

There is an old saying that goes something like this. Some people are great because they do great deeds. Some people are great because they take credit for the great deeds done by others. Some people have greatness thrust them.

These people who have greatness thrust upon them were the right people in the right place at the right time that did what was right. The person that runs into a burning building is such a person that was there at the right time and did what was right.

Some people would say that it was a coincidence that they were there at that time to save these people from the burning building. 1 have said before and I will say it again, I do not believe in coincidence. A coincidence is a seemingly random pattern that turns out to have meaning.

Some people say the human mind is geared to see and detect patterns. They say that when we observe something we can't explain that we try to fit it into some pattern that we can explain. John Nash, a Nobel Prize winner and subject of the movie "A Beautiful Mind," saw patterns everywhere he looked.

I believe we see patterns because they are there. The seemingly randomness of a coincidence is really a pattern that is not at all random. Few people follow such thought to its logical conclusion

It is no coincidence that I wrote this book. I was in the right place at the right time, and I was the type of person to do what was right, write this book. I don't expect to win the Nobel Prize in Economics for writing this book. I don't want to be considered a hero for waking you up. I also don't want you to be mad at me. I didn't take the money or make it disappear. I'm only the messenger.

They said they didn't want a handout, they wanted a hand up, so I gave them the finger and said "up yours."

In the beginning of this book I warned you not to read it if you didn't want to know what the Money Matrix of the new World Order was. I told you what got me started down the path of researching and writing this book. I gave a brief history of money in America. Then I told you there is no money.

I showed you both the Treasury Department and the Federal Reserve admit that our currency we use today is backed by nothing Thus, money equals nothing. I showed you that Banks don't have any money, only numbers in a computer. I showed you that in the absence of money nobody is rich. I showed you it is impossible to own land. I showed you that you work for nothing and everything you buy costs you nothing.

I showed you that in the Bible, money and greed are the root of all evil. I showed you there is no credit, there are three types of money, that currency is not money, and that only a silver dollar is really a "dollar."

1 explained fractional reserve banking and how it generates currency from nothing. I showed that math proves there is no money and that science and the mechanics of money prove there is no longer any money. I explained what true wealth really is, and it isn't money.

I portrayed a humorous look at what aliens might think of our With the help of Tater, the little cartoon character, I sprinkled humor throughout the chapters. I also used quotes from famous and intelligent people that warned us of the effects of the Money Matrix.

I showed you the rise of the New World Order, told you who was behind it, the monied elite, and how they went about stealing all the money and setting up the money matrix.

I don't expect you to believe what I've told you. That is why I have also included a glossary and a rather hefty bibliography. Go and look for yourself at the web sites, especially of the Treasury Department and the Federal Reserve. Watch the movies and read the books I reference. The Money Matrix is self evident. I don't have to prove it: its very existence proves it!

Some people, who are otherwise intelligeat Americans, are thought to be conspiracy theotorists because they think a few powerful monied clite people covertly control our country, and are out to control the world, for their own greedy evil purposes. I see these people as the ones that are awake to the truth. A government by and for the people must control the people it is by and for. That central mechanism is our finances and the Money Matrix.

Government, the most efficient money irradicating agent known to mankind.

Every human alive today is capable of doing more than they are. We are limited only by ourselves. The Money Matrix is based on a system of rules. It is limited by these rules. These rules do not apply to a freed mind.

Society begins to decline when it stifles itself with limits. Once inside the box no growth can occur outside the box, and the box keeps getting smaller.

Experience is something you learn just after you need it. However, if you think for yourself, you can learn from others experience. In the end, if it's all smoke and mirrors, money is the smoke. Most people can't see beyond the money. What really matters is the reflection in the mirror.

Do you like that person looking back at you? Chances are if you don't, nobody else does either. At the end of the day, that's the person you go to bed with. Are you still trying to grab a handful of smoke? Whatever helps you sleep at night.

A conscience is what hurts when the rest of you feels good.

When my good friend Phil Moncada died, five hundred people attended his funeral. Monetarily, he was not rich. It was his wealth of friends that made him a millionaire. When you die, will a piece of you remain in the hearts of all who knew you? Or will you be remembered as a cheap bastard that only cared about money, if you are remembered at all?

It's up to you. You can be chump change, or you could be the chump that changes the lives around you in some kind way. You've run out of money, but you never ran out of kindness. Your cup ranneth over with continuous and spontaneous acts of kindness!

The purpose of this book is not to fix blame, or even to fix the problem. The purpose of this book is to wake you up to the fact that there is a problem. If you're awake, I've done my job. I'm not here to tell you what to do or how it will end. I'm here to tell you this is the beginning of the end.

Where it goes from here depends on what you decide to do. I have led you to the door. The decision to walk through it is up to you. I am

of the opinion that if you won't stand up for yourself and demand your money, you don't deserve any!

A friend of mine asked me, "What am I supposed to get out of this book?" of the fact that there is no money! If you can't be happy with what you Hopefully, it will help you live a freer, richer, life, fully cognizant have, you can never be happy!

We the unwilling, led by the unknowing, are doing the impossible, for the ungrateful. We have donc so much, with so little, for so long, we are now qualified to do anything with "nothing!"

Did you know you can get a Hummer in the backseat of a Honda?

BILL GATES AND WARREN BUFFETT

Several weeks before this book was to go to the printers, Bill Gates, the richest man in the world, and Warren Buffet, the second richest man in the world stunned the world by announcing they were giving away their fortunes to charity. Bill Gates is perhaps America's most generous philanthropist, but Warren Buffett had previously said his estate would be dealt with after his death. It is interesting to me that both men thought the dollar would drop in value two years earlier and were hedging their bets against the dollar.

Why would the two richest people in the world suddenly decide to give away billions of dollars? I asked myself that question and came up with several possibilities. By giving away their fortunes to charity they gain a huge tax write-off. This keeps a currency wasting government from getting their grubby hands on it and wasting it or worse, losing track of it!

By giving it to charity, they get to do some good with this resource and they get to choose the good that gets done with it. Governments are notorious for making bad or personal interest decisions when it comes to spending someone else's currency.

If they give it away now, before the currency devalues farther or goes away altogether, full value of the nothing can go to helping others who have no nothing. They were correct in betting that the value of our currency will soon go way down.

As I have said before, nobody needs more than they need. They can donate it away because they truly don't need it. It does no good to sit there, it's only good is realized in the action of using it. To spend their worthlessness for good is a worthy cause.

It also sets an excellent example for the other Billionaires as to what they should do with their excess excesses. The government does not like people to have more currency resources than them. That is why they went after Howard Hughes in the late 1960's, and why they went after Bill Gates and his company Microsoft at the turn of the millennium. for a generation are throwing in the towel. Who will the governmen Now the men who moved our economy and productivity forward pick on next? My guess would be Wal-Mart and the Walton family. However, that is another story. In the mean time, my hat is off to Bill Gates and Warren Buffett for doing the right thing. Bravo!

GLOSSARY

<u>Abrogate</u> - to abolish by authoritative action/ to do away with.

<u>Absolute</u> -free from imperfection, perfect.

<u>Absolute Value</u> - the numerical value of a real number irrespective of sign.

<u>Absolute Zero</u> - a hypothetical temperature characterized by complete absence of heat and approximately minus 459.69 degrees F. /The point at which all molecular activity stops.

<u>Abstract</u> - difficult to understand/ insufficiently factual.

<u>Absurd</u> - lacking order or value/ ridiculously unreasonable! meaningless.

<u>Abundance</u> - relative degree of plentifulness/ an ample quantity! affluence, wealth.

<u>Abundance Theory</u>- There is enough money for everyone, so there is no reason why you shouldn't get as much as you want.

<u>Accept</u> - to make a favorable response to/ to regard as proper, normal,

or inevitable.

<u>Accord</u> - to assign as a portion/ to confer something on as an award.

<u>Accounting</u> - the system of recording and summarizing business and financial transactions in books and analyzing, verifying, and reporting

the results/ the principles and procedures of accounting.

<u>Accounting Unit Dollar</u> - token dollar, imaginary accounting unit used to denominate United States currency.

<u>Accretions</u> - the increase of land by the gradual or imperceptible actions of natural forces/ the process of growth.

<u>Acolyte</u> - one who attends or assists.

<u>Acquire</u> - to get as one's own/ to come into possession or control of often by unspecified means.

<u>Addition</u> – increase/ the act or process of adding, especially the operation of combining numbers so as to obtain an equivalent simple quantity.

<u>Additional</u> - the result of adding more/ increase.

<u>Ad valorem tax</u> - a tax imposed on the arbitrary and subjective value of property.

<u>Advance</u> - to supply or furnish in expectation of repayment/ a provision of something (as money or goods) before a return is received: also, the money or goods supplied.

<u>Advantage</u> - Benefit, gain.

<u>Advantaged</u> - Superiority of position or condition.

<u>Affluent</u> - flowing in abundance, copious/ having a generously sufficient and typically increasing supply of material possessions.

<u>Afford</u> - to be able to bear the cost of.

<u>Agrarian</u> - Related to agriculture/ Farming

<u>All</u> -As much as possible/ nothing but, only the whole of one's possessions.

<u>Allot</u> - To assign as a share or portion.

<u>Allowance</u> A share or portion allotted or granted for personal or household expenses.

<u>Alms</u> - Something (as money or food) given freely to relieve the poor.

<u>America </u>- Land of the free.

<u>Amortize</u> - to provide for the gradual extinguishment of usually a mortgage, by contribution to a sinking fund at the time of each periodic interest payment.

<u>Amount</u> - the total number or quantity/ a principal sum.

<u>Amplitude</u>- The quality or state of being ample/ Fullness.

<u>Anachronistic</u>- Out of place/ chronologically.

<u>Analogy</u> - Inference that if two or more things agree with one another in some respect, they will probably agree in others.

<u>Annuit Coeptis</u>-God shines on our endeavors.

<u>Ante </u>- An amount paid in advance.

<u>Arbitrage</u> - Simultaneous purchase and sale of the same security in order to profit from price discrepancies.

<u>Arithmetic</u>- A branch of mathematics that deals with computation and

calculation.

Artifice - Clever or artful skill.

Assess - To make an official valuation of something.

Assessment on deposits - The FDIC insurance fee that banks pay for each $100 of deposits.

Asset - the entire property of all sorts of a person, subject to the payment of his debts.

Bail - Money given as security in exchange for release of a prisoner. Bailment- The hiring of another person for safekeeping of property. Property is held in trust by one person for the benefit of another person. The holder is called the bailee, the beneficiary is the bailor.

Bale - Great evil.

Bank - An establishment for the custody, loan, exchange, or issue of currency, for the extension of credit, and for facilitating the transmission of funds.

Bank Money - A medium of exchange consisting chiefly of checks and drafts.

Bank Note - A promissory note issued by a bank payable to bearer on demand without interest and acceptable as money.

Bank Paper - Circulating Bank Notes.

Bank Roll - Supply of money, funds.

Bankruptcy - A process designed to eliminate debts.

Barter - Wealth traded by direct exchange, one commodity for another.

Bearer - One holding a check, draft, or other order for payment especially if marked payable to bearer,

Belong - To be the property of a person or thing

Benefit - A payment or service provided for under an annuity or pension plan to be useful or profitable to.

Benefactor - The person designated to receive the income of a trust estate/ the person named (as in an insurance policy) to receive proceeds or benefits.

Bequeath - To give or leave by will especially property to hand down.

Bequest - Legacy.

Bestow - To convey as a gift.

Bill - An itemized list of fees or charges.

Bill of credits - Paper document issued as legal tender by the government on its authority and credit, redeemable in specie at a future day, and designed to circulate as money.

Bimetallism -Two metal currency (gold and silver).

Bonus Money - or an equivalent given in addition to what is strictly due/ Dividend/ A sum in excess of what was expected.

Booty - Plunder taken on land as distinguished from prizes taken at sea/ a rich gain or prize.

Borrow -To receive with the implied intention of returning the same or an equivalent.

Bribe - Money or favor given or promised to a person in a position of trust to influence his judgment or conduct.

Bullion - Gold or silver metal.

Business - Includes all activities engaged in or caused to be engaged in with the object of gain, benefit or advantage, direct or indirect.

Buyer - Purchaser, one who buys.

By tale - A libelous report or piece of gossip/ an intentionally untrue story/ an imaginative narrative of an event/ story.

Capital - Any asset used in combination with labor to produce wealth/ the value of accumulated goods/ net worth.

Cash - Ready money/ paper currency backed by something of value such as gold or silver or platinum.

Cashier's check - A check drawn by a bank on its own funds and signed by the cashier.

Cause - Something that brings about an effect or a result.

Change - Money in small denominations received in exchange fee an equivalent sum in larger denominations/ coins of low denomination money returned when a payment exceeds the amount due.

<u>Chaos</u> - Chasm, abyss/ a state of utter confusion.

<u>Charge</u> - To set or ask a given amount as a price/ to postpone payment on a purchase by recording as a debt.

<u>Charitable</u> - Benevolent goodwill towards or love of humanity! helpfulness toward the poor and needy.

<u>Charitable Organization</u> - Any entity organized and operated exclusively for charitable, philosophical, scientific, testing for public safety, literacy or educational purposes, or to foster national or international amateur sports competition, or for the prevention of cruelty to children or animals, provided that no part of the entity's net earnings goes to the benefit of any private shareholder or individual.

<u>Chattel</u> - A piece of personal property.

<u>Check</u> - A written order to a custodial third party, usually a bank or credit union, to pay transfer on a stated date a stated amount of currency from one person's account to a stated recipient. A check is not currency and only represents funds on deposit.

<u>Chrematistics</u> - A collection of statistics.

<u>Clear</u> - Free from obligation or encumbrance.

<u>Clinometric</u> - Inclines or inclined.

<u>Clout</u> - Influence.

<u>Cogent</u> - Appealing forcibly to the mind or reason presented in such a way that brings out pertinent and fundamental points.

Coin - A piece of metal with its commodity type, weight and fineness stated on its face; an item of intrinsic value based in the unconditional, historical domain and often used as a medium of exchange. / Monetized bullion or other forms of money manufactured from gold, silver. platinum, palladium, or other metals now or in the future and used as a medium of exchange in the United States or in any foreign nation.

Coincidence – The occurrence of events that seem to happen by accident, which really turn out to have a meaningful point or conclusion.

Collateral – Used as security for payment of a debt/ property pledged by a borrower to protect the interests of the leader.

Commerce - Any kind or type of exchange of goods, production or property, or the rights to property offered for a consideration to the general public at large.

Commercial Paper - Used as a means of trade in commerce.

Common law - Unwritten law based on custom and precedent

Commodity - Something useful or valuable, an economic good such as a product of agriculture or mining.

Compensate - To be equivalent to, counterbalance.

Compensation - Something that constitutes an equivalent or recompense, payment, renumeration.

Concept - An abstract or generic idea generalized from particular instances.

Conscience - Sensitive regard for fairness or justice.

<u>Consideration</u> - An act of forbearance or the promise thereof done or given by one party in return for the act or promise of another as payment for services.

<u>Contribute</u> – To give or supply in common with others free of obligation.

<u>Contrived Sale</u> – A commercial transaction executed in a extraordinary manner for the purpose of evading the national sales and use tax otherwise due.

<u>Convertibility</u> -Capable of being exchanged for a specified equivalent in another currency or security.

<u>Convertibles</u> – Capable of being exchanged for a specified equivalent in another currency or security.

<u>Corporeal</u> - Having, consisting of, or relating to a physical material body.

<u>Cost</u> - The amount paid or charged for something to have as a price.

<u>Counterfeit</u> - To imitate or copy closely especially with interest to deceive, especially something of value such as currency or Rolex watches.

<u>Coupon</u> - A statement of due interest to be cut from a bearer bond when payable and presented for payment/ a certificate of a purchase redeemable in premiums.

<u>Craft</u> -Skill in deceiving to gain an end/ an occupation or trade.

<u>Credit</u> - Imaginary demand/ reliance on the truth or reality of something; belief; faith/ a negative sum extended for the purpose of buying now and paying later.

<u>Credit Note</u> - Paper document denominated in token dollars, United States Treasury credit note.

<u>Currency</u> - That which circulates as a medium of exchange, a common article for bartering, anything that is in immediate, continuous and widespread use as money.

<u>Custody account</u> - A fiduciary account of general warrant deposits whereby rights to deposited funds remain vested in the depositor.

<u>Debag</u> - To reduce the intrinsic value of (a coin) by increasing the base metal content/ to reduce the exchange value of (a monetary unit).

<u>Debauch</u> - To corrupt, debase.

<u>Debit</u> - A record of indebtedness

<u>Debs</u>- A state of owing/ something owed, obligation/a common-law action for the recovery of money held to be due/ a negative quantity. Deface- To mar the external appearance of, disfigure.

<u>Deflation</u>- A debasement of the monetary system. A decrease in the volume of currency such that there is less currency bidding for goods and services within a free market, tending to force market prices lower. Excessive supply for available demand.

<u>Delusions</u>- A false belief regarding the self or persons or objects outside the self that persists despite the facts.

<u>Demand</u>-For the individual, demand is the desire for wealth (goods and services) coupled with the ability to pay. For society as a whole, aggregate demand varies according to desire for wealth (goods and services) and the

quantity of currency in circulation. When currency is offered in trade or commerce, currency is demand.

Denomination- A value or size of a series of values or sizes (as of money).

Depression- A period of low general economic activity marked especially by rising levels of unemployment.

Derivative- A financial instrument, traded on or off an exchange. the price of which is directly dependent upon (that is, "derived from") the value of one or more underlying securities, equity indices, debt instruments, commodities, other derivative instruments, or any agreed upon pricing index or arrangement (for example, the movement over time of the Consumer Price Index or freight rates). Derivatives involve the trading of rights or obligations based on the underlying product, but do not directly transfer property. They are used to hedge risk or to exchange a floating rate of return for fixed rates of return. In short. derivatives are bets that banks can legally make. The leverage is so great that interest rates moving in the wrong direction (against the bet) by even a quarter point can wipe out a bank's total capital.

Desire - To long or hope for, to express a wish for. Direct tax-Any tax levied on people or property. Discount- A reduction made from a regular or list price. Divesting. To dispose of property, rid.

Dollar - A unit of weight, as construed in the U.S. Constitution and in the Coinage Act of 1792, equal to 371and a quarter grains; equivalent to 24.0566 grams or 0.77344 troy ounces of fine silver in the form of a coin. The unit of value of the United States of America monetary system.

Donate - To make a gift of to contribute to a public or charitable cause.

Draft - An order for the payment of money drawn by one person or bank against another.

Due - Owed as a debt/ having reached a date at which payment is required/ payable.

Eagle - A gold coin containing one troy ounce of gold, an easily recognizable standard United States coin which may be used as money.

Far mark - To designate for a specific use.

Eccentric - Deviating from an established pattern or from accepted usage or conduct.

Economics - A social science concerned chiefly with description and analysis of the production, distribution, and consumption of goods and services.

Edifice - A large or massive structure.

Effect - To bring about, often by surmounting obstacles! something that inevitably follows an antecedent (as a cause or agent).

Efficacy - The power to produce an effect.

Eminent Domain - A right of a government to take private property for public use by virtue of the superior dominion of the sovereign power over all the lands within its jurisdiction.

Empirical - Originating in or based on observation or experience.

Encumbrance - A claim (as a mortgage) against property. Endogenously-Growing from the inside.

Energy - Natural power vigorously exerted/ the capacity for doing work.

Enjoy - taking pleasure or satisfaction in, to have for one's use, benefit, or lot.

Enumerate - To ascertain the number of, count.

E Pluribus Unum - One composed of many; specifically, a national government formed by uniting many states.

Equitable interest - Having or exhibiting equity.

Equity - The money value of a property.

Equity Jurisdiction - Justice according to natural law or rights the money value of property or of an interest in property in excess of chains or liens against it.

Equivalent - Virtually identical in effect or function, equal in amount or value.

Ersatz - An artificial and inferior substitute (such as a Federal Reserve Note instead of a real dollar).

Essence - Something that exists, real.

Ether - A medium that in the undulatory theory of light, permeates all space and transmits transverse waves.

Euro - Currency of the European Union, similar to the U.S. Federal Reserve Note Dollar, except that it is partially backed by gold.

Exchange - The act of giving or taking one thing in return for another trade

the amount of the difference in value between two

currencies.

Exchange Value - Instantaneous parity of a thing at the time of the exchange.

Exigency- A state of affairs that makes urgent demands.

Exist - To have real being whether material or spiritual.

Ex nihilo - From or out of nothing/ either.

Expediency - To accelerate the process or progress of

Expense - Something requiring the expenditure of money.

Expenditure - An expense.

Expensive - Commanding a high price and especially one that is not based on intrinsic worth or is beyond a prospective buyer's means.

Easements - One that champions or advocates.

Expropriate - To deprive of possessions or proprietary rights/ to transfer the property of another to one's own possession.

Extort - To obtain from a person by force or undue or illegal power.

Extra - More than is due, usual, or necessary/ additional.

Face value - The value indicated on the face (as of a postage stamp or a dollar bill or coin).

Faith - Firm belief in something for which there is no proof.

<u>Fascism</u> - The nation above the individual with centralized autocratic government, severe economic and social regimentation.

<u>Federal Reserve</u> - Twelve banks set up under the Federal Reserve System to hold reserves and discount commercial paper for affiliated banks in their respective districts.

<u>Federal Reserve Note</u> - Paper document denominated in token dollars; a token note having only exchange value; a type of U.S. currency adopted by custom and through the imposition of legal tender laws; direct obligation of the United States; fiat money; scrip; currency issued by the Federal Reserve.

<u>Fees</u> - A fixed charge.

<u>Felonies</u>- Forfeiture of fees.

<u>Fiat</u>- A sanction, decree/ money not convertible into coin or specie of equivalent value (as in fiat dollar).

<u>Fiat money</u> - Paper documents or token coins, normally issued by governments and made legal tender by fiat or statutory law, not redeemable in specie; an item of exchange value based in the conditional, future domain; accepted by the issuer as compensation for taxes, fees, duties of debts, accepted by others in anticipation of future exchanges.

<u>Fiduciary</u> - Depending on public confidence for value or currency. such as fiat money.

<u>Figure</u> - A number symbol, numeral, digit/ to calculate.

<u>Finance</u> - The obtaining of funds or capital.

Financial - Relating to money.

Finite - Having definite or definable limits.

Foisted - To force another to accept by stealth or deceit.

Forfeit - To lose the right to by some error offense, or crime/ the subject of confiscation as a forfeit.

Fortune - Prosperity/ possession of material goods/ wealth.

Free - Without charge, not costing or charging anything.

Free market - One in which any individual may exchange their products or services by competitive bidding, open to all, without constraint.

Frequency - The fact or condition of occurring frequently/ the number of times that a periodic function repeats the same sequence of values during a unit variation of the independent variable.

Fulfill - To bring to an end/ to measure up to, satisfy, to convert into reality/ to develop the full potentialities.

Funds - A sum of money.

Fungible - Goods and commodities that are identical with other goods and commodities of the same nature. (Comparing apples to apples and oranges to oranges).

Gain - Resources or advantage acquired or increased/ the obtaining output over input/ to get possession of, usually by industry, merit or craft.

Gainful - Profitable.

General warrant deposits - Fungible deposits allowing banks to return property like-for-like.

Generous - Liberal in giving.

Get - To gain possession of earn/ to obtain by way of benefit or advantage/ to become affected by/ to seek out and obtain/ to receive by way of punishment/ to acquire wealth/ to leave immediately.

Get ahead -To achieve success.

Get by - To make ends meet, survive/ to succeed with the least possible effort.

Gift - Something voluntarily transferred by one person to another without compensation.

Give - To put into the possession of another for his use/ to yield possession of by way of exchange/ to dispose of for a price/ to inflict as a punishment/ to suffer the loss of (sacrifice)/ to offer as appropriate or due (especially to something higher or more worthy)/ to apply freely to offer as a pledge to cause a person to catch by contagion or infection/ to allow one to have or take.

Give away - Something given away freely.

Give and take - The practice of making mutual concessions. Giving- The act of delivering without compensation.

Glean - To gather (as information) bit by bit/ to pick over in search of relevant material/ to find out, learn, ascertain.

Gold - A malleable ductile yellow metallic element that occurs naturally and is used in coins, jewelry and dentures. Money.

Gold certificate - A document certifying that a like amount of its face denomination in gold eagles is on deposit with and held in trust for its immediate redemption at the U.S. Treasury or at a designated agent of the U.S. Treasury.

Gold eagle - U.S. gold coin with the symbol of an eagle.

Gold Standard - A monetary standard under which the basic unit of currency is defined by a stated quantity of gold and which is usually characterized by the coinage and circulation of gold, unrestricted convertibility of other money into gold, and the free export and import of gold for the settlement of international obligations.

Graft - To get by illicit gain.

Grant - To bestow or transfer formally, to give possession or title of by deed, usually with no obligation on the part of the receiver.

Gratuity - Something given voluntarily or beyond obligation usually in return for good service/ a tip.

Greed - Excessive or reprehensible acquisitiveness/ avarice/ insatiable desire for wealth or gain.

Green back - Dollar bills/ a legal tender note issued by the U.S. Treasury.

Gresham's Law - Bad forces out good money.

Groceries - Food or drink advertised or marketed for human Consumption and sold in the same form, condition, quantities, and packaging as is commonly sold by grocers, such as: cereals and cereal products; milk and milk products; meats and meat products; fish and fish products; sugars, sugar products and sugar substitutes; coffees and coffee substitutes; teas, cocoa and cocoa products, carbonated and non- carbonated soft (nonalcoholic) drinks; spices, condiments and salt; or any combinations of food products or food product substitutes, whether sold prepared or unprepared. The term does not encompass chewing gum, cocktail mixes, alcoholic drinks, proprietary medicines, lozenges, tonics, ice, vitamins and other dietary supplements, or food or food products not for human consumption such as pet food. Nor does it encompass food or drink served or furnished in or by cafes, restaurants, lunch counters, cafeterias, delicatessens, hotels, drugstores, social clubs, nightclubs, cabarets, resorts, snack bars, caterers, carryout shops, and other like places of business, whether fixed or mobile, such as pushcarts, motor vehicles or other mobile facilities, at which prepared food or drink is regularly sold; not food or drink vended by machines for a vendor, nor food or drink furnished, prepared, or served for consumption on or near the premises of the retailer although such food or drink is sold on a "take out" or "to go" order and is bagged, packaged, or wrapped and taken from the premises of the retailer.

Gross National Product - The total value of the goods and services produced in a nation during a specified period, such as a year.

Have -To hold in possession as property/ to acquire or get possession of/ obtain to experience especially by submitting to, undergoing, or suffering/ to entertain in the mind/ allow/ to take advantage of, fool, trick/ be entitled to.

Hawala - An ancient practice where people transfer money without paperwork by using money traders who have counterparts in other countries.

Hedge - To protect oneself from losing by a counter balancing transaction/ as a defense against financial loss/ to minimize the risk of a bet.

Hoard - To keep for oneself, usually in mass quantities.

Hollow - Having a cavity within/ deceivingly lacking in real value or significance/ lacking in truth or substance/ cavity, hole.

Ignorant - Lacking knowledge or comprehension or education/ uninformed, unaware.

Illusion - The state or fact of being intellectually deceived or misled/ perception of something objectively existing in such a way as to cause misinterpretation of its actual nature.

Impossible - Incapable of being or of occurring/ incapable of being done, attained, or fulfilled.

Imposture - The act or practice of deceiving by means of an assumed character or name/ fake, counterfeit.

Income - A gain or recurrent benefit usually measured in money that derives from capital or labor/ the amount of such gain received in a period of time.

Incorporeal - Of, relating to, or constituting a right that is based upon property (as bonds or patents) which has no intrinsic value.

Increase - Addition or enlargement in size, extent, quantity.

Indebted - Owing money.

Indemnities - Security against loss.

Indian Giver - One that gives something to another and then takes it back.

Indirect tax - Any tax levied on an activity or event.

Industry - A department or branch of a craft, art, business, or manufacture, especially one that employs a large personnel and capital especially in manufacturing/ manufacturing activity as a whole.

Inertia - A property of matter by which it remains at rest or in uniform motion in the same straight line unless acted upon by some external force.

Infinitesimal - A variable that takes on values arbitrarily close to zero/ immeasurably or incalculable small.

Infinity - Unlimited extent of time, space, or quantity boundless.

Inflation- A debasement of the monetary system. An increase in the volume of currency such that there is more currency bidding for goods and services within a free market, tending to force market prices higher. Excessive demand for available supply.

Inflection- The act or result of curving or bending; bend/ to look inside yourself or alter your perception.

Inherent - Existing as an essential characteristic.

In rem - Against the thing. In rem taxes are against property and not people.

Integer - Any of the natural numbers, the negatives of these numbers, or zero.

Interest - Right, title, or legal share of something/ a charge for borrowed money generally a percentage of the amount borrowed. Intrinsic value

Inherent value usually related to cost of production.

<u>Investment</u> - A possession, as property, acquired for future income or benefit.

<u>Inveterate</u> - Firmly established by long persistence/ confirmed in a habit.

<u>Irredeemable</u> - Not convertible into specie at the pleasure of the holder/ inconvertible, not terminable by payment of the principal.

<u>Jurisprudence</u> - The science or philosophy of law/ a system of law.

<u>Kinetic</u> - Of or relating to the motion of material bodies and the forces and energy associated therewith/ energizing, dynamic.

<u>Lawful</u> - Authorized, sanctioned/ not contrary to nor forbidden by law, constitutional.

<u>Lawful money</u> - Lawful money of account, specie, silver dollars, eagles.

<u>Legal</u> - Done or performed in accordance with the forms and usages of law, or in a technical manner. An act may be legal but, if not constitutional, it is not lawful.

<u>Legal-tender</u> - Default medium of exchange, forced use of a government specified medium of exchange when parties to a mercantile transaction fail to specify a specific medium of exchange.

<u>Levy</u> - Assessing and collecting a tax or payment.

<u>Lien</u> - A charge upon real property for the satisfaction of some debt ordinarily arising by operation of law/ the security interest created by a mortgage.

Liquid assets- Quickly convertible to cash.

Laodicean- Ancient tribe of bankers.

Loot - To rob on a large scale/ something of value taken by force.

Lot - Share, fortune/ a considerable quantity or extent.

Love - A score of zero in tennis.

Lucre - Money.

Luxury - Rich surroundings/ something desirable, but costly to get.

Magnitude - Great size or extent/ spatial quality, size/ a numerical quantitative measure expressed usually as a multiple of a standard unit.

Mamon - Material wealth or possessions.

Manufacture - The operation of producing a new product, article, substance, or commodity different from and having a distinctive name, character, or use from it's constitute raw or prepared materials.

Marauders - Those who roam about and raid in search of plunder.

Mark - Any of various old European units of weight used especially for gold and silver, equal to about eight ounces or one half taler.

Market value - A price at which both buyers and sellers are willing to do business.

Material - Of or relating to the production and distribution of economic goods.

Mathematics - The science of numbers and their operations, interrelations, combinations, generalizations, and abstractions, and of space configurations and their structure, measurement, transformations, and generalizations.

Matrix - Something within which something else originates of develops.

Matter - The substance of which a physical object is composed/ material substance that occupies space and has weight, that constitutes the observable universe, and that together with energy forms the basis of objective phenomena.

Means - Resources available for disposal, especially material resources affording a secure life.

Medium of exchange - Currency/ an intermediate used during trade or commerce/ an expediency accepted in an exchange/ that which is used as money in an exchange.

Meek - Submissive.

Merit - Character or conduct deserving reward, honor, or esteem/ to be worthy of or entitled to, earn/ reward due.

Millionaire - One whose wealth is estimated at a million or more dollars.

Minions - A servile dependent/ one highly favored/ idol.

Mirage - Something illusory and unattainable/ delusion.

Modulation - A regulating according to measure or proportion.

Monetary - Of or relating to money.

<u>Monetize</u> -To coin into money/ to establish as legal tender.

<u>Monetization</u> - The act of creating and introducing currency into circulation through debt.

<u>Monetization fee</u> - Payment required for the monetization of debt, pseudo interest.

<u>Money</u> - A psychological creation/ a concept/ the mental image of that which is generally accepted as a medium of exchange/ gold.

<u>Money Madness</u> - The pursuit of money by any and all means without regard to the consequences to oneself or others/ a radical infection of the Money Matrix.

<u>Money Order</u> - An order issued by a post office, bank, or telegraph office for payment of a specified sum of money usually at another office.

<u>Multiplication</u> - A mathematical operation that at its simplest is an abbreviated process of adding an integer to itself a specified number of times and that is extended to other numbers in accordance with laws that are valid for integers.

<u>National debt</u> - The debt load of a government of a sovereign nation.

<u>Natural law</u> - A body of law or a specific principle held to be derived from nature and binding upon human society in the absence of or in addition to positive law.

<u>Natural number</u> - The number one or any number (3, 12, 432) obtained by repeatedly adding 1 to this number.

<u>Need</u> - Being in want/ poverty.

Nefarious - Flagrantly wicked or impious.

Note - Certified claim on wealth/ a written or printed paper acknowledging a debt and promising payment.

Nothing - Not anything, nothing.

Novus Ordo Seclorum - (Latin) A new order of the ages. (New World Order).

Number - A unit belonging to an abstract mathematical system and subject to specified laws of succession, addition, and multiplication.

Numeral - A conventional symbol that represents a number.

Numerous - Consisting of great numbers of units or individuals.

Numismatics - The study or collection of coins, tokens, and paper money and sometimes related objects (as medals).

Obligation - A debt security (as a mortgage or corporate bond). commitment (as by a government) to pay a particular sum of money.

Obtain - To gain or attain usually by planned action or effort.

Ownership - To have or hold as property, possess, the exclusive right to possess, enjoy, and dispose of a thing.

Paradigm - Pattern (new paradigm emerges, new pattern emerges).

Parlay - To increase or otherwise transform into something of much greater value.

Parsimonious - Frugal to the point of stinginess, stingy, niggardly. Pay-To give money to in return for goods or services rendered.

Payee - The one to whom money is paid.

Payment - Discharge of an obligation or debt by delivery of value, usually lawful money. The execution and delivery of negotiable papers (instruments) is not payment unless it is accepted by the parties in that sense (UCC 3-410).

Payer - One that pays or is responsible for paying a bill or note. Pecuniary-Consisting of or measured in money.

Perception - A mental image, concept, (personal view point),

Person - Any individual, firm, partnership, joint adventure, corporation, estate, or trust, or any group or combination acting as a unit, but not a governmental unit, and the plural as well as the singular number.

Personal property - Exclusive individual ownership of private property.

Phree - Anything you buy or pay for using worthless Federal Reserve Notes.

Pilfer - To steal stealthily in small amounts and often again and again.

Pip - One of the dots used on dice and dominoes to indicate numerical value.

Pirating - To reproduce without authorization especially in infringement of copyright, invention, production, or conception. To take something that does not belong to you usually by force.

Place value - The position of a figure in relation to others of a row or series, especially the position of a digit within a numeral (in 316 the figure 1 is in the tens place).

<u>Plausible</u> - Appearing worthy of belief.

<u>Plow back</u> - To retain profits for reinvestment in a business.

<u>Plunder</u> - To commit robbery or looting/ to take by force.

<u>Poor</u> - Having little or no money.

<u>Posited</u> -To assume or affirm the existence of/ postulate.

<u>Possess</u> - To enter into and control firmly.

<u>Potential</u> - Existing in possibility, capable of development into actuality.

<u>Poverty</u> - Lacking the means of providing the material needs or comports/ the state of one who lacks a usual or socially acceptable amount of money or material possessions.

<u>Precious metal bullion</u> - Any refined precious metal, such as gold, silver, platinum and palladium, which is in a state or condition where its value depends primarily upon its precious metal content and not its form.

<u>Premium</u> - A sum over and above a regular price as an incentive.

<u>Price</u> -Value, worth/ the quantity of one thing that is exchanged or demanded in barter or sale for another/ the amount of money asked for an item/ the cost at which something is obtained.

<u>Price controls</u> - Also price fixing - The setting of prices artificially such as producers or governments, contrary to free market operations.

<u>Price Fixing</u> - Same as price controls. The setting of prices artificially such as producers or governments, contrary to free market operations.

<u>Principal</u> - A matter or thing of primary importance, also a capital sum placed at interest, due as a debt, or used as a fund.

<u>Priori</u> - Earlier in time or order/ taking precedence.

<u>Private property</u> - Everything subject to ownership, not denominated as real estate/ an individual's right or interest in things, either corporeal, meaning moveable and tangible things such as animals, furniture, merchandise, etc., or incorporeal, meaning rights to intangible things such as personal annuities, stocks, shares, patents, copyrights, etc...

<u>Prize</u> - Something exceptionally desirable.

<u>Problem</u> - A source of perplexity, distress, or vexation.

<u>Profit</u> - A benefit, advantage or gain, particularly a pecuniary gain of excess returns over expenditures, accruing to an owner through the use or exchange of their property, or their rights to property, other than an individual's personal labor, barter or trade.

<u>Profligacy</u> - Wildly extravagant, grossly self-indulgent expenditure.

<u>Progressive tax</u> - A levy which collects more from those better able to pay.

<u>Promulgated</u> - To make known or public by open declaration/ proclaim usually to make known a new law.

<u>Property</u> - Everything that is subject to ownership, corporeal or incorporeal, tangible or intangible, visible or invisible, real, private or personal/ something owned or possessed.

Property rights - Any type of right to specific property.

Prophet - Disappearance of material sense before the conscious facts of spiritual Truth/ one who utters divinely inspired revelations.

Prosper - To achieve economic success.

Prosperity - The condition of being successful.

Public utility - A business organization performing a public service and subject to special governmental regulations. The Federal Reserve might be considered a public utility.

Purchase - The transfer of property or property rights from one person to another by voluntary act or agreement in exchange for a valuable consideration/ to obtain by paying money or its equivalent.

Purchase price - The cost or consideration paid the purchaser, exclusive of any direct tax imposed by territorial, state, or local government and exclusive of the national sales and use tax.

Purchaser - Person who acquires property or rights to property in commerce for a valuable consideration/ buyer/ vendee.

Purchasing power - The ability to purchase goods and services, or the amount of goods and services that one unit of money can buy.

Quantum - Quantity, amount.

Real - Having substance, not fake/ a former monetary unit of Spain.

Real estate - Land and those things erected or growing upon it, such as buildings, fences or crops. The term embraces items such as light, plumbing and heating fixtures when permanently attached.

Reality - The totality of real things and events in actual fact.

Recession - A period of reduced economic activity.

Recompense - To give something to by way of compensation/ to pay for.

Regressive tax - An onerous levy, one which unduly burdens poorer families and individuals less able to pay.

Rendered - To make available.

Renumerate - To pay an equivalent to for a service, loss, expense.

Resonance - A vibration of large amplitude in periodic stimulus of the same or nearly the same period as the natural vibration period of the system/ a quality of richness or variety.

Resonate - To have a repetitive pattern that resembles resonance. Retailer- Person doing a retail business, known to the trade and public as such, and selling in commerce to any user or consumer/ also called vendor or seller.

Retail sale - All sales other than wholesale sales.

Return -To produce or yield profit as a payment for labor, investments, or expenditures.

Revelation - The act of revealing to view or making known. An enlightening or astonishing disclosure.

Revenue - The total income produced by a given source.

<u>Rich</u> - Having abundant possessions and especially material wealth.

<u>Sale</u> - The transfer of ownership of and title to property from one person to another for a price.

<u>Salvation</u> - The realization of the supremacy of infinite mind over all, bringing with it the destruction of the illusion of sin.

<u>Satisfaction</u> - Fulfillment of a need or want/ a source or means of enjoyment/ compensation for a loss/ the discharge of a legal obligation.

<u>Sawbuck</u> - A ten-dollar bill.

<u>Scratch</u> - Slang for money or funds.

<u>Scrip</u> - Provisional certificate; evidence that the holder or bearer is entitled to receive something.

<u>Secular</u> - Of or relating to the worldly or temporal/ not overtly religious/ relating to a long term of indefinite time.

<u>Securitization</u> - The issuance of bonds backed by some asset.

<u>Seigniorage</u> - Revenue from printing money/ the difference, which may be positive or negative, between the face value of specie (coin). silver or gold certificates, or fiat currency and its commodity value in a free market.

<u>Selfish</u> - Concerned exclusively with oneself, concentrating on one's own advantage, pleasure, or well-being or welfare without regard for others.

<u>Sell</u> - To give up property to another for money or other valuable consideration/ to deliver the personal services of for money.

<u>Seller</u> - One that offers for sale/ any person who transfers. property or property rights by sale in commerce; a merchant, a retail dealer, a supplier, a retailer, a vendor; one who offers a service or buys to sell.

<u>Severance Pay</u> - An allowance usually based on length of service that is payable to an employee on termination of employment.

<u>Share</u> -To divide and distribute in shares/ one's full or fair portion/a part allotted or belonging to one or a number owning together property/ any of the equal portions into which property or invested capital is divided such as stock in a corporation.

<u>Silver certificate</u> - A document certifying that a like amount of its face denomination in dollars of coined silver is on deposit with and held in trust for its immediate redemption at the U.S. Treasury or at a designated agent of the U.S. Treasury.

<u>Quarter Silver dollar</u> - A coin containing a dollar weight - 371 and a quarter grain of silver, an easily recognizable standard United States coin which may be used as money.

<u>Slave</u> - A person held in servitude as the chattel of another.

<u>Smithereens</u> - Fragments, bits. Something- A person or thing of consequence.

<u>Source</u> - Point of origin or creation.

<u>Sovereign</u> - Freedom from external control/autonomy.

<u>Spatial</u> - Occupying or having the character of space.

<u>Specie</u> - Money in coin form usually of silver or gold.

Spoils - Plunder taken from an enemy in war or the victim in robbery/loot.

Spot - A small quantity or amount/ involving immediate cash payment.

Spurious - Of falsified or erroneously attributed origin/ forged, fake, false, bastard.

Stagnation - Motionless, stable, dull, inactive.

Stake - An interest or share in an undertaking (as a commercial venture).

Steward - A fiscal agent/ one employed in a large household or estate to manage domestic concerns (supervision of servants, collection of rents, and keeping of accounts).

Stewardship - The individual's responsibility to manage his life and property with proper regard to the rights of others.

Stingy - Not generous/ unwilling to share with others.

Stipend - A fixed sum of money paid periodically for services of to defray expenses.

Stratagem - A cleverly contrived trick or scheme for gaining an end/ skill in ruses or trickery.

Substance - Physical material from which something is made or which has discrete existence/ material possessions.

Subterfuge - Deception by artifice or stratagem in order to conceal.

Succession - The act or process of following in order, sequence, the act of becoming beneficially entitled to property of a deceased person.

Sum - An indefinite or specified amount of money.

Sundries - Miscellaneous small articles, details, or items. Supply- Goods and services/ wealth held by the community at large.

Surplus - The amount that remains when use or need is satisfied.

Sustained - To give support or relief to/ to supply with sustenance/ suffer/ support.

Symbol - Something that stands for or suggests something else by reason of relationship, convention, or accidental resemblance/ a visible sign of something invisible.

Symbolism - The practice of using symbols, especially by investing things with a symbolic meaning by expressing the invisible or intangible by means of visible representation.

Symptom - Something that indicates the existence of something else/ a slight indication.

Taint - Corrupt/ to affect with putrefaction/ a contaminating mark.

Tale - An intentionally untrue story.

Taler - Any of numerous silver coins used as currency in certain Germanic countries between the fifteenth and nineteenth centuries.

Tangible - Capable of being perceived by the sense of touch.

Tax - Either a fee payable by the purchaser of property or of property rights subject to taxation, or an aggregate amount of fees due from the taxpayer, as the context may require.

Taxpayer - Any person obligated for taxes payable, to be collected or due.

Temporal - Of or relating to earthly life.

Tender - Any offer to settle a debt or obligation with any accepted medium of exchange accompanied by means for fulfillment of that offer.

Thing - Whatever may be possessed or owned or be the object of a right.

Tip -To give a gratuity/ a gift or sum of money tendered for a service performed or anticipated.

Token - Something that serves as what it is not.

Token coin - A piece of metal intended for use as currency, issued at j a nominal or face value normally far in excess of its commodity value United States clad coins and subsidiary coins of base alloys.

Token dollar - Imaginary accounting unit dollar/ debt/ an artificial creation, irredeemable in specie.

Trade - The business of buying and selling or bartering commodities / an exchange of property without use of money.

Trade Dollar - A U.S. silver dollar weighing 420 grains 900 fine issued 1873-85 for use in oriental trade.

Transmogrification - To change or alter greatly and often with grotesque or humorous effect.

Treasury - The government department in charge of finances, and especially the collection, management, and expenditures of public revenues.

Treasury bill - Obligation of the U.S. Treasury for a specified term of three, six or twelve months from the date of issue, bearing no interest but sold at a discount.

Treasury bond - Paper document issued by the government as evidence of long-term indebtedness.

Treasury certificate - Obligation of the U.S. Treasury generally maturing in one year on which interest is paid by coupon.

Treasury credit-note - United States currency/ paper document denominated in token dollars, designed to circulate as money, having exchange value, irredeemable, with limited legal-tender character, authorized by Congress of the United States, issued by the U.S. Treasury bearing no interest and spent into circulation through voluntary acceptance/ an obligation of the United States/ fiat money.

Treasury note - Obligation of the U.S. Treasury, with a maturity of one to five years and interest paid by coupon.

Trust - A property interest held by one person for the benefit of another.

Umpteen - Indefinitely numerous.

Unit - Any specified or determinable amount or quantity adopted as a standard of measurement/ unity/ one.

Usury - An unconscionable or exorbitant rate or amount of interest.

Valuable - The monetary worth of something.

Value - A numerical quantity that is assigned or is determined by calculation or measurement.

<u>Vendee</u> - Purchaser.

<u>Vendor</u> - Seller.

<u>Viceroy</u> - The governor of a province who rules as a representative of the sovereign.

<u>Virtual</u> - Being such in essence or effect though not formally recognized or admitted.

<u>Virtual Wealth</u> - Potential wealth to be created through future production and assumed to currently exist for accounting purposes/ wealth that could be created provided all requirements for its production existed, (the chickens that were counted before they hatched).

<u>Void</u> - Containing nothing/ empty space.

<u>Volume</u> - The amount of a substance/ the degree of loudness or intensity.

<u>Wad</u> - A roll of paper money/ money.

<u>Wage</u> - A payment usually of money for labor or services usually according to contract and on an hourly, daily, or per week basis.

<u>Wager</u> - A sum of money risked on an uncertain event/ a bet.

<u>Waif</u> - A piece of property found but unclaimed/ stolen goods thrown away by a thief in flight/ something found without an owner. especially by chance.

<u>Want</u> - To fail to possess, especially in customary or required amount/ lack/ to have a strong desire for/ to suffer from the lack of, to wish or demand the presence of/ to be needy or destitute/ to have or feel need/ grave and

extreme poverty that deprives one of the necessities of life.

<u>Warrant</u> - A document that authorizes a person to pay or deliver to another and the other to receive money or other consideration/ a short term obligation of a government body issued in anticipation of revenue/ an instrument issued by a corporation giving to the holder the right to purchase the capital stock of the corporation at a stated price either prior to a stipulated date or at any future time.

<u>Wealth</u> - Abundance of valuable material possessions or resources/ a profusion of abundance/ all goods and resources having economic value.

<u>Welfare</u> - Government benefits concerning the improvement of the welfare of disadvantaged social groups.

<u>Well-being</u> - A state of being happy, healthy, or prosperous.

<u>Wholesaler</u> - Person doing regularly organized wholesale or jobbing business, known to the trade as such and selling to retail merchants, jobbers, dealers, or other wholesalers for resale.

<u>Whompum</u> - Native American shell money.

<u>Will</u> - A legal declaration of a person's mind as to the manner in which he would have his property or estate disposed of after his death/ the legal written instrument of the will.

<u>Wit</u> - Reasoning power.

BIBLIOGRAPHY

http://en.wikipedia.org/wiki/Money http://en.wikipedia.org/Flex dollars

http://en.wikipedia.org/Bretton Woods Conference http://en.wikipedia.org/Franklin D. Roosevelt

http://en.wikipedia.org/wiki/Law or Conservation of Mass http://en.wikipedia.org/wiki/Wall Street Crash 1929 http://en.wikipedia.org/wiki/National Socialist German Workers Party

http://en.wikipedia.org/wiki/Charles E. Hughes http://en.wikipedia.org/wiki/Woodrow Wilson

http://en.wikipedia.org/wiki/World War One

http://en.wikipedia.org/wiki/Zimmermann Telegram

http://en.wikipedia.org/wiki/RMS Lusitania

http://en.wikipedia.org/wiki/French Revolution

http://en.wikipedia.org/wiki/Mexican-American War

http://en.wikipedia.org/wiki/Spanish-American War

http://en.wikipedia.org/wiki/Philippine-American War

http://en.wikipedia.org/wiki/Adolf Hitler

http://en.wikipedia.org/wiki/World War II

http://en.wikipedia.org/wiki/List of World War II Conferences

http://en.wikipedia.org/wiki/Arcadia Conference

http://www.marxists.org/golssary/terms/c/a.htm

http://nesara.org/articles/index.htm

http://nesara.org/articles/not yours to give.htm

http://nesara.org/articles/rabbits/htm

http://www.findlaw.com/casecode/constitution/ http://nesara.org/main/dictionary.htm http://quotes.liberty-tree.ca/QuotesByCat! Read Form&Restrict to Money

http://nesara.org/artickes/faq money and currency.htm http://nesara.org/articles/coinage act of 1792.htm http://www.reformation.org/rome steals us lands.htm http://www.libertyhaven.com/regulationan dpropertyrights/bankingmoney http://www.binioncollection.com/Silver Dollars.htm http://www.lib.umich.edu/govdocs/jfkco/co/11110lhtm

http://www.ronscurrency.com/retype.htm

http://www.harrybassfoundation.org/cnhist.asp

http://www.coin-newbies.com/articles/gold was never illegal.html

http://www.moneyfactory.com/documents.cfm/18/113

http://www.moneyfactory.com/document.cfm/18/106

http://www.moneyfactory.com/document.cfm/18/116

http://www.moneyfactory.com/document.cfm/18/107

http://www.moncyfactory.com/document.cfm/18/110

http://www.moneyfactory.com/document.cfm/18/120

http://www.wooden-nickel.net/history/

http://www.ex.ac.uk/-RDavies/arian/government.html

http://www.ex.ac.uk/-RDavies/arian/northamerican.html

http://www.amergold.com/vault/uspeacesilverdollars.shtml

http://www.coinfacts.com/silverdollars/1804dollars/ http://www.coin-newbies.com/articles/stamps for money.html http://pa.essortment.com/morgandollars

http://www.digitalhistory.uh.edu/database/

articledisplay.cfm?HHID=108 http://www.coins.nd.edu/colcoin/

colcoinIntros/Sp-silver.intro.html

http://www.dederalreserve.gov/faq.htm

http://www.fbi.gov/lobref/historic/famcases/sutton/sutton.htm http://www.positiveatheism.org/mail/em19613.htm http://www.ustreas.gov/education/faq/currency/legal-tender.html

http://nesara.org/articles/nine tenths purc.htm

http://www.ezresult.com/article/Gresham'sLaw

http://historymatters.gmu.edu/d/5829

http://www.hartford-hwp.com/archives/41/415.html http://www.lewrockwell.com/north/north 219.html

http://www.uhuh.com/laws/donnedl/co/1933/EO6102.TXT

http://www.goldsheetlinks.com/production2.htm http://www.law.com/jsp/article.jsp?id=1046288235244 http://www.the-privateer.com/1933-gold-confiscation.html

http://www.icp.utm.edu/n/natlaw.htm

http://www.thebiblespeaks.com/Articles/

Donts/Materialism/greed.htm http://www.acts17-11.com/money.html

http://www.surfinthespirit.com/charity/reap-what-you-sow.shtml

http://www.Keyway.ca/htm2003/20030312.htm

http://www.gotquestion.org/taxes.html

http://www.floridbaptistwitness.com/639.article http://www.theadvent.ort/Mission200/porter.html http://www.essortment.com/greedybiblecovrdqm.htm http://www.thetain.ort/studies/ten.html http://www.mustardseed.net/html/toriches.html

http://www.mustard seed.net/html/topoverty.html

http://www.christinyou.net/pages/greed.html http://www.studylight.org/con/utb/view.cgi?number=T4167 http://www.nccusa.org/poverty/biblespeaks.html http://www.family.org/cforum/fosi/gambling/abp/

a0029493.cfm

http://www.bible.ca/s-gambling.htm

http://www.incommunion.org/misc/iv.asp

http://www.mospat.ru/text/econception/id/5535.html

http://www.nysscpa.org/prof library/guide.htm

http://www.quickmba.com/accounting/fin/double-entry/ http://www.cardratings.com/creditater.html

http://www.nolo.com/lawcenter/ency/ articlecfm/objectID/1FF752c2-

http://www.studylight.org/enc/isb/biew.cgi?number=T7048

http://www.studylight.org/con/ntb/view.cgi?number=T221

http://www.studylight.org/con/ntb/view.cgi?number-T3934

http://www.studylight.org/con/ntb/view.cgi?number-T3919

http://nesara.org/wiifm/index.htm

http://fx.sauder.ubc.ca/PPP.html

http://nesara.org/articles/theyellowbrickroad.htm

http://nesara.org/articles/anewtheoryofmoneyl.htm

http://nesara.org/articles/anewtheoryofmoney2.htm

http://nesara.org/articles/back to basics1.htm

http://nesara.org/articles/back to basics3.htm

http://nesara.org/articles/back to basics2.htm

http://nesara.org/articles/back to basics4.htm

http://nesara.org/articles/barter trade commercel.htm

http://nesara.org/articles/barter trade commerce2.htm

http://nesara.org/articles/anewtheoryofmoneyl.htm

http://nesara.org/articles/anewtheoryofmoney2.htm

http://nesara.org/articles/anewtheoryofmoney3.htm

http://nesara.org/articles/anewtheoryofmoney4.htm

http://nesara.org/articles/anewtheoryofmoney5.htm

http://nesara.org/articles/anewtheoryofmoney6.htm

http://nesara.org/articles/anewtheoryofmoney7.htm

http://nesara.org/articles/letters from college main.htm

http://nesara.org/articles/letters from college01.htm

http://nesara.org/articles/letters from college02.htm

http://nesara.org/articles/letters from college03.htm

http://nesara.org/articles/letters from college04.htm

http://nesara.org/articles/letters from college05.htm

http://nesara.org/articles/letters from college06.htm

http://nesara.org/articles/letters from college07.htm

http://nesara.org/articles/letters from college08.htm

http://nesara.org/articles/letters from college09.htm

http://nesara.org/articles/letters from college10.htm

http://nesara.org/articles/rabbits-banking.htm

http://nesara.org/articles/rabbits-money and currency.htm

http://nesara.org/articles/conspiracies and games.htm

http://nesara.org/articles/practical virtual wealth1.htm

http://nesara.org/articles/practical virtual wealth2.htm

http://nesara.org/articles/practical virtual wealth3.htm

http://nesara.org/articles/practical virtual wealth4.htm

http://nesara.org/articles/practical virtual wealth5.htm

http://nesara.org/articles/practical virtual wealth6.htm

http://nesara.org/articles/practical virtual wealth7.htm

http://nesara.org/articles/abstract.htm

http://nesara.org/articles/understanding moneyl.htm http://nesara.org/articles/understanding money2.htm

http://nesara.org/articles/understanding money3.htm

http://nesara.org/articles/understanding money4.htm

http://nesara.org/articles/understanding money5.htm

http://nesara.org/articles/understanding money6.htm

http://nesara.org/articles/understanding money7.htm

http://nesara.org/articles/understanding money8.htm

http://nesara.org/articles/understanding money9.htm

http://nesara.org/articles/their lips are moving 1.htm

http://nesara.org/articles/their lips are moving 2.htm

http://nesara.org/articles/their lips are moving 3.htm

http://nesara.org/articles/their lips are moving 4.htm

http://nesara.org/articles/their lips are moving 5.htm

http://nesara.org/articles/their lips are moving 6.htm

http://nesara.org/articles/personal private public.htm

http://nesara.org/articles/Let them eat cake 1.htm

http://nesara.org/articles/Let them eat cake 2.htm

http://nesara.org/articles/negotiating with the warden1.htm

http://nesara.org/articles/negotiating with the warden2.htm

http://nesara.org/articles/negotiating with the warden3.htm

http://nesara.org/articles/negotiating with the warden4.htm

http://nesara.org/articles/negotiating with the warden5.htm

http://nesara.org/articles/to talk of many things1.htm

http://nesara.org/articles/to talk of many things2.htm

http://nesara.org/articles/to talk of many things3.htm

http://nesara.org/articles/to talk of many things4.htm

http://nesara.org/articles/to talk of many things5.htm

http://nesara.org/articles/pie in the sky1.htm

http://nesara.org/articles/pie in the sky2.htm

http://nesara.org/articles/pie in the sky3.htm

http://nesara.org/articles/pie in the sky4.htm

http://nesara.org/articles/pie in the sky5.htm

http://nesara.org/articles/pie in the sky6.htm

http://nesara.org/articles/pie in the sky7.htm

http://nesara.org/articles/new equations.htm

http://douglas7eberman.net/money.html http://bible-history.com/isbe/l/
inheritance/ http://deadlysins.com/sins/index.htm

http://metamind.us/members/stevemoyer/email/1075695203.htm

http://bibletools.ort/index.cfm/fuseaction/ Topical.show/RTD/cgg/
ID/254 http://www.metlife.com/Applications/corporate/ WPS/CDA/
PageGenerator/0.1674

http://ftc.gov/bcp/conline/edcams/credit/yer free reports.htm

http://www.math.com/school/subject1/lessons/SIUILIDP.html

http://mathforum.org/K12/mayan.math/ http://fn2.freenet.edmonton.

ab.ca/-martinh/soddy88.htm http://www.bu.edu/wcp/Papers/Econ/EconShep.htm

http://encarta.msn.com/media 461577350/ Benjamin Franklin Quick Facts/ http://landru.i-link-2.net/monques/mmm2.html http://www.josephnewman.com/Heqt and Thermodynamics.html http://www.emc.maricopa.edu/faculty/farabee/ BIOBK/BioBook Enerl.html

http://www.economics.utoronto.ca/munro5/ http://www.silver-investor.com/prop.htm

http://www.prisonplanet.com/022904rfidtagsexplode.html http://www.multied.com/documents/Clayton.html http://business-Law.freeadvice.com/trade regulation/anti trust act.htm

http://www.harwich.edu/depts/history/pp/gilded/tsld054.htm

http://canadianeconomy.gc.ca/english/ economy/1944 Bretton Woods.html http://econ161.berkeley.edu/Politics/whynotthegoldstandard.html

http://econ161.berkeley.edu/TCEH/Slouch Gold8.html http://fame.org/HTM/Vicira EdwinWhatisa DollarEV-002.HTM http://www.elev.frb.org/annual/essay.htm http://www.gold-eagle.com/greenspan011098.html

http://www.polyconomics.com/searchbase/files13.html http://www.ucc.ie/law/irlii/statutes/1999 4.htm http://www.federalreserve.gov/General Info/fract/sect01.htm

http://www.federalreserve.gov/GeneralInfo/fract/sect02.htm http://www.federalreserve.gov/GeneralInfo/fract/sect11.htm http://www.investopedia.com/terms/brettonwoodsagreement.asp http://www.pbs.org/fmc/timeline/stockmarketcrash.htm

http://www.conservativeusa.org/co/1933/co6260.htm http://www.strike-the-root.com/columns/chkoreff/chkoreff1.html http://www.brainyhistory.com/years/1933.html http://www.themomoryhole.org/war/debs-speech.htm http://www.onwar.com/aced/mike/mexicousa1916.htm http://www.edu.uiuc.edu/courses/edpsy317/sp03/

development-maps/human-development

http://www.ebookapprentice.com/profits/ incalucofyourproduct.html

http://www.snopub.com/cgi-bin/forum/

webbbs_config.pl/read12097

http://www.snopub.com/cgi-bin/forum/

webbbs_config.pl/read12098 http://www.thinkingmanagers.com/
management/perceived-value.php http://www.diakrisis.org/oprah
Winfrey.htm http://www.businessweek.com/magazine/ content/04 48/
b3910414.htm

http://www.army.mil/cmh/books/wwii/sp1943-44/chapter6.htm http://
home.wanadoo.nl/cclinks/abtf/beatge-1.html http://history.acusd.edu/
gen/WW2Text/ declaration united nations.html http://oldfraser.lexi.net/
publications/critical issues/1999/amero/section 01.htm http://oldfraser.
lexi.net/publications/critical

issues/1999/amero/section 02.htm

http://oldfraser.lexi.net/publications/critical

issues/1999/amero/section 03.htm

http://oldfraser.lexi.net/publications/critical

issues/1999/amero/section 04.htm

http://oldfraser.lexi.net/publications/critical

issues/1999/amero/section 05.htm

http://oldfraser.lexi.net/publications/critical issues/1999/amero/section
06.htm http://oldfraser.lexi.net/publications/critical issues/1999/amero/
section_07.htm

http://oldfraser.lexi.net/publications/critical issues/1999/amero/
section_08.htm

http://oldfraser.lexi.net/publications/critical issues/1999/amero/section
09.htm

(AP) articles from the Billings Gazette U.S. Statistical abstract Webster's
dictionary Knight Ridder News

Newsweek, April 25, 2005 pg. 29.

Columbia encyclopedia.

Marketwatch by Andrea Coombes.

Ask Marilyn, Parade, 711 Third Ave., New York, NY 10017. 7 Steps To Getting Rich: How to think like a millionaire, by Jorge A. Colon.

Jeff Brown, Personal Finance.

Don McAlvany's reports, 166 Turner Drive,

Durango, CO 81303/ www.mcalvany.com The United States Treasury Bureau of Engraving. R.J. Samuelson - The fading "Wealth effect" threatens economy. 10-12-05.

South Florida Sun-Sentinel - Personal savings plunge to all-time low in U.S. 8-27-05.

The Washington Post - Social Security in flux. 8-14-05. Market Watch by Paul B. Farrell - Get a

Millionaire Mindset. 3-20-05.

Casper Star-Tribune - Walton heir dies in plane crash. 6-28-05. The Wall Street Journal - Love & Money, by Jeff D. Opdyke. The Lewis & Clark Journals - "to live for mankind". Aug 18, 1805, Lewis. Amazing Facts & Quotes, by Gail Brooks, Carrie Depaoli, and Barbara Wies. http://quotes.liberty-tree.ca/quotes.nsf/Quotesbycat ReadForm&RestrictToCatagory=Money.

SONGS

Billy Joel - Moving Out (Anthony's Song) Billy Preston - Nothing From Nothing

The Beatles-Can't Buy Me Love, Lennon/McCartney. Abba - Money Money Money

Charlie Daniels - Long Haired Country Boy. Tennessee Ernie Ford - 16 Tons, author Merle Travis.

MOVIES

A Million To Juan, Directed by Paul Rodriquez, written by Robert Grasmere & Francisca Matos.

Escape From L.A. Dir. by John Carpenter, written by WGA & John Carpenter.

The Matrix, Dir. & written by Andy & Larry Wachowski.

Matchstick Men, Dir. by Ridley Scott, written by WGA & Eric Garcia (Book) Nicholas Griffin (Screenplay).

Never Ending Story, written by Michael Ende.

Fight Club, Dir. by David Fincher, written by WGA & Chuck Palahniuk (Book) Jim Uhls (screenplay).

The Assassination of Richard Nixon, Dir. by Niels Mueller, written by Kevin Kennedy & Niels Mueller.

Trading Places, Dir. by John Landis, written by Timothy Harris & Herschel Weingred.

ABOUT THE AUTHOR

Phillip Tilley was raised in rural Montana. He has a diploma in small business management, trained as a financial planner for American Express, and operated several businesses including mail order, jewelry manufacturing, janitorial, and micro-business consulting. After working as the supervisor of the Environmental Sciences department of a major hospital he became a member of Who's Who World Wide of Environmental Scientists in 1993. His military career includes the National Guard, inactive National Guard, Army Reserve, inactive Army Reserve, and the regular Army where he was a member of an elite Special Operations Unit. He attended officer candidate school at the Montana Military Academy and tested for a job with the CIA.

Phillip is a workaholic often holding down two or three jobs at the same time. He has written several articles and booklets on American Business. Four years of research went into the creation of this book.

www.ingramcontent.com/pod-product-compliance
Lightning Source LLC
Chambersburg PA
CBHW071322210326
41597CB00015B/1310